Instructor's Manual and Test Bank

Invitation to Public Speaking

FOURTH EDITION

Cindy L. Griffin
Colorado State University

Prepared by

Rev. Louis Serio, MDiv, JD

Elizabeth Nelson

WADSWORTH
CENGAGE Learning™

Australia • Brazil • Japan • Korea • Mexico • Singapore • Spain • United Kingdom • United States

WADSWORTH
CENGAGE Learning·

ISBN-13: 978-1-111-34810-6
ISBN-10: 1-111-34810-3

Wadsworth
20 Channel Center Street
Boston, MA 02210
USA

Cengage Learning is a leading provider of customized learning solutions with office locations around the globe, including Singapore, the United Kingdom, Australia, Mexico, Brazil, and Japan. Locate your local office at: **www.cengage.com/global**

Cengage Learning products are represented in Canada by Nelson Education, Ltd.

To learn more about Wadsworth, visit **www.cengage.com/wadsworth**

Purchase any of our products at your local college store or at our preferred online store **www.cengagebrain.com**

Printed in the United States of America
1 2 3 4 5 6 7 14 13 12 11 10

Contents

Acknowledgments viii

Preface ix

Suggested Course Schedules 1

    Fifteen Week Schedule 2
    Sixteen Week Schedule 4
    Ten Week Schedule 7
    Summer Five Week Schedule 9

Service Learning 11

Chapter One: Why Speak in Public? 14
    Goals 14
    Outline 14
    End of chapter activities and discussion questions 17
        Review Questions and Activities 17
        Web Activities 20
        InfoTrac College Edition Activities 21
        Interactive Student and Professional Speech Videos 22
        Additional Exercises and Resources 23
        Supplemental Bibliography 23

Chapter Two: Effective Listening 25
    Goals 25
    Outline 25
    End of chapter activities 27
        Review Questions and Activities 27
        Web Activities 29
        InfoTrac College Edition Activities 29
        Interactive Student and Professional Speech Videos Website 30
        Additional Exercises and Resources 31
        Supplemental Bibliography 35

Chapter Three: Developing Your Speech Topic and Purpose 37
    Goals 37
    Outline 37
    End of chapter activities 40
        Review Questions and Activities 40
        Web Activities 42
        InfoTrac College Edition Activities 42
        Interactive Student and Professional Speech Videos 43
        Additional Exercises and Resources 44
        Supplemental Bibliography 51

Chapter Four: Your Audience and Speaking Environment 53
   Goals 53
   Outline 53
   End of chapter activities 58
      Review Questions and Activities 58
      Web Activities 60
      InfoTrac College Edition Activities 61
      Interactive Student and Professional Speech Videos Website 62
      Additional Exercises and Resources 62
      Supplemental Bibliography 67

Chapter Five: Gathering Supporting Materials 69
   Goals 69
   Outline 69
   End of chapter activities 73
      Review Questions and Activities 73
      Web Activities 74
      InfoTrac College Edition Activities 75
      Interactive Student and Professional Speech Videos 76
      Additional Exercises and Resources 76
      Supplemental Bibliography 87

Chapter Six: Developing and Supporting Your Ideas 89
   Goals 89
   Outline 89
   End of chapter activities 93
      Review Questions and Activities 93
      Web Activities 94
      InfoTrac College Edition Activities 96
      Interactive Student and Professional Speech Videos 96
      Additional Exercises and Resources 97
      Supplemental Bibliography 99

Chapter Seven: Reasoning 101
   Goals 101
   Outline 101
   End of chapter activities 104
      Review Questions and Activities 104
      Web Activities 105
      InfoTrac College Edition Activities 105
      Interactive Student and Professional Speech Videos 106
      Additional Exercises and Resources 107
      Supplemental Bibliography 112

Chapter Eight: Organizing and Outlining Your Speech 114
   Goals 114
   Outline 114
   End of chapter activities 117
      Review Questions and Activities 117

Web Activities 119
InfoTrac College Edition Activities 119
Interactive Student and Professional Speech Videos Website 120
Additional Exercises and Resources 121
Supplemental Bibliography 126

Chapter Nine: Introductions and Conclusions 127
Goals 127
Outline 127
End of chapter activities 129
Review Questions and Activities 129
Web Activities 131
InfoTrac College Edition Activities 131
Interactive Student and Professional Speech Videos Website 132
Additional Exercises and Resources 133
Supplemental Bibliography 135

Chapter Ten: Language 136
Goals 136
Outline 136
End of chapter activities 139
Review Questions 139
Web Resources 140
InfoTrac College Edition Activities 141
Interactive Student and Professional Speech Videos 142
Additional Exercises and Resources 143
Supplemental Bibliography 147

Chapter Eleven: Delivering Your Speech 149
Goals 149
Outline 149
End of chapter activities 154
Review Questions 154
Web Resources 156
InfoTrac College Edition Activities 157
Interactive Student and Professional Speech Videos 158
Additional Exercises and Resources 158
Supplemental Bibliography 163

Chapter Twelve: Visual Aids 165
Goals 165
Outline 165
End of chapter activities 170
Review Questions and Activities 170
Web Resources 171
InfoTrac College Edition Activities 172
Interactive Student and Professional Speech Videos 172
Additional Exercises and Resources 173
Supplemental Bibliography 179

Chapter Thirteen: Informative Speaking 180
    Goals 180
    Outline 180
    End of chapter activities 183
        Review Questions and Activities 183
        Web Activities 184
        InfoTrac College Edition Activities 184
        Interactive Student and Professional Speech Videos 185
        Additional Exercises and Resources 186
        Supplemental Bibliography 195

Chapter Fourteen: Invitational Speaking 196
    Goals 196
    Outline 196
    End of chapter activities 199
        Review Questions and Activities 199
        Web Activities 201
        InfoTrac College Edition Activities 201
        Interactive Student and Professional Speech Videos 202
        Additional Exercises and Resources 203
        Supplemental Bibliography 228

Chapter Fifteen: Persuasive Speaking 230
    Goals 230
    Outline 230
    End of chapter activities 234
        Review Questions and Activities 234
        Web Activities 235
        InfoTrac College Edition Activities 236
        Interactive Student and Professional Speech Videos 237
        Additional Exercises and Resources 238
        Supplemental Bibliography 251

Chapter Sixteen: Persuasion and Reasoning 253
    Goals 253
    Outline 253
    End of chapter activities 258
        Review Questions and Activities 258
        Web Activities 259
        InfoTrac College Edition Activities 260
        Interactive Student and Professional Speech Videos Website 261
        Additional Exercises and Resources 261
        Supplemental Bibliography 270

Chapter Seventeen: Speaking On Special Occasions..272
    Goals...272
    Outline...272
    End of chapter activities...274
        Review Questions and Activities...274
        Web Activities...275
        InfoTrac College Edition Activities...275
        Interactive Student and Professional Speech Videos Website.......276
        Additional Exercises and Resources..276
        Supplemental Bibliography..278

Appendix: Speaking in Small Groups 279
    Goals...279
    Outline...279
    End of chapter activities...281
        Review Questions and Activities...281
        Additional Exercises and Resources..282
        Supplemental Bibliography..284

Test Bank 286

Acknowledgments

First, I want to thank Cindy Griffin for creating *Invitation to Public Speaking*, and for her ongoing wisdom and guidance to students and instructors of public speaking. Thank you as well to Larry Goldberg of LarryTotalBooks, Inc. and to Rebekah Matthews of Wadsworth, Cengage Learning, for placing confidence in me to complete this project. Finally, I want to express gratitude to my entire family for their patience and support while I completed this project.

- Rev. Louis Serio, MDiv, JD.

Preface

Welcome! We are very pleased that you have chosen *Invitation to Public Speaking* as your textbook for the basic public speaking course. This manual provides both experienced and new instructors ideas and new approaches to public speaking, while still adhering to some traditional approaches. In fact, this is the unique feature of the textbook; it brings together the traditional and the contemporary, providing a space for diversity of thought, approach, and perspective, while introducing the discipline to new ways of teaching public speaking. Please feel free to use this instructor's resource manual as a guide to make your course a success. Realize that the activities in this manual, although numerous, are not exhaustive and that there are many more ways in which you can adapt certain activities to fit the unique environment in which you teach, be that at a university, community college, traditional classroom, or a web-based classroom.

The first part of this manual consists of sample schedules for a variety of courses (semester, quarter, and summer). Included in the outlines are examples of different units you can teach along with different types of speeches. Also included in part one is a discussion about possible service learning options that you may be interested in pursuing in your course.

The second part of the manual includes chapter-by-chapter outlines as well as a list of goals for each chapter, discussion and review questions, activities and assignments, and extra resources where relevant. Included within the informative, invitational, and persuasive chapters are sample outlines from student speeches and sample critique forms. Included in this section is a fairly new speech type emerging from invitational rhetoric: the invitational speech (Chapter 14). Because this is a relatively recent speech type, we have included additional information in this chapter (frequently asked questions, extra resources, and suggestions) to facilitate teaching this speech type.

Enjoy the textbook and the ancillaries, which have been developed specifically for the unique needs of the public speaking instructor using the 4ᵗʰ edition of Cindy Griffin's *Invitation to Public Speaking*. It is our hope that this text will provide a space for all approaches to public speaking, keeping a connection to the tradition, while also opening a space for new approaches.

Suggested Course Schedules

Each instructor will have a slightly different approach to organizing their course. In what follows, we offer a range of course schedules for faculty operating under a traditional semester system (15-16 weeks), a quarter system (10 weeks), and a summer course schedule (4-5 weeks). Each semester system will also vary with regard to contact hours (which are specified with each course outline). Note that the samples illustrate the range of speeches that can be taught in a term as well as speech lengths. These schedules are adapted for a class of 22-24 students and reflect both spring and fall semesters, allowing for spring and winter breaks. Other holidays such as Martin Luther King, Jr., Day, Labor Day, and Independence Day are included in the samples.

Suggestions for syllabus writing: Having a day-by-day schedule for public speaking will help keep students on track and faculty organized. An excellent way to conceptualize creating the syllabus is to ensure that each lecture teaches students the skills they will need to be successful for the upcoming speech. You will notice that with each schedule shown here, the lecture material does exactly that. Note, too, that in some of the samples, the readings are assigned as units, while other samples reflect a chapter-by-chapter model.

Certain speeches should be worth more points than other speeches. The more skills you add to each speech type, the more points a speech should be worth. Because students have so many assignments due at the end of a term, try assigning the speech with the most point value as the second-to-the-last speech and ending the semester with a speech that is worth fewer points. For example, students tend to like ending the course with the commemorative speech (worth fewer points than a persuasive, invitational, or group speech) because it is weighted less heavily than the other speech types and, it ends the semester on a positive and fun note. You may want to experiment with different options, semester to semester, to find the sequence that works best for you and your students. Finally, when determining the length of time for each speech and the number of days you will need, always provide a few minutes extra for feedback after speeches.

Some colleges have high attrition rates. Thus, be aware that you can be flexible and reschedule speaking days or add an extra lecture day. If your attrition rate is high, you also can plan for impromptu speeches with time left on speaking days. Having students "workshop" their speeches if you push back speeches for a day also can be very valuable. "Workshopping" simply means that students can bring in drafts of their speeches to show to a small group and get feedback on structure, clarity, research, audience adaptation, etc. You can also implement the textbook activities specified in the end of the chapter review questions, or any of the exercises that appear in this manual.

1

FIFTEEN WEEK SCHEDULE
Meeting twice a week for 75 minutes

The following sample syllabus is for a fifteen week spring semester (no finals week). This course is structured in such a way that students will find a new challenge with each speech type. For instance, the diagnostic speech is only the first speech; therefore the reading is only foundational reading. The informative speech will have the expectation of visual-aides and more research; therefore the reading reflects these expectations, etc. The time allotment for each speech is also indicated, but these time limits can be flexible depending on your expectations. This schedule also allows for a spring break.

Day 1 —   Introduction to the course

Day 2 —   **Unit One** (read chs. 1 and 2): Lecture/Discussion
               Assign diagnostic speech

Day 3 —   **Unit One wrap-up** (have all reading done)
               Assign informative speech

Day 4 —   **SPEECHES: *DIAGNOSTIC (2-3 minutes)***

Day 5 —   **SPEECHES: *DIAGNOSTIC (2-3 minutes)***
               Unit Two (read chs. 3, 4, 6, 9-11, 13): Lecture/Discussion

Day 6 —   **Unit Two continued**
               Tentative: Guest Speaker about local area nonprofits for service learning option

---

Day 7 —   **Unit Two continued** (have all reading done)
               Due: Informative speech topic sheet

Day 8 —   **SPEECHES: *INFORMATIVE (4-6 minutes)***

Day 9 —   **SPEECHES: *INFORMATIVE (4-6 minutes)***

Day 10 —   **SPEECHES: *INFORMATIVE (4-6 minutes)***
               Unit Three (read chs. 5, 7, 8, 12, 15 & 16): Lecture/Discussion (if there is time)
               Assign persuasive speech

Day 11 —   **Unit Three continued** (continuing reading): Lecture/Discussion

Day 12 —   **Unit Three continued** (continue reading)
               Study guide for exam
               Due: Persuasive speech topic sheet

vii. **Context** *is the environment or situation in which a speech occurs* (pg. 11).

V. Building Confidence as a Public Speaker

1. **Communication apprehension** is what we often call nervousness before a speech (pg. 12).

2. People who are apprehensive about communicating with others have **trait anxiety** (pg. 12).

3. People who are apprehensive about communicating with others in a particular situation have **state or situational anxiety** (pg. 12).

4. A list of suggestions from Ch. 1 for building confidence as a public speaker:

    i. Do your Research (pg. 14).

    ii. Practice your speech (pg. 14).

    iii. Have realistic expectations (pg. 14).

    iv. Practice visualization and affirmation.

      visualization is the process in which you construct a mental image of yourself giving a successful speech (pg. 15).

      affirmations are positive motivating statements (pg. 16).

      The technique of **cognitive restructuring** is the process that builds confidence by which one replaces negative thoughts with positive thoughts (pg. 16).

    v. Connect with your audience (pg. 17).

End of the Chapter Activities and Discussion Questions

The following questions and activities can be found at the end of Chapter One.

Review Questions and Activities

1. Who are the most compelling speakers you have encountered? Why did they speak: Did they decide, were they asked, or was it required? What issues did they discuss? How do these issues relate to the public dialogue discussed in this chapter? What made these speakers such strong presenters?

Either during lecture or as a homework assignment, ask students to think of speakers they have heard or they know about. Let them know they can be speakers that have passed on or that are still alive. You can also prompt students to speak about people in their community that may not be "famous" but still are very effective speakers within certain communities. For instance, students may use pastors and/or priests, athletic coaches, or leaders of service organizations as examples.

2. This chapter presented Deborah Tannen's notion of the argument culture. What is your perception of this culture? Have you been exposed to public communication as an argument? What were your reactions to this kind of interaction? If the people engaged in this interaction were to communicate civilly, what specific things would change?

One way to prompt students to think about the idea of an argument culture is to have them think about the arguments they hear on many television shows, see in movies, or witness on the internet. You could even have them think of arguments they have with roommates, friends, family, etc. Ask students to consider how they felt listening to these arguments, how much communication actually occurred, and how "effective" the argument was (what were the results, for example). Ask them how many times they back away from an argument, because they are more comfortable with a different style of communication. If they do not like to back away, ask them why. Be sure to show respect for all perspectives and to validate the different styles of interaction.

3. Make a list of the issues you find interesting and have followed for some time. Who spoke publicly on those issues? If you don't know who gave speeches on these issues, spend time in the library and on the Internet finding these speeches. How do these speeches affect your own positions on these issues? How does this activity shape your perception of the unending conversation discussed in this chapter?

This activity is especially effective if it is assigned as a homework assignment, particularly if students are attempting to locate speeches in the library or on the internet. You also can have students turn this in as a short paper, or as a prompt for possible speech topics. Once the students complete the assignment, in class, make a list on the board of the various issues that get raised and ask students which of these issues they would decide to speak out about, which they might choose for a speech assignment, and which they would like to hear another student give as a speech in class. Discuss with them how the speeches on these issues contribute to the public dialogue.

4. What cultural background or gender influences do you think will become (or already are) a part of your speaking style? Are these similar to those discussed in this chapter? If they are different, identify the differences and how they affect communication. Discuss this topic in your own public speaking class so that you and your classmates begin with recognition of the differences you will encounter as you all give speeches.

These questions can be easily addressed in a class discussion after lecturing about gender and cultural differences. Emphasize to students that not ALL men and women, or individuals from a given cultural group communicate identically, but it is still very important to discuss these issues. Generalizations serve a purpose in bringing these issues to the forefront and they enable us to have open discussions about the influences that impact our speaking style. Try to highlight the differences in positive ways, rather than hold one style as better than others.

5. Set aside fifteen minutes of alone time the day before your first speech. Take time to visualize that speech as the process is described in this chapter. Go through each step carefully and in detail. Do not rush or overlook any aspect of the speech process. After you give your speech, compare having visualized the speech and your level of nervousness to a situation in which you were nervous but did not visualize. Was the visualization helpful in reducing your nervousness? Why or why not?

Students can work in pairs on the sharing of the differences between the visualization and the actual speech process.

6. Either alone or with a friend, list or discuss the negative self-talk you use to describe your ability to give speeches. Identify the specific negative phrases you use and turn them into positive affirmations. Be realistic in reframing your negative self-talk into positive self-talk, using the examples in this chapter as a guide.

Remind students not be judgmental of the negative self-talk of themselves or others, reminding them that all people do this. Emphasize converting negative self-talk into positive affirmations.

6. As you listen to other students give their speeches, see if you can find similarities and differences between them and you. This will help you find points of connection with your audience, one of the techniques for reducing your nervousness before a speech. It also will help you stay audience centered.

    These differences and similarities are for the individual student's benefit. Remind them that they are not to be shared with the students who are observed.

8. If you are assigned your first speech, check out Speech Studio to see other students' first speeches. Or record your speech and upload it to Speech Studio. Ask your peers for their feedback—what feedback could you use to help improve your speech before you give it in class?

    Encourage students to become familiar with Speech Studio and to explore this new tool.

Web Activities

1. **Public Dialogue Consortium**

   Go to http://www.publicdialogue.org/?p=155 to explore the seven principles that the Public Dialogue Consortium lists for developing dialogue in communities. How does public speaking prepare you to enact these principles in your community? What issues in your community would benefit from increased dialogue?

   The idea of a public dialogue is being discussed in many arenas (see the resources listed at the end of this chapter for additional reading). You can have students log on to this website and read the principles, then compare them to the idea of a public dialogue discussed in this chapter. How do the seven principles influence the kinds of topics they choose for speeches and the ways they present those topics? In addition, many instructors assign a first speech topic (research a local organization, for example, and present the services that organization provides in an informative speech). Ask students to discuss how each of the seven principles are reflected in the information they are gathering about a specific agency or organization. For instance, principle #4: "We believe there should be support from the top for initiatives from the bottom" can be illustrated by a student who may volunteer for the Untied Way. The campaign associates working for The United Way work closely with community leaders in order to establish positive relationships so that these leaders will see the importance of giving back to the community in supporting programs for at risk youth, or seniors, etc. The key here is to have students identify how these seven principles are being put into practice.

2. **Thinking About Audience**

   Send students to their online resources for *Invitation to Public Speaking* for an activity that will help students learn more about audience. Additionally, students can watch a video clip by Mike Piel that will provide for them a strong example of audience centeredness.

3. **Randall Arauz**

   Go to http://www.goldmanprize.org to read about and listen to more about how Costa Rican, biologist, Randall Arauz, drew international attention to the inhumane and environmentally catastrophic shark finning industry, making his country the international model for shark protection through his experiences with public speaking. Who are some other people who have spoken to address an urgent need? What are some urgent needs in your community? Who might address them?

   This activity can be another that is appropriate for students who are doing service learning in the public speaking course. If you have students do a research paper on a particular speaker, Randall Arauz would be a great person for students to learn more about. An example of another person who spoke because of an urgent need was Judy Sheppard, Mathew Sheppard's mother. If some of your students have not been in the community for long, then have them generate ideas of people from their hometowns who have spoken because of an urgent need.

5. **Joseph Welch**

   Go to http://www.americanrhetoric.com/speeches/welch-mccarthy.html to listen to a clip from Joseph Welch's speech. This clip will help you appreciate the power of his speech. What has been the impact of McCarthyism? How can speakers today avoid the extremes of the McCarthy era?

   If you have internet access from your classroom, you can show this clip during class. Lead a class discussion about this clip, and have students respond to the above questions. Note: you may need to provide students with some background about McCarthy.

6. **Convening Public Dialogue**

   Purpose: To think about how you can help start a public dialogue in your community.
   Directions: Go to http://www.beyondintractability.org/essay/dialogue/
   Learn how in dialogue, participants explore the presuppositions, beliefs, and feelings that shape their interactions; they discover how hidden values and intentions control people's behavior and contribute to communication successes and failures. Has there been an issue in your area you would like to see addressed? How might you organize a meeting to address this issue? What skills do you have that would make you a successful convener?

   If you are assigning a speech topic, using service learning as an option in your course, or you are assigning a small group speech, this activity can be useful. In small groups, have students identify issues in which they might convene a public dialogue. This may be an issue that affects students on campus or something urgent in the community. Students might give a series of speeches on these issues, or even work on putting together a meeting to dialogue with community members to rally support for this issue or to generate solutions to the problem. Have students put into practice the ideas they read from this website.

InfoTrac College Edition Activities

1. **InfoTrac College Edition Activity 1.1: Defining Public Speaking**

   Purpose: To illustrate the differences between public speaking and other forms of communication.
   Directions: Use InfoTrac College Edition's PowerTrac to search for a speech that interests you in *Vital Speeches*. As you read the speech, consider the following: What makes this speech different from other forms of communication? Can you identify the components of the speaking model discussed in this chapter? What style of communication is the speaker using (argument versus dialogue). Was the speech audience centered? How can you tell? Do you think the speaker effectively raised awareness about his or her topic with the audience?

   You can assign this activity as homework. Students may have difficulty accessing a speech they will think is interesting. Give them some assistance in brainstorming ideas for speeches. For instance several students know about the former governor of Minnesota, Jesse Ventura, primarily because of his wrestling career. Mention to students if they know who Ventura is, to access one of his speeches to determine if, in fact, he is as effective a politician as he might have been a wrestler. Or ask them to think about their favorite athletes, politicians they may find interesting or may criticize, or famous writers like Toni Morrison who give speeches.

21

2. **InfoTrac College Edition Activity 1.2: The Speaking Model**
   Purpose: To apply the speaking model to a contemporary speech.
   Directions: Use InfoTrac College Edition to find a speech in *Vital Speeches*. Now, consider the components of the public speaking model. Who is the speaker? What is the relationship between the speaker and the audience? What is the speaker's message? What do you know about the audience? Was the audience supportive or hostile to the speaker? What type of feedback do you think the audience gave the speaker?

   For ideas to help students determine which speech to select in Vital Speeches, *refer to InfoTrac College Edition Activity 1.1. You can assign this question as a homework assignment. You can also assign students a specific speech, and have them work with partners or small groups of 3-4.*

3. **InfoTrac College Edition Activity 1.3: Deciding to Speak**
   Purpose: To consider the various reasons for speaking.
   Directions: Use InfoTrac College Edition to locate three speeches in *Vital Speeches*. Compare and contrast these speeches, and determine the reasons each speaker had for giving the speech. Are these people speaking on matters of importance because they have unique experiences to share, or some combination of these reasons? In what ways do these speakers add to the public dialogue? If you've spoken in public, why did you choose to do so? What future speaking experiences do you anticipate?

   This activity can be a larger homework assignment or even a short paper. You can encourage students to locate three different speeches by three different individuals, about the same topic, incident, or issue. For instance, students can look up speeches given by different people after the September 11 attacks. One speaker can be George Bush. Another speaker can be a leader from the Muslim faith, and another speaker can be a survivor, police officer or fire fighter. Have students respond to the above questions. On the due date of the activity, have students share their responses and observations in class.

Interactive Student and Professional Speech Videos

1. **Mike Piel Video Clip**
   As you watch Mike Piel speak, consider the ways in which he remains audience centered throughout his speech. How does he stay audience centered in this clip? Can you list specific phrases he uses that indicate he is considering his audience as he speaks?

   Show this video clip in class as an example of how a speaker uses particular phrases to remain audience centered. You can have students write those phrases down as they listen, and then discuss as a group. As well, discuss the importance of language in remaining audience centered.

Additional Exercises and Resources

1. **Controversial Topics List**
   Ask students to generate a list of the most controversial issues that are part of the public dialogue locally or nationally. Record their ideas on the board or an overhead. Discuss with them whether they would decide to speak out about any of these issues and in what situations. Then, select an issue and using the idea of a dialogue rather than an argument, discuss the many ways this issue could be approached and framed. Wrap up the activity by asking them to consider the ideas generated as possible speech topics for a speech they might give in the class.

2. **Styles of Communication**
   Discuss with students the different styles of communication presented in this chapter that are specific to cultures (many of the resources listed in the supplemental bibliography will help you with this discussion). What specific differences do they notice, and what are the strengths and weaknesses of those differences? Discuss whether, if they use these culture-specific styles of communication, they might include them in their speeches. What are the benefits or disadvantages of including them in their speeches?

3. **Service Learning**
   If you are incorporating service learning in your class, introduce the idea during this first lecture. Identify the agencies you have selected and the topics students will be researching and speaking on. Encourage them to consider volunteering with agencies they feel connected to, or want to learn more about. Frame your discussion as giving students a structured opportunity to enter the public dialogue outside the classroom and then to bring those issues back into the classroom in their speeches to the class.

Supplemental Bibliography

Axtell, Roger E. Gestures: The Do's and Taboos of Body Language Around the World. New York: Wiley, 1998.

> The solid examples provided by this book will help when discussing how culture can influence speaking style and what is acceptable and not acceptable.

Boyd, Stephen D. and Lanita Bradley Boyd. Attention: The Art of Holding Your Audience in the Palm of Your Hand. Ft. Thomas, Kentucky: Ajalon Press, 2009.

> The Boyds' book gives eighteen valuable strategies for assuring that your audiences pay attention when you speak. Chapters cover paying attention to Preparation, Overcoming Stage Fright, Your Audience, Organization, Opening and Closing, Stories, Delivery, Persuasion, Credibility, the Words You Speak, Humor, Visuals, Handouts, Ceremonial Speeches, Special Situations, Common Sense in Speaking, Question and Answer Sessions, and Getting Better Even When You Are Good.

Cushner, Kenneth, and Richard W. Brislin. <u>Intercultural Interactions: A Practical Guide.</u> Thousand Oaks: Sage, 1996. 2nd ed.

This resource offers a wealth of examples of how communication differs across cultures. The examples provide excellent models for speaking about the relevance of communication in real life situations.

Dowis, Richard. <u>The Lost Art of the Great Speech: How to Write One, How to Deliver It</u>. New York: American Management Association, 2000.

Dowis offers many examples throughout the book of both historical and contemporary speeches that have had significant power and impact on audiences. This fresh look at how influential public speaking can be may help you impart the importance to your class.

Ford, Wendy S. Zabava, and Wolvin, Andrew D. "The Differential Impact of a Basic Communication Course on Perceived Competencies in Class, Work, and Social Contexts." *Communication Education*, 42 (1993): 215-223.

This article demonstrates how the course in basic public speaking can help students improve their communication skills in public speaking, small group, and interpersonal settings, as well as improve their overall self-confidence.

Gudykunst, William B. and Kim, Young Yun. <u>Communicating With Strangers: An Approach to Intercultural Communication</u>. 3rd ed. New York: McGraw-Hill, 1997.

Gudykunst and Kim offer a comprehensive discussion of the need for and the processes of communication. This book is an excellent resource for a lecture and discussion of the importance of communication and its basic forms. The text also provides study questions in each chapter.

Kearney, Pat, Plax, Timothy G., <u>Public Speaking in a Diverse Society</u> / Second Edition, Mayfield Publishing Co. 1999.

This introductory public speaking text integrates discussion of cultural influences on communication with instruction in public speaking theory and practice. Cultural influences are considered in all areas of public speaking, from selecting topics and evidence to using particular styles of verbal and nonverbal communication.

Robinson , Audrey Ph. D. *Ethics Blog*
http://ezinearticles.com/?5-Top-Causes-of-Fear-of-Public-Speaking&id=4980741

This scientific researcher and small business entrepreneur in internet marketing offers advice and tips on handling fear in public speaking in a number of e-zine articles.

Rubin, Rebecca B. and Graham, Elizabeth E. "Communication Correlates of College Success: An Explanatory Investigation." *Communication Education*, 37 (1988): 14-27.

This article shows the real life benefit of the course in that it shows that communication experience, like that gained in a public speaking course, is related to higher college GPA.

Chapter Two: Effective Listening

Chapter Goals

Chapter two introduces students to the importance of effective listening. Students should have an understanding of the following concepts by the end of this chapter:

- To explain why listening to others is important
- To identify the reasons we sometimes fail to listen to others
- To implement strategies for becoming a more careful listener
- To implement strategies for becoming a more critical listener
- To implement strategies for becoming a more ethical listeners
- To describe how the roles of the speaker and listener are related

Chapter Outline

I. **Why listen to others?** (pg. 21).
   a. When we listen to others, we confirm the humanity, presence, and worth of that person.
      i. **Confirmation** *is recognizing, acknowledging, and expressing value for another individual* (pg. 21).
      ii. Hearing is different from listening.
         1. **Hearing** *refers to the vibration of sound waves on our eardrums and the impulses that are then sent to the brain* (pg. 22).
         2. **Listening** *is the process of giving thoughtful attention to another person's words and understanding what you hear* (pg. 22).
            a. To listen to others is to confirm them because you have made an attempt to understand their message.
            b. When you listen to another's words, you recognize those words as expressions of that person's experiences, values, and beliefs.

II. **Why we sometimes fail to listen** (pg. 22).
   a. There are several reasons we fail to focus our attention and listen to others.
      i. **Interference** *is anything that stops or hinders a listener from receiving a message* (pg. 22).
         1. **Listener interference** *occurs when listening is impeded based on our own bad habits* (pg. 22).
         2. **Speaker interference caused by information** *can affect the audience's ability to listen in direct ways* (pg. 23).
            a. A **listenable speech** *is considerate and delivered in an oral style, meant to be heard rather than read.* (pg. 23).
            b. **Considerate speeches** *ease the audience's burden of processing information* (pg. 23).
         3. **Speaker interference caused by language** *results from a speaker who uses language that is unclear* (pg. 25).

a. The speaker's language use can be too **formal or technical** too **casual**, too **non-inclusive**, or too **cluttered**. (pg. 25).
   i. **Jargon** *is language used by a special group or for a special activity* (pg. 26).
b. **Casual language** can also be difficult to listen to (pg. 26).
   i. **Slang** *is an informal nonstandard vocabulary, usually made up of arbitrarily changed words* (pg. 26).
   ii. **Colloquialism is** *a local or regional informal dialect or expression* (pg. 26).
   iii. **Euphemism** *substitutes an agreeable or inoffensive expression for one that may offend or suggest something unpleasant* (pg. 26).
c. **Non-inclusive Language** can be words that seem to refer only to certain groups of people (pg. 27).
   i. **Gender-inclusive language** *recognizes that both women and men are active participants in the world* (pg. 27).
   ii. **Culturally inclusive language** *respectfully recognizes the differences among the many cultures in our society* (pg. 27).
   iii. **Spotlighting** *is the practice of highlighting a person's race, ethnicity, sex, sexual orientation, physical ability, etc. during a speech, resulting in language that is not culturally inclusive* (pg. 27 -28).
d. **Verbal clutter** is *extra words in a sentence that do not add meaning* (pg. 30).

4. **Interference caused by differences** can also contribute to a failing to listen (pg. 31).
   a. **Speech style can affect listening,** including accents, tonal, and rhythmic qualities, stuttering, nonnative speakers of a language, and gender speech differences (pg. 31).
   b. **Background and occupation can affect listening,** including differences in race, ethnicity, nationality, regional upbringing, religion, education, occupation, and economic status (pg. 31).
   c. **Appearance can affect listening** including styles of dress, height, weight, hair, body adornment, and speaker's posture (pg. 31).
   d. **Values can affect listening** because speakers and audience members will not always agree on which values are "worthy" and "good," "wrong" and "bad" (pg. 31).

III. **How to listen carefully** (pg. 32).
   a. **Listen to the speaker's purpose** (pg. 32).
   b. **Listen for the main ideas** (pg. 33).
   c. **Listen for supporting evidence and sources** (pg. 33).
   d. **Write down new words, ideas, and questions** (pg. 33).
   e. **Listen for the conclusion** (pg. 33).
   f. **Offer nonverbal feedback** (pg. 33).

IV. **How to listen critically** (pg. 33).
   a. **Critical listeners** *listen for the accuracy of a speech's content and the implications of a speaker's message* (pg. 33).

26

V. **How to listen ethically** (pg. 35).
   a. **Ethics** *refer to the study of moral standards and how those standards affect our conduct* (pg. 35).
   b. An **ethical listener** *considers the moral impact of a speaker's message on one's self and one's community* (pg. 35).
   c. In order to listen ethically, listeners must **suspend judgment** throughout a speech (pg. 35).
       i. Ethical listeners are willing to enter an "opinion holding pattern" for the duration of a speech.
       ii. They are willing to listen to a speaker's message without assigning "right" and "wrong" to it.
   d. In order to listen ethically, you must **assess the information** you hear, and, at times, respond to the speaker's message (pg. 36).
       i. Listeners can respond during the speech or in a conversation with the speaker and other audience members after the speech is given.
       ii. Even if they do not agree with a speaker's position, ethical listeners join the public dialogue so they can better understand a position, explore differences, and share their views.
VI. **Speakers as listeners: Adapting to your audience** (pg. 36).
   a. **Audiences who are uninterested** may not want to listen to your message (pg. 36).
       i. The audience can become interested if you make your introduction and main points compelling, dynamic, and innovative.
       ii. You can also be attentive to your audience's particular biases.
   b. **Audiences who are distracted or disruptive** (pg. 38).
       i. Take a moment to explain any distractions that you may be causing. The chapter has several suggestions for how to address various behaviors.
   c. **Audiences who are confused** (pg. 38).
       i. If an audience is confused because of you, slow down, explain with more detail, reduce the number of main points in the speech, alter language, use all of the three listening styles.
   d. **Audiences who plan their responses rather than listen** (pg. 39).
       i. Acknowledge their eagerness to participate and recognize it as a positive sign of interest.
       ii. Make a space for conversation at the close of the speech.

End of the Chapter Activities and Discussion Questions

The following activities and questions can be found at the end of Chapter Two.

Review Questions and Activities

1. Identify the times you have listened to confirm others. Were you able to recognize, acknowledge, and express value for another individual? Did you do this verbally or nonverbally? Now identify the times you listened with "guns loaded." What are the differences between the two types of listening? Do you prefer one over the other? Why?

This activity can be conducted as an in class discussion when introducing the concept of confirmation or you can place students in groups of 3-4. Have them respond to the questions listed here, and have them generate examples of how they would confirm others in their future speeches (if they have an idea of topics they will address). When students address the above questions, encourage them to identify specific phrases or nonverbal signals that were confirming. For instance, phrases such as "I understand," "That's a great point," and, "I have not experienced that in the same way, but your perspective is very insightful," are examples of confirming verbal responses. Confirming nonverbal signals might be such responses as nodding the head, eye contact, smiling, moving closer to the audience, etc.

2. Monitor your listening for a day and write down five ways your listening failed. How might you change these bad listening habits?

   Students can turn this in as a homework assignment or as extra credit. On the due date, have students discuss as a class their observations. A variation to this activity would be to have students monitor their listening during speeches and respond to the above questions. You can also have students who are speaking address some of the reasons they felt listening might have failed during their own speeches. You then can discuss how they might attempt to use some of the strategies to help their audience listen more effectively in future speeches.

3. Attend, watch, or listen to a speech given by someone very different from you. Pay attention to how you manage the listening interference that comes from differences. Can you listen non-judgmentally? Can you accommodate different speech styles, mannerisms, dress and backgrounds? How are you able to listen even though differences may be present?

   This activity is particularly effective given the last presidential race. The race for the 2008 elections features much public discussion about gender and race given presidential candidates Hillary Rodham Clinton and Barack Obama. Many students became interested in discussing whether the USA would have seen its first "female" president or its first African-American president. Discussions about how gender and race are perceived in public speaking can be a great learning opportunity for students. This activity also can be turned in as a homework assignment. On the due date of the assignment, take time in class to have students share their responses to the speakers they observed. Some students may see the same speakers but have different perspectives. As they share their responses, be sure to also emphasize the importance of listening critically and ethically.

4. What kinds of slang, jargon, or euphemisms do you use in your everyday interactions at school, at work, or at home? Make a list of some of the unique expressions you use and define each word or phrase on your list. Now think about your next speech topic and your audience. What would be the benefits or the drawbacks of using slang, jargon, or euphemisms in your speech?

   Use these questions as an in class activity. Have students take a few minutes to write out the definitions of slang, jargon, and euphemism, as well as a few examples of each. Then, have them partner up with a classmate, or place them into small groups of 3-4. Have them share their examples with their classmates and discuss how these expressions might come up in their next speeches. Many students will assume that their classmates will know the terms they are using. This can be an excellent opportunity for students to give each other feedback about what may and may not be clear in their next speeches.

5. Review the definition of ethical listening. What is the role of ethical listening in the public dialogue? Do you believe it is your responsibility to listen ethically? Do you think you can suspend judgment and listen to, assess, and respond to the information? Explain your answers.

This question can be used as a homework assignment or assigned as extra credit. Students may be challenged by the notion of suspending judgment and assessing and responding to information. Chapter 4 (Your Audience and Speaking Environment) will help students to further understand the differences in perspectives among audience members and speakers, so you might want to introduce some of that material here, or have them read ahead in the text. When discussing the ideas of suspending judgment and assessing the information presented, encourage students to be aware not only of their thought processes and the content of their questions, but also of their tone of voice and inflection when they ask and answer questions because disagreement and disapproval can come across quite easily in one's voice. The concept of ethical listening is very important in all speeches, but takes on a very direct role during the open dialogue of the invitational speech, so you may want to return to this activity in Chapter 14.

Web Activities

1. **Interfering with the Message**
   Purpose: To learn how speakers can make it difficult to listen.
   Directions: Use InfoTrac College Edition to find several articles on topics that interest you. To what degree do the authors present information that is too complicated? Too basic? To what degree does their language interfere with your ability to read the articles? Is the language too technical? Too causal? Too narrow? Too cluttered?

This activity can be particularly useful for students when working on their own outlines. Often, students are challenged by simplifying some of their language and removing the verbal clutter from their own speeches. Have them read the articles critically and generate specific statements that would reduce clutter and add clarity to the articles. For those students you assigned the same article, have them compare the changes they would make and explain their choices. This can be a good activity to conduct at the library if you have a library day scheduled.

InfoTrac College Edition Activities

1. **InfoTrac College Edition Activity 2.1: Sharpening Your Listening Skills**
   Purpose: To think critically about information that speakers present.
   Directions: Use InfoTrac College Edition's PowerTrac to search for several speeches that interest you in *Vital Speeches*. Do the speeches include words that are new to you? What do they mean? What questions do you have about the content of the speeches?

Initially, students will be challenged by determining which speech to look for. Assist them by reminding them of any speeches that may have been on television. Did any of their favorite athletes participate in commencement speeches or fundraising speeches? Most of the speeches in Vital Speeches *will be current, but some students may want to use historical speeches. If using historical speeches keeps their interest, then encourage them to do so. Remind them to record any new words and to look up their definitions. Encourage them to attend to the content of the speech and to bring questions about that content to class. On the day this assignment is due, take some time to discuss students' observations in class making a list of new words and similar questions about content, if there are any.*

Interactive Student and Professional Speech Videos Website

1. **Video Clip 1: Tiffany Birsco: Encouraging Effective Listening**
   As you watch Tiffany's speech, consider how well she helps her audience listen to her speech. In what ways is her introduction compelling, dynamic, and innovative? How do you think it encouraged her audience to continue listening to her?

   This video clip will be very useful for students to watch before their next speech so as to observe what these concepts look like and sound like in practice. You can have students respond to the above questions as a class after they view the video clip. If students felt that the speaker was not very effective, then ask them to specify how she could have been more effective—what changes would they suggest?

2. **Video Clip 2: Barbara Bush's Speech at Wellesley College**
   In her speech, how did Barbara Bush deal with the differences between her and her audience? How did she acknowledge differences in speech style or appearances? How did she invite others to consider her values? How did she assume an invitational stance?

   Show this video clip in class and then place students with partners or in small groups. Have students respond to the questions listed here. If you have time, show the clip a second time. Often times, students will get more out of a video clip if they are able to see it twice. Remind students that everyone may have a slightly different perspective on the speech. Encourage students to specify why they felt she adapted well to certain styles by using specific examples (evidence) from the clip. Often students will respond "Yes, it was good" but may not provide the why or how it was good— encourage them to do so. Students can also consider Barbara Bush's inclusive language and delivery in this clip.

3. **Video Clip 3: President Bush's Address to the Nation on October 7, 2002**
   As you watch President Bush's speech, consider his speech's purpose and main points. How did he connect or relate main points? What evidence did he provide to support his main points? Also consider his delivery. Did it suit the content of his speech?

   This activity works well as an in-class assignment and a review of the material introduced in Chapter 2 and a preview of Chapter 4 (Speech Topics and Purposes). Place students in groups of 3-4 and use the handout appearing at the end of this chapter to give to students to follow along as they watch the video clip. Have them then work together responding to the questions above. After giving students about 20 minutes in class, have them discuss their observations with the class as a whole. This activity may run over to the next class day given the time it will take to show the video, the group work time, and the discussion time.

Additional Exercises and Resources

1. **"Irritating Listening Habits" Activity.**
   This is a role-play activity in which you place students into groups of four. Using the **10 Irritating Listening Habits** list from Web Link Activity 2.1, write the irritating habits on index cards. These will serve as instructions for students role playing as members of the audience. On other index cards, list the principles of effective listening from this chapter. Finally, you will want to have four speaker index cards, instructing the students who will role play the speaker to practice effective listening skills. Tell students not to reveal their instructions to each other. Distribute the cards among the groups and then give the groups about 5-8 minutes to role play. Have a discussion afterwards about students' reactions to each other and strategies they used, or could have used, to be more effective listeners. The following are examples of information you can have on each card (keeping in mind you can create your own instructions as you deem appropriate).

   <u>Index card #1: The Speaker</u>
   Begin to speak to your group about a topic that is important to you. Remember to use the strategies outlined in chapter 3 about how to listen effectively as a speaker. Those strategies include: paying attention to the introduction and main points; managing a distracted audience by asking questions or assigning a quick activity; explaining any distractions that may result from your own accent or unusual style of dress; explaining unusual terms or unfamiliar language or subject matter; acknowledging that there will be a question and answer session at the end of the speech.

   <u>Index Card #2: Audience member</u>
   As the speaker presents information do the following: interrupt the speaker, rush the speaker as if they are wasting your time, get ahead of the speaker and finish his or her thoughts.

   <u>Index Card #3: Audience member</u>
   As the speaker presents information do the following: do not look at the speaker, show interest in something other than the conversation, do not respond to the speaker's request.

   <u>Index Card #4: Audience member</u>
   As the speaker presents information listen effectively, critically and ethically. Be sure to also confirm the speaker when appropriate.

2. **Listening Styles Activity.**
   Place students into groups of 3-4. Give each group a listening style (experiential, auditory, and visual) and a topic (they can make one up or you can select one that is relevant to the public dialogue). You can also put this information on index cards to hand out to students. Ask each group to generate ideas for how they would present that topic to someone with that specific listening style. Have the groups share their ideas with the class, without revealing which listening style they were given. Have the class guess which listening style the group was assigned. Lead a discussion about which ideas were most effective and how ideas can be improved.

31

3. **Gender-Neutral Language**

Without introducing the topic of gender-neutral language, start this component of the lecture with the following scenario: *"A father and son are in a serious car accident. The son is rushed to the emergency room. The doctor looks at the son and states 'I can't operate . . . this is my son.' . . . Who's the doctor?"* Now it may seem very obvious that the doctor is in fact the mother; however, this scenario still keeps many students guessing because doctors are still often portrayed as men. This can provide an interesting entry into a discussion about gender-neutral language and the roles we assign to people based upon their gender. Also emphasize to students that this becomes a very important issue when they are adapting to a diverse audience. See also Chapter 4 "Your Audience and Speaking Environment" of this manual for additional exercises related to diverse audiences.

4. **Guidelines for Listening Critically**

At the end of this section you will find a handout "Guidelines for Listening Critically." This handout is a modified version of Table 2.3 in the textbook. Using the InfoTrac College Edition, access an article you believe will be helpful for students. Have them access the article as well, or make a copy for them before class. Place them into small groups and have them discuss the article, and practice listening (in this case "reading") critically by using the strategies on the handout. Conclude with a discussion in class about each group's findings.

5. **Un-cluttering the "Colors" Outline**

Give students a copy of the outline of the introduction for the speech "Colors" appearing at the end of this section. Ask students to un-clutter the introduction to this speech. You can have students hand write their changes or retype the introduction before they come to class. Discuss their changes and the strengths and weaknesses of their revisions. Students often will take out less of the clutter than the instructor will, so set aside enough time to discuss your own editing changes and the reasons you might take out more clutter than the students. Another activity working with this outline is included in Chapter 8.

Guidelines for Critical Listening

The following are guidelines for critical listening that you can use when you are an audience member and when you are conducting research for your speeches. See your textbook, Table 2.3, for additional guidelines when engaged in this process.

1. *Are all major arguments developed fully?*

   o Do not present argument without explanation and development.
   o Do not exaggerate arguments or understate their importance.
   o Support major ideas with evidence (examples, statistics, testimony).

2. *Are all major and supporting claims made with credible sources that are as unbiased as possible?*

   o Cite sources for all new information (including who said it, where it was found, when it was found).
   o Verify the credibility of the source if you do not know their credentials (check personally owned websites, for example).

3. *Are the claims realistic and logical and does the speaker acknowledge different perspectives?*

   o Solution claims must clearly show that the solution will work.
   o Cause and effect claims must show that the relationship exists.
   o When presenting a position, do not present your position as absolute or the only one possible.

4. *When speakers make claims that go against your personal experience have you tried to discover why?*

   o Is the difference a result of cultural differences?
   o Is the difference a result of the speaker's research?
   o Are you open to different views of the world?
   o Can you assess the speaker's evidence and reason objectively?
   o Before rejecting the speaker's claims, can you engage the speaker in a civil discussion to find out why your perspectives differ?

5. *Does the argument benefit the speaker more than anyone else?*

   o Identify the speaker's motives in order to understand why they are making particular claims.
   o Consider the impact of the speaker's argument on others.

33

Un-cluttering Exercise

Un-clutter the following introduction for the speech "How Colors Affect Our Lives." If you have read or discussed Chapter 8 (Organizing and Outlining Your Speech), make sure to follow the guidelines for appropriate outline format.

How Colors Affect Our Lives

Introduction

I.   Picture this, it's like a bright yellow fireball into orange and then red. Absolutely fascinating, don't you think?

      A.   In the background electric pink, purple, and white clouds roaming about. All of the magnificent colors swirling together and like slowly slipping behind the indigo mountains; completing yet another beautiful sunset. This sight is just so incredible, you cannot believe just how majestically beautiful the array of colors appear on the backdrop of our sky, you know?

      B.   Seeing colors is definitely like one of the most positive aspects of seeing at all. It is like totally and absolutely fascinating!

II.   My name is Shannon, and I am like here to share with you one of most favorite like hobbies of all time: deciphering how colors affect us all and what not.

      1.   I have researched a lot for this speech. I read like six different books by Faber Birren, Manlio Brusatin, Linda Clark, Leatrice Eiseman, Dorothee Mella and Enid Verity.

            a.   These were all extremely helpful books, okay.

            b.   You would find these books a like totally easy to read, full of like a ton of very valuable and interesting information that relates to just about everyone, even if you think it would not relate to you, you know.

III.   In my speech today, I am going to cover like two main points, okay.

      A.   I will first talk to you about how colors affect our minds and bodies, and what not.

            1.   You may not think that colors affect our minds, but like they totally have an incredible impact on our minds and stuff.

            2.   Colors really affect how we feel inside and what not.

      B.   I am secondly going to talk to you about how colors affect our environment and stuff.

            1.   It is like totally interesting how colors can like affect our environment, you know.

            2.   Just like take a look around our classroom right now, do you notice how color in this situation can affect our environment and stuff. It is absolutely fascinating the power that color has on us, you know.

Supplemental Bibliography

Borisoff, Deborah, and Purdy, Michael. (eds). <u>Listening in Everyday Life: A Personal and Professional Approach</u>. Lanham, MD: University Press of America, 1991.

> This is a comprehensive book on the subject of listening. It includes gender issues in listening, intercultural listening, aspects of listening training, and examples of listening in professional settings.

Borisoff, Deborah, and Merrill, Lisa. <u>The Power to Communicate: Gender Differences as Barriers.</u> Prospect Heights, Ill.: Waveland Press, 1998.

> For an excellent discussion of how gender differences can impact communication, including listening, see this interesting text.

Burley-Allen, Madelyn. <u>Listening: The Forgotten Skill (A Self Teaching Guide).</u> New York: John Willey & Sons, 1995.

> Burley-Allen offers a general book focusing on how to improve personal listening skills. She asks the reader to assess their listening past, barriers to listening well, and offers suggestions for making improvements in personal listening style.

Eadie, William F. "Hearing What We Ought to Hear—The Responsibility." *Vital Speeches of the Day,* 55 (Jul 15, 1989): 587-588.

> Eadie discusses how listening attentively is an important part of participating in a democratic society. This is an interesting resource because it is both a speech and a resource for teaching listening.

Kratz, Dennis M., <u>Effective Listening Skills</u>, Irwin Professional Publishing, 2005.

> Covers the essential listening skills everyone needs to succeed in business including a basic understanding of the communication process, giving and receiving feedback, screening out distractions, listening critically for information and evidence, a

Luke, Robert A Jr. "Improving Your Listening Ability" *Supervisory Management*, 37 (Jun 1992): 7.

> This brief article addresses working professionals with eight questions and suggestions for improving listening skills.

Nichols, Michael P. <u>The Lost Art of Listening</u>. New York: Guilford Press, 1995.

> This excellent book on listening offers wonderful lecture material on the importance of listening, barriers encountered in listening, and ways to improve listening skills. Written for working professionals, this book describes the ten habits of non-productive listeners. It also addresses the benefits of listening such as higher self-esteem, professional and economic benefits, and

interpersonal benefits not usually included in the discussion of why listening is important. These concepts may make the subject more relevant to students and add to a lecture on listening.

Purdy, Michael, http://www.ruderfinn.com/blogs/ethics/2010/01/listening.html Ethics Blog

This University Professor of Communication Studies, at Governor's State University IL, blogs about his belief that listening is a social behavior and therefore falls under the umbrella of ethics. Robertson, Arthur K. *Listen For Success: A Guide to Effective Listening.* Burr Ridge, Ill.: Irwin Professional Publishers, 1994.

Wolff, Florence I. Perceptive Listening. Fort Worth, Tex: Harcourt Brace Jovanovich, 1992.

Wolff offers many interesting ways of discussing listening including "ten axioms about listening," "five power tools of listening," and "three basic concepts to enhance listening comprehension." These lists could help add new energy to lectures and activities about the subject.

Wolvin, Andrew D. and Gwynn Coakley, Carolyn. "A Survey of the Status of Listening Training in Some Fortune 500 Corporations" *Communication Education,* 40 (Apr 1991): 152-164.

For proof that listening is important to future success, this survey found that 59% of Fortune 500 Corporations provide listening training. The article then goes on to describe the types of training being offered.

Zimmerman, Jack and Virginia Coyle. "Council: Reviving the Art of Listening" *Utne Reader*, 44 (Mar 1991): 79-85.

This is an extremely interesting article about how to really listen using the "council process" which comes from Native American tradition. This underlying model moves toward understanding one another rather than establishing hierarchy or dominance.

Chapter Three:
Developing Your Speech Topic and Purpose

Chapter Goals

Chapter Three teaches students how to select topics, narrow their speaking purposes, and write clear thesis statements. As students reach the end of this chapter they should have an understanding of the following goals:

- To identify how context influences speaking goals
- To choose a speech topic whether deciding to speak, being asked to speak, or being required to speak
- To develop clear statements of purpose for a speech
- To develop the thesis statement of a speech

Chapter Outline

I. **How context influences our speaking goals** (pg. 43).
  a. There are several contexts in which we speak publicly.
    i. **Deciding to speak** is the most common reason because we find an issue so important or our experience so relevant that we decide to speak about it.
      1. Before the advent of television, people spoke in churches and town halls, at street corners, and in town squares or centers, and on soapboxes.
        a. In the USA, legislation prevented certain people, like women, to speak publicly until the 1850s.
      2. In educational settings, we give class presentations and participate in student government.
      3. In social gatherings, we offer toasts and congratulations to others.
      4. In community forums, we speak about the environment, population growth, education, and the like.
      5. When people decide to speak, they generally speak about issues central to their lives and well-being.
      6. To decide to speak publicly is to decide you can offer an audience important knowledge or a valuable perspective.
    ii. **Being asked to speak,** the most flattering, occurs when we are asked to share a part of ourselves with others (pg. 43 - 44).
      1. We share our important experiences, our expertise, or our perspectives with others.
      2. We are recognized as experts or at least as someone who has information others want.
    iii. **Being required to speak** can be a regular part of our lives (pg. 44).
      1. You may be required to take a public speaking class.
      2. You may be required to speak in jobs such as marketing or as a tour guide.

3. You may be required to speak to fulfill a civic or legal obligation.
   a. You often must follow strict guidelines.
      i. At work, you may have a specified time and specified speaking goal when giving a presentation at a meeting.
      ii. In a public speaking class, you will be asked to fulfill specific requirements for each given speech assignment.

II. **Choosing your speech topic** (pg. 44).
   a. **A speech topic** *is the subject of the speech* (pg. 44).
      i. With a little systematic thought and inventive organization, speakers often come up with a wide range of interesting speech topics.
      ii. It is important to select a speech topic that is both interesting to the speaker and to the audience.
   b. It is important to consider the different contexts when selecting a speech topic.
      i. **The classroom setting** (pg. 45).
         1. Assigned speeches usually have several constraints because they are given in a classroom setting.
            a. Instructors will give students a *pre-selected purpose*.
               i. You do not have the freedom to select a speech purpose.
               ii. You must select a topic compatible with the purpose.
            b. *Time limits* will be determined by class size.
               i. All students need to have time to give their speeches.
               ii. You may be penalized for going over time.
               iii. You must select and narrow your topic to satisfy the assignment's time limits.
            c. It will be a *highly structured assignment*.
               i. You will be asked to incorporate several specific speech components.
               ii. You will be required to cite a specific number of sources, depending on the speech.
               iii. You will be required to incorporate visual aids, a specific style of language, or use a particular pattern of organization.
            d. The *instructor as* a member of the *audience*.
               i. You will give your speech to an instructor, who is a skilled public speaker.
               ii. You should select a stimulating topic that the instructor will appreciate.
            e. *Class members as an audience*.
               i. They will appreciate your hard efforts because you are all in the same boat.
               ii. They can be a challenge when they want to hear topics the instructor is not interested in hearing.
               iii. Try to avoid commonly used topics.
      ii. **Choosing your topic when you are required to speak** (pg. 45).
         1. Make a list of your interests and give a speech about one of them.
         2. There are several other steps you can take in selecting your speech topic.
            a. Outline the requirements of the speech assignment.
            b. Match your interests to the requirements (pg. 46).
            c. Match your expertise to a speech assignment (pg. 47).

38

      d. **Brainstorming** *is the process of generating ideas randomly and uncritically, without attention to logic, connections, or relevance* (pg. 49).

          i. There are a few **tips for successful brainstorming** (pg. 49).

              1. Let your thoughts go where they will.

              2. Write your ideas down quickly.

              3. Keep your list handy over the course of several days and add to it as new thoughts come to you.

          ii. There are several ways to brainstorm.

              1. *Brainstorming by free association* can occur when sitting at a desk with a pencil and paper, or at the computer and recording all ideas that come to mind (pg. 49).

              2. *Brainstorming by clustering* is a visual brainstorm where you write an idea in the center of the paper, and draw four to five lines extending from it (pg. 50).

              3. *Brainstorming by categories* involves listing several categories and then listing five or six different words under each that fit into the given category (pg. 50).

              4. *Brainstorming and technology* can be used in a few different ways to find a suitable speech topic (pg. 51).

          iii. **Narrowing your topic when you are asked or decide to speak** (pg. 52).

              1. You want to be sure you clearly understand what the topic is and what is expected of you as a speaker.

              2. Ask yourself the following questions to help you with clarity of focus:

                  a. What *exactly* is the topic of the speech?

                  b. Can I discuss the topic in the time allowed?

                  c. Who is my audience?

III. **Articulating your purpose** (pg. 52).

    a. **The general speaking purposes** *of a speech is its' broad goal* (pg. 52).

      i. The broad goal can be to inform, to invite, and to persuade, or to introduce, commemorate, and accept.

    b. **Specific speaking purposes** *are focused statements that identify exactly what a speaker wants to accomplish with a speech* (pg. 53).

      i. They help speakers narrow the focus of their speech.

      ii. The specific speaking purpose states exactly what you want to accomplish in the speech.

      iii. They indicate what you want your audience to understand or do as a result of your speech, or **behavioral objectives** (pg. 55).

      iv. There a few tips for writing specific speaking purposes effectively.

          1. *State your specific speaking purpose clearly* (pg. 55).

              a. Begin the specific-purpose statements with the infinitive phrases *to inform, to invite, to persuade, to introduce, to commemorate, and to accept.*

              b. The specific speaking purpose should clearly phrase the general purpose and what the speaker hopes to accomplish in his or her speech.

          2. *Keep your audience in the forefront of your mind* (pg. 56).

              a. The specific speaking purpose should clearly reflect the presence of an audience.

b. The specific speaking purpose statement should include the words "*my audience.*"

IV. **Stating your thesis** (pg. 57).

    a. **A thesis statement** *is a statement that summarizes in a single declarative sentence the main ideas, assumptions, or arguments a speaker wants expressed in their speech* (pg. 57).

        i. It is sometimes called a *central idea.*

        ii. It adds focus to the specific purpose because a speaker states, in a single sentence, the exact content of the speech.

        iii. In the thesis statement, a speaker identifies the main ideas of the speech, which become the main points.

        iv. The thesis statement and main points guide speakers in several ways.

            1. They guide your research efforts and selection of supporting materials.

            2. They guide the reasoning in the speech.

            3. They guide the organizational pattern of a speech.

        v. Some instructors like to divide the thesis statement into two sentences:

            1. One that states the thesis (main idea).

            2. The second that lists the main points of the speech (preview).

End of the Chapter Activities and Discussion Questions

The following questions can also be found at the end of Chapter Three in *Invitation to Public Speaking.*

Review Questions and Activities

1. Use the strategies suggested in this chapter to make a list of four different speech topics you might like to speak about. How do you think the classroom setting would affect what you would say about these topics? What would you do to make these topics suitable for a classroom setting?

    This activity can be conducted in class in small groups. Direct students to make their lists and then discuss class reactions to those topics. After giving students time to discuss their perspectives, have the groups report back to the class. This activity should not take a whole class period, but can add to the discussion about the importance of appropriate topic selection.

2. Rewrite the following incorrect specific-purpose statements so that they are correct:

To give 10 percent of your annual income to charity
Barack Obama
Olympic gold medals
Natural disasters
Isn't the level of water pollution in our local river too high?

Students are often challenged by wording specific purpose statements correctly. Use this as a small group activity to give students the opportunity to practice writing specific purpose statements. Place students into small groups of 3-4. If they do not have their books with them, place these incorrect statements on a handout, on a whiteboard or chalkboard, an overhead, or PowerPoint slide. Have each group change these statements into correct specific purpose statements. Give them about 20 minutes, then, have each group share with the class how they reworded these specific purpose statements. If you are teaching this course online, have students post their results. Remind students that they should choose the speaking goal for each of these speeches as they see fit.

3. Make a list of speech topics you might decide to speak about. For each topic, identify why you've decided to speak and who your audience would be. How might your reasons for speaking and your audience affect what you say about your topics? Write a general-purpose and a specific-purpose statement for at least one of these topics. Is this a speech you might give in your speech course? Why or why not?

   You can have students address this question in class in small groups. Or, you can assign this activity as homework and ask them to come to class prepared to share their results with small groups. Have the groups give each other feedback about the appropriateness of the topic, and how well they narrowed down their focus as they wrote their general purpose and specific purpose statements. Let students know that they can turn the ideas from this assignment into one of their first speech assignments, depending on the requirements of the assignment.

4. Practice writing a general and a specific statement of purpose for a speech on each of the following topics: teen violence, mandatory military service, terrorism, bilingual education. Now write a thesis statement for each of these possible speeches and identify the main points for each. Could you choose one of these possible speeches for your next speech? Why or why not?

   *This is can be a very effective small group activity. Place students into small groups. If they do not have their books with them, place these topics on a handout, on the smartboard, chalkboard, or an overhead, or on a PowerPoint slide. Have each group follow the instructions indicated here. Give them about 20 minutes or so to complete the activity. Then, have each group share their results with the class. Phrasing general and specific purpose statements often challenges students. They are also challenged by phrasing thesis statements and determining main points in speeches. This activity can serve as a good review, as well as practice for developing these skills. If you are teaching this course online, have students post their results. Lastly, remind students that they can also choose the speaking goal for each of these speeches as they see fit. **NOTE:** At the end of this chapter you will find a handout that you can give to students to determine topic, general purpose, specific purpose statement, and thesis statement. An explanation also appears in the "Additional Exercises and Resources" section of this chapter.*

5. Check out Speech Studio to see speeches about various topics—do any of them give you ideas for your own speech topics? Or record a speech you're working on, upload it to Speech Studio, and ask your peers for their feedback. What feedback could you use to fine tune your topic before you give your speech in class?

Web Activities

1. **Brainstorming with Technology**
   Purpose: To explore brainstorming with technology
   Directions: To brainstorm topics for your speech, go to the Yahoo website at http://www.yahoo.com. Choose a general category and click on it. Continue clicking on links until you find one that is relatively specific. Did this method help you find a speech topic that you hadn't known about before you started clicking on links? Try this exercise again, this time starting with a different general category. Would some topics you found work better for different types of speeches?

   Although many students are computer literate, most students need a lot of encouragement to access these websites, particularly students who claim they are not computer literate. If you are able to illustrate the ease at which this information can be accessed in the classroom, the more confident and comfortable students will feel. Also, during office hours, access these sites with students to show them that it is fairly easy.

2. **Identifying Thesis Statements**
   Purpose: To identify and evaluate thesis statements
   Directions: Go to the Opinion-Pages website at http://www.headlinespot.com/opinion/oped/
   Read several editorials or letters to the editor. For at least three that you read, identify its specific statement purpose and thesis statement. How effective is each statement in identifying the main points of the writer's argument? Is the thesis statement more specific than the specific statement of purpose?

   This can be a great activity to do in small groups or with partners. Have students read this assignment, and then have them access editorials or letters to the editor before coming to class. Let students know that they will need to print out the information they access. When they come to class, have them share with their group or partners what they discovered. Provide some time for students to discuss their ideas with the class as a whole. Have students talk about the importance of clear thesis statements, and what can occur if thesis statements are not clear. If you are teaching in a learning community with a composition class, this activity can also be very helpful.

InfoTrac College Edition Activities

1. **InfoTrac Activity 3.1: Speaking Publicly**
   Purpose: To understand the constraints and restrictions of various speaking contexts.
   Directions: Use InfoTrac College Edition's PowerTrac to search for three speeches that interest you in *Vital Speeches*. As you read each speech, consider why each person was speaking. Did the speaker decide to speak? Was the speaker asked to speak? Was the speaker required to speak? How did the speaking context constrain what each speaker said? What unique opportunities did each context provide? What was the general purpose of each speech?

   Students are challenged by finding speeches they think are interesting. Prompt students by having them think about politicians with whom they agree or disagree, any celebrities or athletes that may have spoken out on an issue, or events that may have occurred that warranted a speech. Once they have taken this first step and have found the speeches they are interested in, have them respond to the

42

questions listed above. You can have them turn this in as a homework assignment, and/or discuss in small groups, or select one or two to discuss as a full class. Whether as a homework assignment or small group discussion, give students time to discuss their findings with the class as a whole.

2. **InfoTrac Activity 3.2: Creating the Specific Purpose Statement**
   Purpose: To assess a speaker's specific purpose.
   Directions: Use InfoTrac College Edition to locate the speech "Realize Your Dreams" by Barry L. Ray, *Vital Speeches,* August 15, 2001, p. 671. Students can also locate any other speeches that are included in InfoTrac. What is the speaker's specific purpose statement? How clearly is the speaking goal stated? Does the statement keep the audience in the forefront of the speaker's mind? Does the statement use definitive, complete sentences?

   Have students access this article before class and respond to the questions listed here, writing out the answers on a sheet of paper. Encourage students to bring the speech to class on the day you will discuss this activity. During class have students share their findings with the class as you facilitate the discussion. Be sure to ask for specific examples and for specific suggestions for improving the answers the students bring to class.

Interactive Student and Professional Speech Videos

1. **Video Clip 1: President Bush's Speech on September 11, 2001**
   Did President Bush decide to speak after the attacks on New York City and Washington, D.C., on September 11, 2001? Was he asked to speak? Was he required to speak? What were the expectations of his audience on this occasion? To what degree do you think Bush fulfilled those expectations?

   You can address the first few questions listed here before showing the video. Or, have students see the video clip before they come to class, and then come to class prepared to address all of these questions. You can also show the video clip in class, and have students respond to the questions. The best format to address these questions will be in an open class discussion. Note: many students may say that Bush decided to speak. You may also encourage them to explore the reasons he actually was required to speak, explaining that as the president of the United States, he is required to speak when events such as the attacks of September 11 occur.

2. **Video Clip 2: Rebecca Ewing "The Case for Graduated Licensing"**
   As you watch this video clip, listen to the effectiveness of her thesis statement.

   In this video clip Rebecca does a nice job in capturing attention, which then leads her into a clearly developed thesis statement for a persuasive speech. Have students watch the clip and discuss the merits of her first few objectives in the introduction lead well into her thesis statement.

3. **Video Clip 3: Jesse Rosser "Preventing School Violence"**
   As you watch this clip of a speech introduction, listen carefully to how Jesse develops his thesis statement. Is it effective? Why or why not? How will this example help you to develop your own thesis statements, especially for a persuasive speech?

   Have students pay close attention to how Jesse builds into his thesis statement. Emphasize to students the importance of accomplishing the objectives in the introduction of their speech leading into a clearly stated thesis.

43

4. **Video Clip 4: Ogenna Agbim "This is Dedicated: A Tribute to Women in History"**
As you watch this video clip of a speech delivered by Ogeena Agbim, consider how her passion for her topic helps to facilitate her delivery in a commemorative speech.

Students often lose sight of how passion for a topic can contribute immensely to their delivery. Have students watch this speech and discuss how Ogenna's delivery brings her topic to life.

Additional Exercises and Resources

1. **Matching Interests to a Speaking Assignment**
Students will often approach instructors for topic ideas. They often are challenged by topic selection, and will say that they have "nothing important to talk about." As we know, students usually do have something important to say, it's just a matter of helping them identify those topics. Included at the end of this chapter is a handout to help students match their interests to the speech assignment. Photocopy the handout for your students. As they are preparing for their speeches, encourage students who are "stuck" to use the handout.

2. **Matching Expertise to a Speaking Assignment**
Students will often feel that they are not really experts in any area. Give them some examples that may help in showing them they can be experts in certain areas. For instance, if students work retail they may be experts in customer service, and in knowing the ins and outs of certain products. If some students work in restaurants, they may be experts in matching the perfect wine with the perfect meal. If some students are avid hikers or spend a lot of time in the outdoors they may be experts in setting up camp, or knowing the perfect places to camp and hike, or they may know about the history of certain national parks. Many students live on a very tight budget, so they might be experts in budgeting or money management. These ideas, along with the handout at the end of this chapter, can help students to match their expertise to a speaking assignment. Photocopy the handout, and encourage students to use it as they are preparing their speeches.

3. **A Checklist: When you are Asked or Decide to Speak**
At the end of this chapter, you will find a handout to use for this activity. As students prepare their speeches, they may be interested in this checklist to make sure they follow the different tips provided in the textbook. They can use this checklist individually or in groups, but make sure they turn in the checklists so that you can be sure everyone is following the suggestions correctly.

4. **What is the Specific Purpose Statement?**
The more practice students can get phrasing specific purposes and thesis statements, the easier it will be for students to write them on their outlines. Using the handout at the end of this chapter, place students in small groups and have them generate specific purpose statements and thesis statements from the speech topics listed on the handout (you can also do this with the class as a whole). Another option is to have students bring in either of the handouts, "Matching Interests to the Speaking Assignment" or "Matching Expertise to the Speaking Assignment" and, in small groups, help one another generate possible topics, specific purpose statements, and thesis statements. Any of these activities will give them practice in narrowing focus and having the ability to word these statements effectively.

5. **Handout: Selecting a Topic and Identifying the General Purpose, Specific Purpose, and Thesis Statement**

It can be challenging for students to select and then narrow their speech topics, and then to identify their general and specific purposes as well as their thesis statements. Use the handout provided in this chapter to help students in this process. Have students fill this out and turn in this information when beginning to prepare their speeches (you can have them do this for each speech assignment). Provide them feedback on the handout about the appropriateness of topic, and how well they are narrowing their focus for their speech. Students find this feedback quite helpful. They will, of course, need to turn this in well in advance of their speech due-date in order to make changes as needed. Having students consider two topics is especially helpful in case their first choice does not match the assignment requirements. Be sure to give feedback to students on the wording of each of these components (general purpose, specific purpose, thesis statement). Part of what will help them understand these concepts is ensuring that they have the phrasing correct.

Matching Your Interests to a Speaking Assignment

Use this chart to help you match your interests to a speaking assignment.

I like to	*I like to talk about*	*I would like to learn more about*
Possible topics	Possible topics	Possible topics

Matching Your Expertise to a Speaking Assignment

Use this chart to help you match your expertise to a speaking assignment.

I have these special skills	*I have witnessed the following events*	*I have received the following training*
Possible topics	Possible topics	Possible topics

A Checklist:
When you are Asked or Decide to Speak

This handout is a basic checklist to assist you in fine-tuning your focus in a speech when you are asked or decide to speak. Make sure that you can answer each of the questions clearly.

1. **About the Topic**

   If you have decided to speak, do you know what *specific* topic you want to talk about?

   If you have been asked to speak, do you know the *specific* topic your audience wants to hear about?

2. **About the Time Constraints**

   Can you discuss the topic in the time allowed, or do you need to narrow or broaden your scope?

   Is there some aspect of the topic that you may be better able to cover in the time allowed?

3. **About the Audience**

   Who is your audience?

   What is your relationship to them?

   If you have decided to speak, why are you qualified to speak about the topic?

   Will your audience see you as qualified? If not, could you change the topic or strengthen your qualifications in some way?

   If you have been asked to speak, why are you qualified to speak about this topic?

Specific Purposes

Listed below are some general speech topics. Practice writing specific purpose and thesis statements for these topics using the tips provided in your textbook. Note that before you write the specific purpose statement, you will also need to decide on a general purpose.

1. **Topic:** *Housing*

   General Purpose:

   Specific Purpose:

   Thesis Statement:

2. **Topic:** *Travel*

   General Purpose:

   Specific Purpose:

   Thesis Statement:

3. **Topic:** *Careers*

   General Purpose:

   Specific Purpose:

   Thesis Statement:

4. **Topic:** *Financial Aid*

   General Purpose:

   Specific Purpose:

   Thesis Statement:

Topic Choices

Name _____

Refer to Chapter 3 of your text to help you write the following statements.

Topic Choice #1

Topic:

General Purpose:

Specific Purpose:

Thesis Statement:

Main Points:

Topic Choice #2

Topic:

General Purpose:

Specific Purpose:

Thesis statement:

Main Points:

Supplemental Bibliography

Brake, Mike. "9 Steps to Effective Speech-Writing." *Writer's Digest*, 79 (Jul 1999): 40-43.

> Brake emphasizes the importance of identifying the central idea. This short article is useful as a handout or as a resource for your lectures.

Boyd, Stephen D., and Mary Ann Renz. Organization and Outlining: A Workbook for Students in a Basic Speech Course. New York: Macmillan, 1985.

> This workbook begins with exercises for formulating the "focus points" of the speech including the general purpose and the thesis statement.

Dowis, Richard. The Lost Art of the Great Speech: How to Write It, How to Deliver It. New York: AMACOM, 2000.

> Chapters two and three cover the preparation stages of speech writing and offer historical examples. Overall this book is interesting and helpful for almost any aspect of speech preparation.

Lamm, Kathryn. 10,000 Ideas for Term Papers, Projects, Reports and Speeches. New York: Macmillan, 1998.

> When students are convinced they cannot find a topic for their speech, this book can help. It offers over 400 pages of topic suggestions on a wide variety of subjects from sculpture to psychology to foreign policy.

Meriwether, Nell. 12 Easy Steps to Successful Research Papers. Lincolnwood, Ill.: NTC Publishing Group, 1997.

> This handbook takes students through the writing process. Step two "narrowing the subject into a manageable topic" and step six "forming a thesis" are particularly applicable here.

Michalko, Michael. Cracking Creativity: The Secrets of Creative Genius. Berkeley, CA: Ten Speed Press, 2001.

> Students often say that they cannot think of anything they are interested in enough to write a speech about. This book offers suggestions for ways to help students brainstorm and think about new and creative things in which they have an interest.

Rowna, Katherine E. "A New Pedagogy for Explanatory Speaking: Why Arrangement Should Not Substitute for Invention." *Communication Education*, 44 (1995), 236-250.

> This article stresses the importance of the invention process in informative speaking in that careful work during the invention stage can help eliminate potential obstacles to audience comprehension of the message.

Winkler, Anthony C., and Jo Ray McCuen. Writing the Research Paper: A Handbook with Both the MLA and APA Documentation Styles. Publisher Fort Worth, TX: Harcourt Brace College Publishers, 1999.

In this helpful handbook, Chapter 2 covers selecting a topic while Chapter 4 covers developing the thesis.

ProSpeakingPower.com. How to prepare for public speaking with brainstorming: http://www.prospeakingpower.com/how_to_prepare_for_public_speaking_with_brainstorming. Php.

This Free Information Guide promises to Answer All Your Questions About How To Become A Professional Speaker.

Chapter Four: Your Audience and Speaking Environment

Chapter Goals

Chapter four introduces students to the elements involved in adapting their speeches to diverse audiences. Students will also understand the different components that comprise the speaking environment.   At the end of the chapter, students should understand the following:

- To Define what an audience is
- To conduct a demographic audience analysis
- To adapt to an audience that is both a group of diverse people and a unique community
- To Identify the influence of a speaking environment on an audience
- To identify strategies for adapting to audience expectations for a speech

Chapter Outline

I. **When you give a speech, you add your voice to the public dialogue** (pg. 65).
   a. To engage in a **dialogue** *is to interact, to connect, and to exchange information with other people.*
      i. When you engage in a ***public dialogue*** *you recognize that the speaker and the audience are equally important, that both have opinions, feelings, and beliefs.*
      ii. To be a successful speaker, one must acknowledge these realities and listen carefully to the audience before, during, and after the speech.
   b. To be **audience centered** *is to acknowledge your audience by listening to the unique, diverse, and common perspectives of its members before, during, and after the speech.*
      i. This does not mean that speakers say only what the audience agrees with or wants to hear.
      ii. Audience centered speakers understand the positions and perspectives of the audience so they can craft a listenable message.
II. **What is an audience?** (pg. 66).
   a. **Audience** *is a complex and varied group of people the speaker addresses.*
      i. Audiences are far more complex than the definition suggests.
      ii. Modern audiences are composed of a diverse group of people exposed to endless messages from the media, their workplaces, their families and friends, and many other sources.
   b. **Considering an audience as a group of diverse people** (pg. 66).
      i. People are unique because of a combination of culture, upbringing, experiences, personality, and even genetics.
      ii. Consider how audiences view the world by analyzing the following:
         1. **Masters statuses** *are significant positions a person occupies within society that affect the person's identity in almost all social situations.*
            a. A person's master status might include race or ethnicity, gender, physical ability, sexual orientation, age, economic standing, religion or spirituality, and educational level.

    b. They could include positions in society like being a parent, child, or sibling, or being employed or unemployed.

    c. A status is *master* when it profoundly influences a person's identity as well as the way in which he or she is perceived by others.

          i. Whether we intend to or not, we often respond to other people based on one or more master statuses.

         ii. For example, teenagers with rumpled and baggy clothes are often treated differently in a grocery store than are neatly dressed women in their 30s who have children.

    d. Master statuses affect our view of the world because we make judgments based on them, and hence, we see some as more valuable.

          i. U.S. American tends to rank whiteness, heterosexuality, and masculinity higher than color, homosexuality, and femininity.

             1. Because the first three are considered more valuable, and are generally rewarded with higher salaries, more acceptance, and protections, and more personal freedom.

             2. The last three on average are given lower salaries, less acceptance, fewer protections, and greater threats to physical safety.

c. **Standpoints, attitudes, beliefs and values** (pg. 68).

    i. **Standpoint** *is the perspectives from which a person views and evaluates society.*

        1. Members of an audience will have different standpoints, or views of the world.

        2. Audience members will have different master statuses and thus different experiences.

          a. Teenagers often see life as unfairly biased against them.

          b. Mothers often see the world as expecting them and their children to behave perfectly in all situations.

          c. Although master statuses can have a powerful influence on a person's view of the world, master statuses do not determine a person's standpoint.

             i. Not all women believe they need to have children to fully experience womanhood.

            ii. Not all men believe their masculinity is weakened if they are not the primary breadwinners for their families.

        3. Our standpoints are influenced by our culture and in turn, influence our attitudes, beliefs, and values.

    ii. An **attitude** *is a general positive or negative feeling a person has about something.*

        1. Attitudes reflect our likes and dislikes of events, people, or ideas.

        2. Attitudes reflect our approval or disapproval of events, people or ideas.

    iii. A **belief** *is a person's idea of what is real or true or not.*

        1. Beliefs are more conceptual than attitudes.

        2. Beliefs reflect what we think we know about the world.

    iv. A **value** *is a person's idea of what is good, worthy, or important.*

        1. Values reflect what we think is an ideal world or state of being.

        2. Values help us determine whether we think a person, idea, or thing is acceptable in our worldview.

    v. **Ethnocentrism** *is the belief that our own cultural perspectives, norms, and ways of organizing society are superior to others.*

1. We see other cultures as odd, wrong, or deficient because they do not do things the way we do.
2. Speakers who let ethnocentric views come through in speeches run the risk of alienating audiences who do not hold similar views.

d. **Demographic audience analysis** (pg. 69).
   i. A **demographic audience analysis** *is an analysis that identifies the particular population traits of an audience.*
      1. Demographic characteristics include age, country of origin, ethnicity and race, physical ability or disability, family status (parent, child), religion, gender (male or female).
      2. You can ask your audience to fill out a survey that asks about demographic information, attitudes, beliefs, and values.
         a. An **open-ended question** *allows respondents to answer in an unrestricted way.*
            i. An example of an open-ended question might be "What are your reactions to the president's policy on terrorism?"
            ii. Open-ended questions allow the respondent to answer any way they like.
         b. A **closed-ended question** *requires respondents to choose an answer from two or more alternatives.*
            i. Examples of closed-ended questions might be, "Do you support the president's policy on terrorism?" or "On a scale of 1 to 5, with 5 being the highest support, how do you rate the president's policy on terrorism?"
      3. Surveys are good ways to gather information about an audience's beliefs, attitudes, and values. When you construct surveys, follow these guidelines:
         a. Keep your survey short.
         b. Keep your questions short and focused on one idea at a time.
         c. Use clear and simple language.
         d. Keep your own biases out of the survey.
         e. Provide room for respondents to write their comments.
      4. Your goal in analyzing your audience is to give an audience centered speech.
         a. When conducting a demographic audience analysis and considering master statuses, it can be easy to resort to stereotyping.
            i. A **stereotype** *is a broad generalization about an entire group based on limited knowledge or exposure to only certain members of that group.*
            ii. Stereotyping is harmful because we make assumptions based on incomplete information.
            iii. It may seem comforting to predict certain behaviors based on stereotype, but we can usually find many exceptions to any stereotype.
            iv. Speakers need to remember that audiences are a collection of people with unique experiences and personalities.
            v. The speaker also needs to remember that audiences cannot be lumped together into one universal category.

III. **Considering an audience as a community** (pg. 70).
   a. **Voluntary audiences** *find something significant enough to listen to* (pg. 70).
      i. There are several examples of voluntary audiences, including the delegates who attend the Democratic and Republican national conferences every four years, audiences at the Super Bowl victories, audiences gathering to welcome the return of a famous person to their hometown, audiences who gather after tragedies such as the September 11 terrorist attacks or the shootings at Virginia Tech.
      ii. The need to listen unites people with various master statuses and standpoints.
      iii. Voluntary audiences usually have an active interest in your topic.
   b. **Involuntary audiences** *are people who sometimes form an audience because they must* (pg. 71).
      i. Examples of involuntary audiences include students in public speaking courses and employees in mandatory business meetings.
         1. Some involuntary audiences have little or no interest in your topic.
            a. Before giving your speech, discover why your audience is required to attend.
            b. At the beginning of your speech, ask your audience members why they have been asked to listen to you, and address these issues in your speech, if you can.
            c. Confirm the audience if they oppose your topic.
            d. Use **empathy** *by trying to see and understand the world as another person does* (pg. 72).
IV. **Considering your speaking environment** (pg. 73).
   a. The **speaking environment** *or where and when a speaker will speak.*
      i. **Size and physical arrangement** (pg. 73).
         1. Speakers will not be able to change the size of the audience, but can work with the physical setting to create the kind of speaking environment desired.
         2. To stay audience centered with respect to size and place, follow these guidelines:
            a. Consider having the audience stand or sit (in rows, circles, on chairs, or on the floor).
            b. Consider how these decisions will affect your ability to connect with the audience.
            c. Make arrangements to establish a speaking environment ahead of time.
      ii. **Technology** refers to *the tools speakers use to help them deliver their message* (pg. 73 - 74). Students will learn more about presentational aids that rely on technology in chapter 12.
         1. Technology can be as elaborate as a computer and LCD panel, or as simple as a pen and a flip chart.
         2. Technology can also have its drawbacks.
            a. The technology may not function; therefore consider how to present your speech without technology.
            b. To help you to stay audience centered, by keeping your attention focused on delivering your message to your audience in a way that they appreciate.
      iii. Speakers consider **temporal factors,** *issues of time or chronemics, to stay audience centered* (pg. 75).
         1. Speakers should consider the **time of day.**

a. In the morning, audiences tend to be fresher, but they may also be more anxious about the responsibilities they have.
b. At lunchtime, they are hungry and preoccupied with getting some food, or they have just eaten and may be drowsy.
c. In the evening, audiences may be weary and tired from all the work they've done.

2. Speakers should consider **speaking order**.
   a. The first speaker gets the audience when they are fresh, listening more actively, and usually are more willing to process your message.
      i. The first speaker also sets the stage for later speakers.
      ii. He or she also gets to connect with the audience before anyone else does as the audience will sometimes ask more questions of the first speaker.
   b. The last speaker's audience may be tired and weary of processing the information presented by the previous speakers.
      i. The audience may be more inclined to tune out a speaker or leave than to sit and listen to another speech.
      ii. Thus, the last speaker needs to use his or her speech to re-energize the audience and redirect their focus as needed.
   c. Middle speakers have the advantage of a warmed-up crowd, but the disadvantage of an audience that might want to compare information given in their speech with information previously presented.
      i. Thus, engage your audience by making connections to previous speakers.
      ii. Help your audience remember your information by making your own connections to previous speakers.

3. Speakers should consider the **length of the speech**.
   a. Going overtime in a series communicates to an audience that your presentation is more important than the other speakers'.
   b. This can communicate a sense or arrogance, suggesting to an audience that our message is more important than the other speaker's information.
   c. If you are the only speaker, then you may communicate that you do not understand or care about the many demands on an audience's time.
   d. Going over time also can suggest that a speaker is unorganized and cannot prioritize and organize his or her own material.
   e. For more information about time limits students should see chapters 9 and 11.

V. **Adapting to audience expectations** (pg.77).
   a. **Expectations about the speaker**.
      i. Audiences expect the speaker to be competent and credible.
      ii. Acknowledge your own master statuses as a speaker to help your audience understand your perspective.
   b. **Expectations about the form of a speech** (pg. 79).
      i. **Form** *is the creation of an appetite* in the minds of an audience and the *adequate satisfying of that appetite*.
         1. Audiences expect a speech to follow a certain progression of events and those events to progress as they had anticipated.

57

2. Staying audience centered isn't saying only what the audience wants to hear, it is creating an appetite in them to hear what you have to say.

c. **Expectations about speaker-audience discussions** (pg. 80).

    i. Speakers are often expected to make time for question-and-answer sessions at the end of a speech or to manage brainstorming sessions and discussions.

        1. To help you do this, consider why people ask questions.

            a. They want to clarify points.

            b. They want more information about a position you advocated.

            c. They want to satisfy curiosity about an issue or an idea.

            d. They need to identify or establish connections between ideas.

            e. They want to support or challenge ideas presented.

        2. People participate in discussions for many of the same reason they ask questions, but they may also want to restate information to make it clearer, to share a new perspective, or even to dominate the discussion.

        3. In adjusting to audience expectations about discussions, it is helpful to recognize what motivates an audience to attack or challenge a speaker.

            a. When an audience attacks or challenges a speaker it is usually because they doubt the validity of the information or the credibility of the speaker.

            b. When you recognize why the audience challenges you, you are likely to respond appropriately to the challenge.

End of the Chapter Activities and Discussion Questions

The following questions can be found in the *Invitation to Public Speaking* textbook at the end of Chapter Four.

Review Questions and Activities

1. Identify the following statements as true or false:

_____ A dialogue is simply taking turns in a conversation.

_____ When preparing my speech, I need to think more about what I want to say than the background and experiences of my audience.

_____ All cultures and subcultures have the same basic idea of how the world works.

_____ Audiences will interpret my message in just the way I want them to.

_____ To be audience centered, I must say only what the audience wants to hear.

_____ Temporal and situational factors have little effect on my speech.

_____ When I open up my speech for questions or discussion, I lose all control of the flow of communication.

Each of these statements is false. Can you explain why?

Discuss with students each of these questions and the reasons they are false. These questions help students realize that listening to their audience and having an awareness of factors such as culture, setting, etc,. can positively impact their message. During the discussion, try to help students step out of their own frame of reference and acknowledge the diverse perspectives in their audiences. At the end of this chapter, you will find a handout you can give students that includes the above true/false questions. You might have them work in groups answering these questions and identifying key points for a discussion of each question.

2. Consider the times that as an audience member you held a very different standpoint from the other audience members. Consider the times you held a very similar standpoint to other audience members. How did these situations affect your experience? Did the speaker address these differences or similarities? What was the effect of the speaker's actions?

Students can address these questions in class as they are preparing their next speeches. Place students into groups of 3-4. Encourage students to identify strategies that past speakers may have used successfully, and in turn incorporate those same strategies into their own speeches.

3. Discuss with your classmates the differences between voluntary and involuntary audiences. In your public speaking class, you will speak to involuntary audiences. What strategies will you use as a speaker to communicate an audience centered perspective to your audience?

This question can be addressed after lecturing about voluntary and involuntary audiences. Facilitate a discussion with students about strategies they will use to communicate an audience centered perspective, and list them on the board. Students should be able to create a detailed and useful list. Encourage students to provide specific examples. For instance, if one student was considering giving a speech about "abstinence only" being taught in schools, how would the class specifically suggest that student use an audience centered perspective?

4. Imagine you are giving a speech to introduce your audience to rock climbing and to encourage them to take up the sport. Describe how your speech might change for each of the following audiences:

- Thirty sixth graders, voluntarily present
- Thirty corporate executives, asked to attend by their bosses
- Seven pregnant women and their partners, voluntarily present
- Fifteen people over the age of sixty, voluntarily present
- Twelve lower income teenagers who are part of an environmental education program and quite frightened by the prospect of rock climbing
- Your boss at the sporting goods store (you want her to invest more money in supplies for rock climbing)

With your classmates, discuss the changes you would make in your approach, content, and presentation.

Place students into groups of 3-4 and provide each group with one of the above scenarios and have them develop a plan for their specific audience. Encourage students to think of specific examples illustrating how their speech would adapt to each of the audiences above. Have students use specific phrases that would be included in the actual speech they would give for the scenario they were given. You might even have them develop a speech for these scenarios, give the speeches to the class, and then critique one another.

59

5. Consider the room in which your public speaking class is held. Describe the physical setting, options for the placement of speakers, time constraints, and other temporal factors. How is your audience limited or enhanced by these environmental factors? How are *you* limited or enhanced? Identify specific strategies you can use to enhance this environment so your audience is more open to your message and better understands it.

This question can be addressed with the class as a whole after lecturing about the speaking environment. Have students as a group look around the room and generate some ideas. For instance, many classrooms may not have dimmer lights over a podium. This can be challenging when students use PowerPoint because the classroom should not be completely dark, but this is the only option for students if they turn off the lights. Ask students what they would do in this salutation? In some classes, students may use the overhead projector as a "spotlight" to light the room enough to see the audience, and yet not detract from the PowerPoint. NOTE: shining the overhead on the ceiling of the classroom works best so that it is not pointed directly in a speaker's eyes.

6. Do discussions and question-and-answer sessions make you feel nervous? If so, what are your biggest fears regarding these speech elements? Using this chapter as your guide, identify three ways you might ease some of your fears.

If you are incorporating question-and-answer sessions in all speech assignments, have students respond to this question early on in the semester in small groups of 3-4. This question is also appropriate for students to address when they are preparing the invitational speech. Have them identify specific fears rather than general ones and then generate solutions or options for those situations, should they arise.

7. Check out Speech Studio to see how other students acknowledge their audience and speaking environments in their speeches. Or record a speech you're working on, upload it to Speech Studio, and ask your peers for their feedback. What feedback could you use to make your speech more audience centered before you give your speech in class?

Encourage students to work in small groups on this activity.

Web Activities

1. **Learning About Your Audiences**
   Purpose: To learn how to design a survey to give to students in your public speaking class.
   Directions: Although written for media professionals, the online book *Know Your Audience: A Practical Guide to Media Research* at http://www.audiencedialogue.net/kya.html offers excellent advice for creating surveys you might give an audience. Read the first three chapters and create a survey for your class. What did the survey tell you about your class? How will this information influence how you create your speech?

   Some instructor's require students to create surveys, and some leave it up to the student's discretion. For students who are interested in creating a survey for their audience, encourage them to access the above website for tips and options. At times, students like to create surveys for people outside of class or imaginary audiences. Emphasize that the surveys need to be for legitimate groups of people and not just a group of friends who are filling out a survey as a favor.

2. **U.S. Census**
   Visit the website for the U.S. Census at http://www.census.gov, and explore its demographic information. What information on this site might you use in your speech? Of what value is this information to the U.S. government?

   Encourage students to access this website in preparation for their next speech. If you are having a workshop day for students to improve or polish their speeches, have them discuss the demographic information they saw on the website and how they will incorporate the information in their speech. Ask them to get feedback from their groups about the effectiveness of their strategies and share ideas for changes they can make to be even more successful.

3. **Identifying Audiences**
   Purpose: To isolate characteristics of an audience and assess how well speakers adapt to these audiences.
   Directions: Use InfoTrac College Edition's PowerTrac search to find two speeches in *Vital Speeches*. Compare and contrast the audiences for the speeches you locate. How are the audiences similar and how are they different? To what degree does each speaker adjust to the audience?

   You can assign this as a homework assignment or as an assignment in class with a partner. Students may be challenged to determine which speeches to look for. Help them generate ideas by encouraging them to look for speeches made by politicians they admire, or do not admire, athletes they admire, celebrities, etc. On the due date of the assignment, have students share their observations with the class. If you have time, ask students give short presentations about their observations.

4. **Advanced Public Speaking Institute**
   Go to http://www.public-speaking.org/public-speaking-roomsetup-article.htm to read an article about room setup and public speaking. Which of the advice offered in this article is audience centered? Is there any advice in the article that is not audience centered?

   Encourage students to access this website as they practice for their next speech. Some students will be less nervous if they are able to set up the room in a way that is much more comfortable to them. Remind students that not everybody feels comfortable in the same speaking environment. Explore the different possibilities for your own classroom that might make students feel more comfortable when they give or listen to speeches.

InfoTrac College Edition Activities

1. **InfoTrac College Edition Activity 4.1: Being Audience Centered**
   Purpose: To learn how speakers communicate to diverse audiences.
   Directions: Use InfoTrac College Edition to find Don Winkler's speech, "Learning How to Live," in *Vital Speeches* (September 1, 2001), p. 701. In this commencement speech, how did the speaker stay audience centered? Is there something the speaker could have done to be more audience centered?

   This InfoTrac activity is appropriate for a homework assignment. On the due date of the assignment, have students share their observations with the class. Students might not want to be specific, so make sure you have them identify specific strategies used by Winkler. For example, they may answer with

"The speech was very good" or "The speech was not very good . . . I did not like it," but they do not provide the specific reasons they felt the way they did. Encourage students to be very specific about how they would have made changes to be more effective, if they believe the speaker was not effective. If they believe the speaker was quite effective, have them provide specific examples to this effect.

2. **InfoTrac College Edition Activity 4.2: Expectations of a Memorial**
   Purpose: To understand how speakers adapt to their audience's expectations about form.
   Directions: Use InfoTrac College Edition to find Norman Mineta's speech, "Memorial Day," in *Vital Speeches* (August 15, 2001), p. 669. Who does Mineta praise in his speech? Was it appropriate for him to do so? How does the speaker acknowledge the occasion on which he is speaking? Do you think he does so appropriately?

   You can assign this activity as homework. You can also have students work with partners. Ask students to discuss form as "the creation and satisfaction of an appetite in the minds of the audience." Does Mineta actually do this? Why do the students think so, or why not? What specific aspects of form are upheld or violated? Encourage students to provide specific examples from the speech and this chapter in order to support their claims.

Interactive Student and Professional Speech Videos Website

1. **Video Clip 1: Reverend Al Sharpton: 2004 Democratic National Convention**
   Watch this video clip, and consider why going over-time in this speech did not negatively affect Sharpton's speech. In this particular case, consider the important role that a strong delivery and responding to audience feedback play in public speaking. Do you feel that you could deliver a speech as strongly, passionately, and effectively to an audience? What audience do you see yourself addressing in this way?

   You can assign that students watch this speech as a homework assignment, and consider the questions listed. Or, you can also show this video clip in class when you are lecturing about audience and delivery, and have students discuss these questions as a class.

2. **Video Clip 2: The George Bush and John Kerry Debate, 2004**
   Watch this clip, and consider how Bush and Kerry respond to the question asked by the audience. How do they respond to the audience? What do their responses teach you about the importance of audience centeredness? What do you think was most effective and least effective about their responses?

   Encourage students to view this video clip on their own and consider the listed questions. Or, show this video clip in class and have students discuss the listed questions.

Additional Exercises and Resources

1. **Cultural Heritage Exercise**
   In class, give students about 10 minutes to begin preparing a brief speech about their cultural heritage. Place them into groups of 3-4 and have them take 2-3 minutes each delivering their speech. If you have time, let students take a few minutes after each speech for questions-and-answers. After everyone has presented his or her speech, have students (still in their groups) discuss how their own

cultural upbringing influences their communication style, their focus on certain topics, how they react to the audience and how audiences might react to them. After the small group discussion, come together as a class and have students share their observations. This exercise might also work well when done as 1-2 minute impromptu speeches followed by a class discussion after all students have spoken.

2. **Master Statuses and Public Speaking**
   Have students respond to the following questions related to the scenarios offered below: What is the role that master statuses play in these scenarios? How might these speakers' master status affect their audience's expectations? What could these speakers do to address an audience's assumptions and help the audience move past them to focus on the content of their speeches? What are the implications here for public speaking? How might students strategize to make these situations effective public speaking situations, while also remaining audience centered?

   a. Gifty is a 42-year-old, Ghanaian born, citizen of the United States. She holds both a law degree and a Masters of Public Health. When she gives presentations, people often doubt her credibility because she is a soft-spoken woman, small in stature, who speaks with an accent. They think she is very sweet but that she may not really know what she is talking about.

   b. Cynthia is a 35-year-old, white, deaf woman. She is passionately involved in environmental preservation and is a community educator for the World Wildlife Federation. She uses an interpreter when she gives presentations to school groups and service clubs. When she speaks to children, they usually stare at her in awe, and when she speaks to adult groups, they often watch the interpreter rather than her. During the question and answer sessions, almost every audience asks her what it's like to be deaf, to use an interpreter, and how a deaf woman became interested in Animal rights and preservation.

   c. Ghalib is a 40-year-old, Muslim male from Palestine, and a United States citizen. He has a Ph.D. in Political Science, focusing on international policy. He has been in the United States since he was 15. After the September 11, 2001 terrorist attacks, Ghalib went to meet his students for class, and very few attended. He figured it was because they were upset about the tragedy. After about a week, more students began to reappear. Ghalib began a section, which he always teaches, about United States foreign policy. Some students in the class asked him about the U.S. foreign policy in the Middle East. Other students reacted quite negatively toward Ghalib. For the first time, Ghalib's student evaluations were not positive. Several students commented that his accent made it hard to understand him (even though he speaks perfect English), while others commented on how anti-American he was. A few students even commented on how he was pro-terrorist. Ghalib also received crank calls on his office phone.

These scenarios address issues related to gender, ethnicity, nationality, race, and disability. Have students discuss these scenarios in small groups and then as a full class. Be ready to debrief with students because some may have strong reactions to some of these scenarios. Make sure to emphasize the role that master statuses play here, in addition to stereotypes and ethnocentrism. Help students identify specific ways they can address these issues as speakers and as audience members.

3. My Own Master Status

Students sometimes are challenged by the idea of master statuses and the role master statuses can play in their own lives. They may even have trouble identifying their own master statuses and how those affect their standpoints. On the board write the following:

Sex:

Race:

Ethnicity:

Nationality:

Sexual Orientation:

Socio-economic status:

Religion:

Give students about 5 minutes to respond and write about what their life is currently like as a woman or man, or as Jewish or Muslim, or as a Chinese National, etc. Then have students volunteer to share their perspectives. For instance, a student may say *"As a Chinese man here in the United States, I find it easy to gain respect when it relates to academic work. However, when I am in social settings people think I know martial arts, or laugh at me when I find an American woman attractive."* In this response, the student is addressing his master status as a Chinese man and the stereotypes he faces. After a few students respond, have them fill in the blanks again, but this time have them imagine life as a completely different person. If they are a woman, have them write about being a man, etc. After 5 minutes, have students share their responses. For instance, a woman may say *"If I were a man, I would not be afraid to walk to my car at night after class. As a man, I think I would feel safer and more confident."* After several students share their new perspectives, ask them to discuss the implications of their own master statuses for public speaking. Point out that people will have different perspectives on topics, which can be attributed to master statuses and positions in society. Use this as an activity to encourage students to work on being audience centered. **NOTE:** Do not pressure students to share if they choose not to. Call on students who are willing to volunteer. Some students may not feel comfortable sharing a master status in front of the class.

4. Survey Form

Make a copy of the sample survey form at the end of this chapter for those students who are interested in conducting a survey of the class. Encourage students to create their own surveys if this survey does not cover everything they need. Surveys should not take more than a few minutes in class.

True/False Quiz

Identify the following statements as true or false:

_____ A dialogue is simply taking turns in a conversation.

_____ When preparing my speech, I need to think more about what I want to say than the background and experiences of my audience.

_____ All cultures and subcultures have the same basic idea of how the world works.

_____ Audiences will interpret my message in just the way I want them to.

_____ To be audience centered, I must say only what the audience wants to hear.

_____ Temporal and situational factors have little effect on my speech.

_____ When I open up my speech for questions or discussion, I lose all control of the flow of communication.

Citing Sources and Creating a Works Cited Page

Created by
Jennifer Emerling Bone
T. M. Linda Scholz

Citing sources in speeches may be awkward at first; however, it is very important. Citing sources helps a speaker establish their credibility by strengthening information and arguments they have to offer. The following information contains guidelines for citing sources while you are speaking and for creating a works cited page.

Citing Sources While Speaking

You have two options when citing sources while you are speaking: 1) directly quoting a source and 2) paraphrasing a source. Regardless of which you choose, you always need to give credit where credit is due in order to avoid plagiarism.

*Use **Direct Quotes*** when you use the source's content word-for-word.
   ✓ When you directly quote someone, use a quotation that is only a few sentences long; too long a quote causes wordiness and confusion.
   ✓ Make sure that **you are formulating the argument first**, and use direct quotes only as **support for your arguments**.
   ✓ Only use direct quotes when the quote says something better than you can say it.

*Use **Paraphrasing*** when you summarize a source's content into your own words, without changing the original intent or meaning.
   ✓ When you paraphrase, the author and source **still need** to be cited.
   ✓ In the Diana Hacker's *Pocket Style Manual, 3rd ed*, Hacker recommends that to avoid plagiarism you should "set the source aside, write from memory, and consult the source later to check for accuracy" (112).

Specific information must be cited whether you paraphrase or quote directly.
   ✓ The author of the article, book, website, etc.
   ✓ The author's title or credentials (for credibility).
   ✓ The date of the publication or when the website/webpage was last updated or accessed.
   ✓ When you cite a source with only two-three authors, state their last names as they appear in the source.
   ✓ If you cite a source with more than three authors, state the first author followed by the words "et. al."

Creating the Works Cited Page

To create a works cited page, follow the guidelines given to you by your instructor, or use these guidelines, based on the Modern Language Association (MLA) style, recommended by Diana Hacker in *A Writer's Reference*, 4th ed.

✓ Begin your works cited page on a NEW sheet of paper.
✓ Sources in the work cited page are ALWAYS alphabetized REGARDLESS of the type of source.
✓ DO NOT label or categorize the type of source used.
✓ DO NOT number or bullet the sources.
✓ List only sources that are cited in the speech.
✓ Double-space each entry.
✓ Indent additional lines of the same source five spaces.

Because different types of sources follow different rules, use these examples as guidelines:

Book
Author's last name first, title of the book (italicized or underlined), place of publication, publisher, and date.

Griffin, Cindy L. *Invitation to Public Speaking*. Boston, MA: Wadsworth, 2012.

Book by multiple authors
List authors in the order in which they appear on the title page of the book. Reverse the name of ONLY the first author. Then, follow the above guidelines.

Morreale, Sherwin P., Brian H. Spitzberg, and J. Kevin Barge. *Human Communication:*

Motivation, Knowledge and Skills. Belmont, CA: Wadsworth, 2001.

Unknown Author
Begin with the title, but alphabetize by the first word of content or substance. Do not alphabetize by *A, An,* or *The* if this is the starting word (see the sample works cited page for clarification).

The Pocket Oxford Spanish Dictionary. Oxford: Oxford University Press, 1997.

Pamphlet
Follow the rules for citing a book.

World Conference Against Racism: Racial Discrimination Xenophobia and Related Intolerance.

New York: United Nations Department of Public Information, 2001.

Magazine or Newspaper

Begin with the author's name (last name first); title of the article in quotation marks; title of the source (magazine or newspaper) italicized or underlined; date (day, month and year). Put a colon (:) after the year, and then cite the page number/s.

Boyd, Valerie. "The Last Word." *Ms*. 25 Sept. 2000: 80-83.

Journal

Begin with author's name, title of the article in quotation marks, journal title (italicized or underlined), volume number, year of publication in parenthesis, colon following the year, page numbers.

> Keshishian, Flora. "Political Bias in Nonpolitical News: A Content Analysis of an Armenian and
>
> Iranian Earthquake in the *New York Times* and *Washington Post*." *Critical Studies in*
>
> *Mass Communication* 35 (1997): 332-43.

Personal Interview

Begin with the name of the person interviewed, then write "personal interview," and the date of the interview (day, month, year).

> Loeffler-Clemens, Therese. Personal interview. 13 Dec. 2001.

E-mail

Begin with the author of the e-mail, followed by the topic of the e-mail in quotation marks. Then, begin a new sentence and write "e-mail to _____." Follow this with the date received.

> Bone, Jennifer. "Creating a works cited page." E-mail to T. M. Linda Scholz. 14 Dec. 2001.

Television Educational Programs

Begin with the episode title in quotation marks, followed by the program title (underlined or italicized), the network, the local station and city, the broadcast date.

> "Helping Women of the World." *Oprah*. ABC. KMGH, Denver. 3 Dec. 2001.

Internet Sources

Begin with the author, followed by the name of the article in quotation marks, title of the webpage (underlined or italicized), the date of the last update/publication or date accessed, and then the electronic address in angle brackets.

> Holland, Steve. "Bush: U. S. Abandoning Key 1972 Missile Treaty." *KUNC Community Radio
> for   Northern   Colorado.   13   Dec.   2001*
> <http://www.publicbroadcasting.net/kunc/news.newsmain>.

Encyclopedia

List the author of the article, title of the article, title of the encyclopedia/reference work (underlined or italicized), edition number and the date. If the author's name is signed, place first. If the author's name is unsigned, then provide the title first.

> "Paul, Alice." *The New Encyclopedia Britannica*. 15th ed. 2005.

A sample works cited page follows.

Sample Works Cited

Bone, Jennifer. "Creating a works cited page." E-mail to T. M. Linda Scholz. 14 Dec. 2001.

Boyd, Valerie. "The Last Word." *Ms.* 25 Sept. 2000: 80-83.

Griffin, Cindy L. *Invitation to Public Speaking*. Boston, CA: Wadsworth, 2012.

"Helping Women of the World." *Oprah*. ABC. KMGH, Denver. 3 Dec. 2001.

Holland, Steve. "Bush: U.S. Abandoning Key 1972 Missile Treaty." *KUNC Community Radio for Northern Colorado*. 13 Dec. 2001 <http://www.publicbroadcasting.net/kunc/news.newsmain>.

Keshishian, Flora. "Political Bias in Nonpolitical News: A Content Analysis of an Armenian and Iranian Earthquake in the *New York Times* and *Washington Post*." *Critical Studies in Mass Communication* 35 (1997): 332-43.

Loeffler-Clemens, Therese. Personal interview. 13 Dec. 2001.

Morreale, Sherwin P., Brian H. Spitzberg, and J. Kevin Barge. *Human Communication: Motivation, Knowledge and Skills*. Belmont, CA: Wadsworth, 2001.

"Paul, Alice." *The New Encyclopedia Britannica*. 15th ed. 2005.

The Pocket Oxford Spanish Dictionary. Oxford: Oxford University Press, 1997.

World Conference Against Racism: Racial Discrimination Xenophobia and Related Intolerance. New York: United Nations Department of Public Information, 2001.

Supplemental Bibliography

Alexander, Janet E. Web Wisdom: How to Evaluate and Create Information Quality on the web. Mahwah, NJ: Lawrence Erlbaum Associates, 1999.

Alexander writes a solid general book on overall web research and evaluation. The pictures offer an easy way to identify the information being described and might be turned into power point or overhead visual aids for a lecture.

Berkman, Robert I., Find it Fast: How to Uncover Expert Information on Any Subject, 4th ed. New York: Harper Perennial, 1997.

This is a user-friendly guide to all types of research. Not only does this book describe and explain how to use reference sources, the book also helps users to define their needs and organize their research effectively.

Butler, John A. CyberSearch: Research Techniques in the Electronic Age. New York: Penguin Reference, 1998.

Butler covers the range of basic to advanced internet searching. He also offers tips on where and how to find the best information. This resource is a nice supplement to a lecture or a great resource to ask students to find and bring back to class on a library day.

Hacker, Diana and Fister, Barbara, Research and Documentation in the Electronic Age, 5th ed. Bedford/St., Martin, 2010.

Hacker and Fister show how to locate and document sources in the humanities, social sciences, history and sciences. This book includes tips for evaluating sources, a list of style manuals and a glossary of research terms.

Li, Xia. Electronic Styles: A Handbook for Citing Electronic Information, 2nd ed. Medford, N.J.: Information Today, 1996.

Students will no doubt have questions as to how to cite their electronic material. This book is an exhaustive resource for all types of electronic citations.

Mann, Thomas. The Oxford Guide to Library Research. New York: Oxford University Press, 1998.

An up-to-date comprehensive guide to using the library and doing research. Very thorough.

Metter, Ellen. The Writer's Ultimate Research Guide. Cincinnati, OH: Writer's Digest Books, 1995.

While focused on fiction and nonfiction writers, this book has useful information for any researcher. Specific suggestions for improving library research techniques, options for ways to conduct research, and places to find the most useful information are listed. This is not the most detailed book, but covers what most students usually want to know more about.

Radford, Marie L., and Barnes, Susan B., and Barr, Linda R., *Web* Research: Selecting, Evaluating, and Citing. Boston: Allyn and Bacon, 2002.

The authors cover many aspects and issues of web research including search engines, copyright issues, web evaluation criteria, and how to cite sources. This is a good basic book that covers most of the issues you will likely need to address about web research.

Stewart, Charles J., and Cash, William B.. Interviewing: Principles and Practices. Dubuque, Iowa: W. C. Brown Co., 1974.

Although this is an older text, it offers excellent coverage of the foundations of interviewing such as how to phrase questions, different types of interviews, and includes a discussion of communication principles involved in interviews. Sample interviews are also included.

Chapter Six: Developing and Supporting Your Ideas

Chapter Goals

Chapter six introduces students to the importance of developing their ideas, and to support their ideas and arguments with supporting materials. Students should have an understanding of the following goals after the end of this chapter:

- To explain the importance of supporting materials in a speech,
- To identify and provide examples of the five main types of supporting materials,
- To apply tips for using each of the five types of supporting materials effectively.

Chapter Outline

I. When we enter the public dialogue, we take part in a social interaction—one person makes a claim about a topic to an audience, "calling out" to his or her listeners, and they respond to this claim in some way.
- a. **Claim** is an assertion that must be proved (pg. 109).
  - i. When we make claims, we explore and exchange ideas, we respond to one another, and we clarify, refine, and revise our positions.
  - ii. When we communicate our claims ethically and effectively, we stimulate and enhance the public dialogue.
- b. **Evidence** *are the materials speakers use to support their ideas* (pg. 109).
  - i. Evidence comes from the information you gather in your research on the internet, at the library, and in interviews.
  - ii. Your evidence is proof, and it helps you build your credibility, or believability.
  - iii. There are five most common types of supporting material.

II. **Examples** *are specific instances used to illustrate a concept, experience, issue or problem* (pg. 110).
- a. There are several different types of examples.
  - i. Examples can be brief, by using only a word or a sentence or two, or they can be longer and more richly detailed.
  - ii. Examples can be **real,** indicating that the instance actually took place.
  - iii. Examples can be **hypothetical**, indicating that the instance did not take place but could have.
- b. There are several criteria to help decide when to use an example.
  - i. **Use examples to clarify concepts** (pg. 110 -111).
    1. Try to anticipate what parts of your speech might prompt an audience to ask "What do you mean by that?" and use an example to help clarify that given concept.
    2. An example can make something abstract and complex much clearer.
  - ii. **Use examples to reinforce points** (pg. 112).
    1. Consider what parts of your speech might prompt the audience to say "I don't see that it matters."
    2. Examples help audiences recognize the relevance and importance of your points in their own lives.

iii. **Use examples to bring concepts to life or to elicit emotions** (pg. 112).
1. An example can bring a concept to life by providing specific images an audience can picture in their minds.
2. A mental picture can be filtered through an audience's thoughts and experiences to better understand how an issue affects them or someone they know.

iv. **Use examples to build your case or make credible generalizations** (pg. 112).
1. Examples can help someone who thinks "It's not as common or prevalent as you say" to see that it is.
2. If you can cite numerous examples of the prevalence of binge drinkers in college dorms, you can make a stronger claim for binge drinking as a significant problem.

v. **There are several tips for using examples ethically and effectively - See Table 6.1** (pg. 113).
1. *Is the example relevant and appropriate?*
   a. Make sure it refers to the point you are making, not to something else.
   b. Avoid examples that are too graphic, emotional, detailed, or personal for the audience.
   c. Use caution with examples that contain violent details, the manipulation of emotion, overly technical material , or explicit personal detail.
2. *Is the hypothetical example ethical?*
   a. Make sure the hypothetical example represents events or information grounded in fact. Do not mislead or lie to your audience.
   b. An example should be plausible, meaning that it really could be true or have happened.
   c. If you use a hypothetical example, tell your audience it is hypothetical.
3. *Are there enough examples to support your claim?*
   a. If you cannot find more than one example to support your claim, your claim may be unfounded.
   b. When you make a case for the existence of something, you will need quite a few examples.
   c. Avoid generalizing from a single example.
4. *Have you accounted for the counterexamples?*
   a. Counterexamples can make what you say false or weaken your assertions.
   b. You may have to change your claims to explain the counter examples.

III. **Narratives** (pg. 112 - 114).
a. A **narrative** *is a story that recounts or foretells real or hypothetical events.*
   i. There are two different types of narratives.
   ii. **Brief narratives** *also called vignettes, illustrate a specific point.*
   iii. **Extended narratives** *make an evolving connection with a broader point.*
   iv. Stories often reference other stories or rely on parts of other stories to be complete in a process called **intertextuality.**
b. There are several criteria to use when thinking about incorporating narratives into a speech (pg. 114).
   i. **Use narratives to personalize a point** (pg. 114).
      1. Ronald Reagan used stories effectively to make his point in personal ways.

90

2. In the story of Jose Salcido, Reagan drew his audience personally into his argument.
ii. **Use narratives to challenge an audience to think in new ways** (pg. 115).
1. As we tell a story, we share our perspectives with an audience in personal and organized ways.
2. As we listen to a story, we find commonality we had not recognized before.
3. We may gain a new or deeper understanding of an issue, such as an audience member listening to Curtis' speech about Ishmael.
iii. **Use narratives to draw an audience in emotionally** (pg. 115).
1. Facts, statistics and examples are important, but can lack the personalized emotional component of a story.
2. Use a story when you want to draw an audience in emotionally.
iv. **Use narratives to unite with your audience** (pg. 116).
1. When you share a story about an experience that is just like everyone else's experience, you establish common ground with your audience.
2. Because of their content and the personalized way they are told, stories often create a sense of togetherness for speakers and their audiences.
v. **Tips for using narratives ethically and effectively – See Table 6.2** (pg. 116).
1. *Does your narrative make a specific point?*
   a. When telling a story in a speech, make sure it is for a specific reason to make a specific point.
   b. Be sure your narrative has a clear point. Many great stories are available, but not all stories make a point well.
2. *Is the length appropriate?*
   a. Make sure your story fits the time limit for your speech.
   b. Brief stories allow you to make your point quickly and so often fit better into speeches.
   c. An extended story can draw the audience in more fully and with more detail.
3. *Is the language vivid?*
   a. The language should bring the message to life.
   b. The language selected makes a difference in the kind of image created.
4. *Is the delivery appropriate to the story?*
   a. The manner in which the story is told is also significant.
   b. Practice telling your story several times to get pauses, emphasis, gestures and expressions the way you want them.
5. *Is the story appropriate for my audience?*
   a. Is the story too graphic, too personal, or simply inappropriate for a particular audience?
   b. Make sure the stories told ring true for a particular audience.

IV. **Statistics** (pg. 117).
a. **Statistics** *are numerical summaries of facts, figures, and research findings* (pg. 117).
   i. Statistics help audiences understand amounts and percentages.
   ii. Numbers summarize and help audiences make sense of large chunks of information and help people see where something is in relation to other things. Statistics help audiences understand proportions such as half of the people in this organization.
   iii. **There are different types of statistics** (pg. 118 - 120).
   1. Common statistics include totals and amounts, costs, scales and ranges, ratios, rates, dates and times, measurements, and percentages.

a. The **mean** *tells the average of a group of numbers*.
   i. Use a mean when you want to describe averages, patterns, tendencies, generalization, and trends.
b. The **median** *is the middle number in a series or set of numbers arranged in a ranked order*.
   i. It tells you where the midpoint is in your set of data.
   ii. It shows that one-half of the observations will be smaller and one-half larger than that midpoint.
   iii. Use the median when you want to identify the midpoint and make claims about its significance or about the items that fall above or below it.
   iv. The disadvantage of using a median is that significant numbers below and above the midpoint might not be discussed.
c. The **mode** *is the number that occurs most often in a set of numbers*.
   i. Use the mode when you want to illustrate the most frequent or typical item in your data set.
   ii. Use the mode in order to establish the occurrence, availability, demand, or need for something.
b. **There are several guidelines to consider when using statistics** (pg. 121).
   i. **Use statistics to synthesize large amounts of information.**
   ii. **Use statistics when the numbers tell a powerful story.**
   iii. **Use statistics when numerical evidence strengthens a claim.**
   iv. **There are two tips for using statistics effectively.**
      1. Evaluate your statistics carefully.
      2. *Use statistics sparingly.*
c. **Tips for using statistics ethically and effectively – See Table 6.3** (pg. 122)
   i. **How accurate are your statistics?**
   ii. **Can you make your statistics easier to remember by displaying them visually?**
   iii. **Can you make your statistics easier to remember by rounding numbers up or down?**
   iv. **Can you make your statistics easier to remember by grouping similar numbers together?**
   v. **Can you make your statistics easier to remember by translating them into relatable numbers?**

V. **Testimony** (pg. 123).
   a. **Testimony** *is the opinions or observations of others* (pg. 159).
      i. Testimony can take can take on two different forms.
         1. A **Direct quotation** *is an exact word-for-word presentation of another's testimony*.
            a. Direct quotations are often seen as more credible than paraphrasing.
            b. Sometimes a person's words or stories are too long, too complex, or contain inappropriate language for a particular audience.
         2. A **Paraphrase** *is a summary of another's testimony in the speaker's own words*.
      ii. There are three different types of testimony.
         1. **Expert testimony** *is when you use the testimony of someone considered an authority in a particular field.*
         2. **Peer testimony**, *sometimes called lay testimony, is when you use testimony of someone who has firsthand knowledge of a topic.*

92

3. **Personal testimony** *is when you use your own testimony to convey your point.*

    b. There are several guidelines for using testimony in a speech (pg. 125).

        i. **Use testimony when you need the voice of an expert.**

            1. *Be careful about using testimony from biased sources. A* **Bias** *is an unreasoned distortion of judgment or prejudice about a topic.*

                a. **Biased sources** *will have an unreasoned personal stake in the outcome of an issue.*

                b. *An* **objective source** *is someone who does not have a personal stake in an issue and can provide a fair and undistorted view about a topic.*

        ii. **Use testimony to illustrate differences or agreements.**

        iii. **Use your own testimony when your experience says it best.**

        iv. **Paraphrase testimony to improve listenability.**

            1. *Be sure to paraphrase accurately.*

    c. **There are several tips for using testimony effectively – See Table 6.4** (pg. 127).

        i. **Is the source of your testimony credible?**

        ii. **Is the testimony biased?**

        iii. **Have you paraphrased accurately?**

        iv. **Is the testimony connected to your point?**

VI. **Definitions** (pg. 129).

    a. *A* **definition** *is a statement of the exact meaning of a word or phrase.*

        i. *The* **denotative definition** *is the objective meaning you find in the dictionary, the definition of a word on which most everyone can agree.*

        ii. *The* **connotative definition** *is the subjective meaning of a word or phrase based on personal experiences and beliefs.*

    b. There are several guidelines for using definitions in speeches (pg. 130).

        i. **Use definitions to clarify and create understanding.**

        ii. **Use definitions to clarify an emotionally or politically charged word.**

        iii. **Use definitions to illustrate what something is not**.

        iv. **Use definitions to trace the history of a word**.

            1. The **etymology**, *or the history of a word*, allows you to trace the original meaning of a word in order to chart the changes it has undergone.

    c. **There are several tips for using definitions effectively – See Table 6.5** (pg. 131).

        i. *Is the source of the definition credible?*

        ii. *Have you avoided proper meaning superstition?*

            1. **Proper meaning superstition** *is the belief that everyone attaches the same meaning to a word and that you are using that meaning.*

        iii. *Have you actually defined the term?*

End of the Chapter Activities and Discussion Questions

The following questions can be found at the end of Chapter Six.

Review Questions and Activities

1. Consider the examples or narratives you have gathered for your speech. Are they real or hypothetical, brief or extended? Out loud, practice delivering one of your examples or narratives.

Do you feel comfortable with your delivery? Why or why not? Practice delivering this material until it sounds natural and conversational.

This is an activity that can also be conducted in class in small groups of 3-4. Place students in groups, and have them take turns practicing their narratives. Have the students acting as audience members provide feedback to the "speaker." Have students switch roles throughout the activity so that everyone gets practice. Give each student about 3-5 minutes for both delivering the narrative and feedback.

2. Bring the statistics you have found in your research to class. In groups, discuss how you might work with these statistics to present them clearly and ethically to your audience. Identify your means, medians, and modes. Discuss what each of these types of statistics tells or illustrates for your audience, including a discussion of how to avoid misrepresenting an issue with your statistics.

This activity can be conducted in conjunction with #1 above. Have students also discuss ideas on how to visually represent these statistics. If some students have already began work on a visual aid, have them bring in the visual aid to show their group and be given feedback.

3. In what instances might you be an expert and be able to offer your own testimony in a speech? What makes you an expert in this situation and not in others? How could you establish your credibility as an "expert" if you were to use this testimony?

You can have students address these questions during your lecture about the different types of testimony. Take a few minutes during your lecture to address this question, and to have students respond accordingly.

4. Check out Speech Studio to see how other students use supporting materials in their speeches. How appropriate and credible did their materials seem? Or record a speech your working on, upload it to Studio Speech, and ask your peers for their feedback. What feedback would help you use your supporting materials before you give your speech in class?

Web Activities

1. **United States Household Statistics**
   Go to http://www.2010.census.gov/mediacenter/portrait-of-america/us-house-stats.php
   Explore the US household *Statistics*. Search for a statistic on the Census 2010 web site that you can use in your next speech. What can this statistic help you prove or illustrate? How reliable do you think this source is?

   Students are often challenged by finding effective statistics. Encourage students to access this website to help them search for statistics from credible sources.

2. **Who Do You Believe?**
   Purpose: To practice evaluating sources for bias and credibility.
   Directions: Use *InfoTrac College Edition* to locate articles about gun control. First search on the term *gun control,* and then follow the subdivision links to Analysis, Social Aspects, or Laws,

Regulations, and so on, as needed to find relevant articles. (An example of one of the articles you might find is Chitra Ragavan, "Ready, Aim, Misfire," *U.S. News & World Report*, May 21, 2001.) Find quotations in the articles from people who are in favor of gun control and from those who oppose gun control. Are the sources credible? Are the sources biased? Which source was most credible? Why?

This InfoTrac activity can be done partially at home, and in-class for the discussion component. Have students access this website, and find the information indicated here. Ask that the students come to class prepared to discuss their findings. This may work best first in small groups of students. After about 15-20 minutes of discussion, have the class come together as a whole to discuss the overall observations of the group.

3. **Word Origins** Go to Word Origins at http://www.wordorigins.org
   to check out their list of words and their original meanings. Choose the link for the list of words and phrases and locate a word that is familiar to you. What is the origin of the word? How does the word's origin help you to understand the term more fully? Are you surprised at the term's origin?

This can be great website to access, even for your lectures. If you can access the internet from your class room, bring this website up and show students how it works. This can also be helpful for students in any type of speech.

4. **Avoiding Proper Meaning Superstition**
   Purpose: To explore how disputed terms have multiple meanings and how multiple meanings shape our conceptions of ideas.
   Directions: Go to Google at **http://www.google.com** and search on the term "feminism definition." Explore some of the sites Google uncovers to find various meanings of the word feminism. Which of these meanings is new to you? Which do you think is most widely held by your audience? Which source is most credible? How might knowing the differences in meanings for the concept of feminism influence a speech you might give on the topic? Now compare these to the Jackson Katz example in this chapter. Log on to his website, **www.jacksonkatz.com**, and compare the definition you found to Katz's definition. How might you explain these differences in a speech?

This is a great activity to discuss denotative and connotative definitions. Follow the questions suggested above to lead the discussion or consider this alternative: access these websites from the classroom (if you have direct access to the internet) or bring visual aids of print outs from the site. Begin by asking students what they think the definition of the word "feminism" is. Write everything on the board. Then ask students what definitions are denotative and connotative. Next, access the above sites (or show them the material on the sites via your visual aids), and show students the different definitions of the word feminism. Conclude with a discussion of the definitions, the student responses, and the importance of acknowledging denotative and connotative definitions.

InfoTrac College Edition Activities

1. **InfoTrac College Edition Activity 6.1: Tax Cut Beneficiaries**
   Purpose: To better understand the power and limitations of examples used to support claims and clarify ideas.
   Directions: Use InfoTrac College Edition to locate and read Barbara Ehrenreich's article, "People as Props," The Progressive, April 2001. This article discusses President George W. Bush's use of "tax families" as examples of people who would benefit from his 2001 tax cut proposal. Also locate and read Bush's own remarks about his proposal: "Remarks at a Tax Family Reunion in St. Louis," Weekly Compilation of Presidential Documents, February 26, 2001. In his remarks, President Bush referred to the Yahngs as an example of a family who would benefit from his tax cut. Did Bush's example effectively support his claim that tax cuts would benefit Americans? That is, did his example clarify his tax cut proposal, reinforce the point he was making, or draw out the emotions of the audience? Did Bush use his example ethically? Consider the relevance of his example, whether he described enough tax families to support his claim, and whether he accounted for counterexamples.

   This InfoTrac activity can be used as a homework assignment. Have students access these articles, and respond to them in written form. On the due date of the assignment discuss students' responses.

2. **InfoTrac College Edition Activity 6.2: Narratives of Personal Success**
   Purpose: To help you harness the power of narratives for your speeches.
   Directions: Imagine you are giving a speech about entrepreneurship. Use InfoTrac College Edition to search on the term entrepreneurship, and follow the link to Personal Narratives. Look for articles that include narratives you think will help you personalize a point or draw your audience in emotionally. Make sure your narrative is vivid, organized, and of an appropriate length.

   You can assign this InfoTrac activity as an in-class assignment. First, have students access this website as homework. Have them come to class prepared to share some of the narratives they would find useful. You can have students share their narratives in small groups. Toward the end of the activity, come together as a whole and have students share their responses with the class. You also could ask students to deliver an impromptu personal narrative about the narrative they selected.

Interactive Student and Professional Speech Videos

1. **Video Clip 1: Ann Richards' Eulogy for Barbara Jordan**
   In her eulogy for former U.S. representative Barbara Jordan, former Texas governor Ann Richards describes how Jordan sought government help to remove a gate that a neighbor had built across the public access road to her house. Richards used the example to give her audience a better sense of Jordan and her character. Are there other examples Richards uses in the speech? Do the examples help to create a mental image of Jordan? What examples might be an effective form of support in a eulogy?

   Show this video clip in class and have students discuss the effectiveness of Richards' examples. Did Richards follow the guidelines suggested in this chapter for incorporating examples into the speech? If so, was she effective? If not, what could she have done differently? Be sure to get specific examples and reasons from the students and discuss ways they can incorporate the techniques Richards used (or could have used) into their own speeches.

2. **Video Clip 2: Chelsey Penoyer, "Mike" narrative**
Watch Chelsey's video clip, and pay close attention to how she uses narrative to set up her speech. How does she deliver the narrative? Does Chelsey illustrate the reasons why to use narratives in speeches? What makes her use of narrative effective?

Show this powerful clip during class, and have students discuss the questions listed here. Emphasize to students how narratives can also be used successfully in an introduction as an attention getter.

3. **Video Clip 3: John McCain Speech to Democrats at the 2004 National Republican Convention**
Watch this clip and focus on ways that McCain addressed his audience and how he attempted to create unity through his use of language.

You can show this video clip in class and address the questions listed here.

4. **Video Clip 4: Sarah Brady's Address to the 1996 Democratic National Convention**

In her speech to the 1996 Democratic National Convention, Brady explains that each year 40,000 Americans are killed and 100,000 wounded, by guns. She makes her argument for gun control more compelling by informing her audience that every two hours, a child is killed by a gun.

Show this video clip in class. Does Brady use statistics effectively? Does she follow the guidelines suggested in this chapter for incorporating statistics into a speech? If so, was she effective? If not, what could she have done differently? Be sure to get specific examples and reasons from the students and discuss ways they can incorporate the techniques Brady used (or could have used) into their own speeches.

Additional Exercises and Resources

1. **Cartoons and Claims**
Bring several newspapers to class (or have students bring several newspapers to class). Have students look through the editorial sections of the papers. Ask them to identify the claims made in the editorials. You can also refer students to any political cartoons in the paper and see if they can identify the type of claims being made. If you have access to the internet from your classroom, you can also access the New Yorker Magazine's Cartoon Archive at www.cartoonbank.com. There are several cartoons from which to choose for this activity to be conducted in class.

2. **Narratives and September 11, 2001**
The following are different activities you can conduct regarding narratives by using students recall their experiences with the September 11, 2001 terrorist attacks.

   a. Have students recall stories they heard about the September 11, 2001, attacks on New York City and Washington, D.C. Have students respond to the following questions: Who were the stories about? Why do the students think the media used the stories they did (emotional appeal)? Did the stories have more impact when told by the people who directly experienced the incident, by family members, or by anchors on the news? Was there a difference? If so, what were those differences? Did the stories personalize a point for the students, challenge

97

the student to think in new ways, draw the student in emotionally, and/or function to unite Americans, Muslims, and Afghans?

b. Bring in any news coverage of the September 11, 2001 attacks, particularly the specials about specific victims. Have students read (or view, if you have videotapes of the coverage) a few of the stories, and discuss the impact of those particular narratives. Do they view the narratives differently now that a couple of years or so have passed? If they do, how so? What narratives could they use to make specific arguments or points and what would those arguments or points be?

c. Access different politician speeches related to the September 11, 2001 attacks. After students read these speeches, ask them to consider whether the particular politicians use stories in their speeches about particular victims? Do the politicians use stories about Osama Bin Laden and his followers? If so, what purpose might those narratives have served? Were the narratives always used ethically?

3. **Visually Representing Statistics on PowerPoint**
PowerPoint is a software program that can enhance students' visual aids. It is also quite simple to create graphs, charts, etc. to visually represent statistical information. At the end of this chapter you will find a handout with basic instructions on how to access graphs and charts on PowerPoint. A complete version of how to access PowerPoint and create slides also appears in Chapter 14, Visual Aids, of this manual.

Visually Representing Statistics on PowerPoint

When working with statistical information you may want to create graphs to visually represent your statistics. Use the following steps to help you do this:

I.   Go into **INSERT** and choose **NEW SLIDE.**
  A.   Select any of the slide options that show charts/graphs.
  B.   Click on **DOUBLE CLICK TO ADD CHART.**
  C.   Enter the appropriate information.

II.   If you do not want the bar graph, you can switch to any type of chart/graph you prefer.
  A.   When you first access the new chart/graph slide, go to **CHART** on the menu bar.
  B.   Click on **CHART TYPE.**
  C.   Select from any of the chart/graph types (either **STANDARD TYPES** or **CUSTOM TYPES**).

III.   You can also animate your graphs.
  A.   Click on **CHART** on the menu bar.
  B.   Scroll down and click on **CHART OPTIONS.**
  C.   Read the labels and choose what you prefer.

Supplemental Bibliography

Allen, James. Inference From Signs: Ancient Debates About the Nature of Evidence. New York: Oxford University Press, 2001.

Allen offers a historical perspective on the use of evidence in arguments. Although not really for classroom use, this book is for someone who is curious about the historical background of the subject and wants to use that in their lecture.

Crossen, Cynthia. Tainted Truth: The Manipulation of Fact in America. New York: Simon & Schuster, 1994.

Case studies, many of which appeared in popular media, of the misuse of evidence are presented in this book. These examples could be used to get students to think about evidence they encounter every day, and to get them to begin to evaluate and question that evidence.

Foss, Karen, and Foss, Sonja K.. "Personal Experience as Evidence in Feminist Scholarship." *Western Journal of Communication*. 58 (Winter 1994): 39.

This is a brief, but important article about the use of personal experience as evidence and the issues involved in doing so.

Kazoleas, Dean C. "A Comparison of the Persuasive Effectiveness of Qualitative versus Quantitative Evidence: A Test of Explanatory Hypotheses." *Communication Quarterly*. 41 (Winter 1993): 40-50 .

Two main categories of evidence, statistical and narrative, are discussed. Kazoleas examines attitude change resulting from both types. This article shows that both kinds of evidence are effective, and that students need not only focus on quantitative information in their speeches.

Langellier, Kristin M. "Personal Narratives: Perspectives on Theory and Research." *Text and Performance Quarterly*, 9 (1989), 243-276.

Langellier discusses how narratives allow marginalized voices to be heard. This is a good foundational article on the use of personal narrative in communication.

Nakayama, Thomas. "Disciplining Evidence." *Western Journal of Communication*. 59, (Spring 1995): 171.

Nakayama's discussion of the narrowness of typical evidence used in research (evidence is limited to that which pertains to white men) and the need to broaden evidence used in order to offer a wider and more comprehensive perspective is very provocative. Assigning this article or summarizing it for them could get students to think about their own perspectives and limitations presented in their research.

Robinson, Grady Jim. "Did I Ever Tell You About the Time": How to Develop and Deliver A Speech Using the Power of Stories to Persuade and Captivate Any Audience. New York: McGraw-Hill, 2000.

This book is helpful in learning how stories can be a powerful part of speeches, in that they are memorable, they can affect listeners more powerfully than other means of support, and they provide an additional means of understanding material. Many helpful exercises, examples, and tools are included to make storytelling a bigger part of the speaking process.

Rosteck, Thomas. "Narrative in Martin Luther King's I've Been to the Mountaintop." *Southern Communication Journal*, 58 (1992), 22-32.

Rosteck examines how the use of an existing narrative (a well known story) engages listeners, elicits reactions, comments on social and political issues, and acts as an invitation to action. These concepts can be presented in class as powerful reasons to use narrative and myth as evidence.

Scheidel, Thomas M. "On Evidence." *Western Journal of Communication,* 58 (Winter 1994): 66.

Scheidel writes an interesting article about how to use evidence in academic research that could, either summarized or assigned as reading, offer new perspectives and insight on the use of evidence.

Ziegelmueller, George W., and Dause, Charles A. <u>Argumentation: Inquiry and Advocacy</u>. Englewood Cliffs, N.J., Prentice-Hall, 1997.

Chapters four and five of this book present different types of evidence and also tests of evidence, offering excellent supplemental information for lectures or in class activities.

Advanced Public Speaking Institute "Public Speaking: Storytelling Do's,

www.public-speaking.org/public-speaking-storydo-article.htm

Chapter Seven: Reasoning

Chapter Goals

Chapter seven addresses the importance of sound reasoning in speeches when entering the public dialogue. Students should have an understanding of the following goals after the end of this chapter:

- To identify and apply Aristotle's three modes of proof
- To describe the five patterns of reasoning used to construct sound arguments
- To test the strength of claims with Toulmin's map of reasoning
- To apply tips for reasoning ethically

Chapter Outline

I.   Sound **reasoning** plays a central role in your preparations to enter the public dialogue.
    a.   Speakers accomplish sound reasoning when they use the three forms of proof defined by the Greek philosopher **Aristotle** (pg. 135).
        i.   **Logos** *refers to the logical arrangement of evidence in a speech.*
        ii. **Ethos** *refers to the speaker's credibility.*
        iii. **Pathos** *refers to the emotional appeals made by a speaker.*
    b.   Reasoning helps an audience make **inferences**, the mental leaps we make when we recognize that a speaker's evidence supports his or her claims.
    c.   In the public dialogue, an **argument** *is a set of statements that allows you to develop your evidence in order to establish the validity of your claim.*

II. **Patterns of reasoning** (pg. 136).
    a.   There are five patterns of reasoning most useful for beginning public speakers.
        i.   **Inductive reasoning, or reasoning from specific instances,** *is a process of reasoning that uses specific instances, or examples, to make a claim about a general conclusion* (pg.136).
            1.   Induction is sometimes called *argument by example*.
            2.   It is best used when you can identify patterns of evidence that indicate something is expected to happen again or should hold true based on previous experience.
            3.   There are two ways in which you can use inductive reasoning.
                a.   State your claim (general observation) first and then offer supporting instances.
                b.   Present the instances first and then make the claim.
            4.   There are three **guidelines** for using inductive reasoning (pg. 138).
                a.   Make sure you have enough examples to make your claim.
                b.   Make sure your generalizations are accurate.
                c.   Support your inductive arguments with statistics or testimony.
                    i.   Avoid **anomalies**, *or exceptions to a rule.*
                    ii. Avoid **hasty generalizations** *or reaching a conclusion without enough evidence to support it* (pg. 138).

101

        b.   Use this pattern when speech topics follow a sequence of first, second, third.

    2. **Spatial pattern** *arranges ideas in terms of location or direction* (pg. 160).

        a.   Arranging ideas from left to right, top to bottom, or inside to outside, helps an audience visualize the relationship between ideas or the structure of something.

        b.   Spatial relationships can be abstract, like eating according to the food pyramid.

        c.   Spatial relationships can also indicate the location of real things or places.

    3. **Causal pattern** *describes a cause-effect relationship between ideas or events* (pg. 161).

        a.   Speeches organized according to a causal pattern will have two main points.

           i.   If the effects have already happened, you can present the effects first.

          ii.   You also can organize the speech presenting the cause first, followed by the effects.

        b.   Regardless of the order of your main points, causal patterns are useful when your topic describes an event or situation and its consequences.

    4. The **problem-and-solution pattern** *identifies a specific problem and offers a possible solution* (pg. 161).

        a.   This pattern is common in persuasive speeches.

        b.   The problem-and-solution pattern has only two main points.

           i.   The problem main point needs to be addressed first.

          ii.   The problem is then logically followed by a solution main point.

    5. The **topical pattern** *allows one to divide a topic into subtopics, each of which addresses a different aspect of the whole topic* (pg. 162).

        a.   When a topical pattern of organization is used, ideas can be organized by following a progression of ideas that suits the topic best.

           i.   The principle of *primacy* can be used, which is putting the most important idea first.

          ii.   The principle of *recency* can be used, which is putting what the speaker most wants the audience to remember last.

        b.   This pattern helps a speaker organize a speech that does not fit into any of the other types of patterns.

  ii. There are three **tips for preparing main points** (pg. 163).

    1. First, **keep each main point separate and distinct.**

    2. Second, **word your main points consistently**.

    3. Finally, **devote the appropriate coverage to each main point**.

III. **Connectives** *are the words and phrases used to link ideas in a speech* (pg. 165).

  a. Four types of connectives are considered here.

    i. **Transitions** *are phrases that indicate you are finished with one point and are moving on to a new one.*

    ii. **An internal preview** *is a statement in the body of the speech that details what a speaker plans to discuss next.*

    iii. **An internal summary** *is a statement in the body of the speech that summarizes a point you've already discussed.*

iv. **A signpost** *is a simple word or statement that indicates where you are in your speech or highlights an important idea.*

IV. **The preparation outline** *is a detailed outline of your speech that helps you evaluate the organization of your idea* (pg. 168).

    a. The preparation outline includes various components.

        i. **Title, specific purpose and thesis statement** (pg. 168).

        ii. **Introduction** (pg. 169).

            1. The introduction should do four things.

                a. Capture the attention of the audience.

                b. Reveal the topic of the speech.

                c. Establish the speaker's credibility.

                d. Preview the main points of the speech.

            2. Speakers should summarize their introductions in outline form rather than including the full text of the introduction.

        iii. **Main points, subpoints, and sub-subpoints** (pg. 169).

            1. **Main points** *are the most important ideas addressed in a speech and they make up the body of the speech.*

            2. A **subpoint** *develops an aspect of a main point.*

            3. A **sub-subpoint** *goes deeper to develop an aspect of a subpoint.*

            4. Points are organized according to the principle of **coordination**, *or arranging points into successive levels, with the points on a specific level having equal importance.*

        iv. **Conclusion** (pg. 171).

            1. The conclusion should satisfy two goals.

                a. Signal the ending of the speech.

                b. Reinforce the thesis statement by summarizing the main points.

            2. In an outline form, the conclusion is not a word-for-word transcript, but a summary of what a speaker will say.

        v. **Connectives** (pg. 171).

            1. Write out the full connectives instead of outlining them.

            2. Connectives are included between the major sections of the outline.

            3. When included in the body, connectives should be in-between main points to help the speaker move from one point to the next.

        vi. **Works cited** (pg. 172).

            1. When citing sources, follow the guidelines listed in Chapter 7 of the textbook or follow the specific guidelines required by the instructor.

            2. Unless otherwise indicated by the instructor, students should include only the materials cited in the speech.

    b. There are a few **tips for preparing the preparation outline** (pg. 172).

        i. *Use complete sentences.*

        ii. *Label the introduction, body, conclusion and connectives.*

        iii. *Use a consistent pattern of symbols and indentation.*

            1. Outlines are based on principles of **subordination** or *ranking ideas in order from the most to the least important.*

            2. The most common way to indicate subordination in an outline is to use a traditional pattern of symbols and indentations.

                a. Main points are labeled with capital Roman numerals.

                b. Subpoints are labeled with capital letters, or lower case letters (this will be dependent upon auto formatting that occurs on your computer).

c. Sub-subpoints are labeled with Arabic numerals.

d. Indentations help a speaker to visually indicate the subordination of ideas.

    i. The main ideas are set farthest left.

    ii. Each level of sub-ideas is indented progressively farther to the right.

  iv. ***Divide points into at least two subpoints***.

  v. ***Check for balance***.

V. The **speaking outline**, sometimes called *speaking notes, is a condensed form of the preparation outline that you use when speaking* (pg. 178).

a. You will almost never memorize a speech or read it from a manuscript.

b. Your outline might include the full text of quotations, statistics, names, and other material you want to remember exactly.

c. The most effective speakers make frequent eye contact with their audience and speak directly to them.

d. There are several **tips for preparing the speaking outline** (pg. 179).

  i. ***Use key words and phrases.***

  ii. ***Write clearly and legibly.***

  iii. ***Add cues for delivery.***

VI. **Note cards** (pg. 180).

a. Some speakers use note cards instead of a speaking outline.

  i. There are a few guidelines for using note cards.

    1. Use key words and phrases and place no more than five or six lines on each card.

    2. Write clearly and legibly.

    3. Use only one side of the card.

    4. Number each card so they can be easily reordered if they get mixed up.

    5. Put cues for delivery on the cards so you can see them.

    6. Give the cards a low profile when the speech is being delivered.

End of the Chapter Activities and Discussion Questions

The following questions can be found at the end of Chapter Eight.

Review Questions and Activities

1. Write a specific purpose, thesis statement, main points, and sub-points for a speech on a topic of your choice. Now mix up those main points and sub-points, and try to deliver a sketch of the speech to your classmates. Can they follow your organization? Why or why not?

This activity can work well as an impromptu speaking activity. Give students time to write out their thesis statement, main points, and sub-points for the speech. Encourage students to respond with a speech they are considering giving in class. Then, have students deliver an impromptu version of the mixed up speech. Or, have students write out the thesis, main points, etc., mix them up, and then trade with another student. Give students time to sort out the mixed up version, then, call on each student to "present" the mixed up version, their revisions, and to give an explanation for why they would organize the speech in the way they have (you can ask them to name their organizational pattern, the kinds of reasoning they might use, and so on).

2. Choose one of the following topics: "M & M's®" candy, "Valentine's Day," or "finals week." Using each of the five patterns of organization discussed in this chapter, write a specific purpose, thesis statement, and main points, for a speech about the topic you chose. What is the emphasis in each speech, depending on its organizational pattern?

   This activity can work well as an in-class assignment. Place students into small groups and give each group a specific topic (or have the students choose their topic). Direct the students to follow the instructions and write an outline for each of the organizational patterns. You can use a variation of the handout that appears in Chapters 2 and 4 of this manual for the specific purpose, thesis statement, and main points. Narrowing down main points will consistently challenge students. The more practice and feedback they get, the more successful they can be in their speeches. At the end of the activity have students provide some examples for the class.

3. In class, write a possible speech topic on a three-by-five-inch card or a strip of paper. Pass your topic to your instructor. Your instructor will select several topics, ask you to get into groups of five, and distribute a topic to each group. With your group, write the specific purpose, thesis statement, and main points for a speech. Also write connectives for the speech, including each of the four types of connectives discussed in this chapter. Now deliver the sketch of your group's speech to the class (be sure to use your connectives).

   Place students into small groups, and follow the instructions included here. This activity can be very helpful for students after you have lectured about each of these concepts.

4. Imagine you're going to give a speech describing your day from breakfast through dinner. Prepare a preparation outline for this speech. Make sure your outline includes the title of your speech, your specific purpose and thesis statement, an introduction, four main points with at least two subpoints per main point, connectives, and a conclusion.

   Divide students into small groups of about 4 and work together or individually to create the preparation outline. Have students give each other feedback on how effectively the preparation outline was constructed. It would also be useful to have a sample outline for students to use as a model. There are some sample outlines included here in the Instructor's Manual and in the textbook.

5. Using the preparation outline from question 4, construct a speaking outline for your speech on your day. Add delivery cues as needed. Discuss the differences between your preparation outline and your speaking outline. What are the strengths and weaknesses of each?

   In connection with 4 above, have students follow the directions included in this question in their small groups. After they are finished, have them discuss the last part of the question, and to address how their speeches will be adapted according to the group feedback provided.

6. Check out Speech Studio to see how effectively other students organized their speeches. Can you identify the organizational patterns they used? Or record a speech you're working on, upload it to Speech Studio, and ask your peers for their feedback. What feedback could you use to fine tune your speech organization before you give your speech in class?

Web Activities

1. **One Voice**
   Access http://www.onevoicemovement.org/to gather additional information about PeaceWorks. Consider how members of this organization might use the different patterns of organization for different speeches they may give. How is this useful to you as you prepare speeches in relation to service learning?

   You can assign students this activity as homework. Upon their return to class, have them discuss what they discovered while navigating through this website. This activity can help prepare students to effectively structure their speeches if they are giving speeches in conjunction with service learning.

2. **Business Council for Peace**
   Access www.bpeace.org. By exploring this website you will learn how this organization assists women in areas of conflict build businesses to sustain their families. Additionally, this organization creates jobs for other individuals in different countries, and helps to strengthen and foster peace.

   Encourage students to access this website through CengageNOW, particularly if you are requiring a service learning component to your basic public speaking course. As they navigate through the website have them consider ways in which they would develop a speech about this organization. Instruct them to consider the different patterns of organization that they would use to help structure the information that emerges in this website. For example, can they use the topical pattern of organization if giving an informative speech about this organization? How would they use the problem and solution pattern?

3. **MLA and APA Citation Styles**
   http://www.aresearchguide.com/styleguides.html can be useful to you as you develop your preparation outline. There are different style manuals that instructors require for the proper citation of sources. This website can provide the guidance you need and simplify the process.

   Students often struggle with and confuse how to cite sources properly within their outline, in their works cited/bibliography, and during their speech. Direct them to this web connect resource to assist them in this process.

InfoTrac College Edition Activities

1. **InfoTrac College Edition Exercise 8.1: Assessing Clarity**
   Purpose: To appreciate the importance of organization.
   Directions: Use InfoTrac College Edition's PowerTrac feature to find two speeches from *Vital Speeches*. Compare the organization of the two speeches. Which speech was better organized? To what degree was it easier to follow the ideas of the more organized speaker? What suggestion would you give the speaker who wasn't as organized?

   This activity can be done as a homework assignment. Finding speeches they find interesting will challenge students. Prompt students by having them think about politicians with whom they agree or disagree, any celebrities or athletes that may have spoken out on an issue, or events that may have occurred that warranted a speech. Once they have taken this first step, have them search on InfoTrac.

Students will need some time to complete this activity. On the due date of this activity, have students report to the class some of the speeches they read and the observations they made.

2. **InfoTrac College Edition Exercise 8.2: Using Transitions**
   Purpose: To identify and appreciate a communicator's use of transitions.
   Directions: It's important for speakers to use transitions, and it is also necessary for writers to use transitions to help their readers. Use InfoTrac College Edition to locate two articles on a topic of your choosing. Identify the transitions used in each article. Which article used more effective transitions? How did the transitions help you better understand each article?

   Assign this activity ahead of time and, on the due date of the assignment, have students report their observations to the class. Ask students to name the specific types of connectives used (internal summary, preview, etc.). This activity does not take too much time to complete and is especially useful if you are teaching in a learning community.

Interactive Student and Professional Speech Videos Website

1. **Video Clip 1: Student Speech: Organization of Main Points**
   Watch Cindy's speech about the proper way to fold a flag. What are her main points? What are her subpoints? What organizational pattern does she use? How effective is this pattern for her particular topic?

   Show this video clip in class and have students respond to the questions asked here. Remind students that this speech was given by a student taking her first public speaking course, just like them, rather than a professional speaker. Inform them, too, that this speech was given in class, then re-taped only once, so that they can get a sense of what a real speech looks like, rather than a very rehearsed one. Also emphasize to students that different speakers may choose different elements on which to focus. Remind them to always keep in mind their speaking goal and the specific purpose and thesis statements. Encourage students to critique Cindy's speech for its strengths as well as its weaknesses, if the students see any portions of the speech they might "copy" or wish were done differently.

2. **Video Clip 2: Student Speech, Jeff Malcolm, Chronological Organization**
   Watch how Jeff Malcolm uses a chronological pattern of organization in his speech. What are his main points? Is it easy to follow his organization? What are the advantages of using this pattern? What are the disadvantages?

   Show this video in class and have students respond to the questions asked here. It is often helpful for students to see examples of the different patterns of organization. You may also want to generate more examples of the different patterns of organization as illustrated by previous student speeches. Your examples can be very specific to your own speech assignments, which can be very helpful for students. If you are conducting service learning as an option, refer to the end of the chapter for a list of examples illustrating the different patterns of organization as they can relate to speeches about local area nonprofit agencies. Remind students, as in #2, that Jeff's speech was given in a public speaking course similar to the one they are taking (rather than as a professional speaker).

3. **Video Clip 3: Student Speech, Damien Beasley, Citing Sources**
   As you watch the video clip of Damien giving his speech, consider how he handles his sources. Does he cite sources in this clip? How effectively does he provide information about the sources he used?

It is particularly helpful for students to watch an example of a student citing sources in his or her speech. Be sure to emphasize to students what your specific expectations are when they cite sources. Other examples of students citing sources are found throughout many of the video clips included on the web connect website.

Additional Exercises and Resources

1. **Transition Words and Phrases**
   Go to http://owl.english.purdue.edu/handouts/general/gl_transition.html to read a list of transition words and phrases you can use to guide your audience creatively through your speech. Some of these words are signposts, and some could be useful in transition sentences. Listen to your everyday conversations with people. What transition words are used? Are you more likely to hear transition words in formal discussions or informal conversations?

   Have students access this website for their own reference. This website can prove to be particularly helpful for students when creating different connectives. This website can also be helpful for composition students who are taking both speech and composition at the same time.

2. **Plagiarism: Its Nature and Consequences**
   Go to http://www.lib.duke.edu/libguide/plagiarism.htm to read Duke University's description of plagiarism and its consequences. What is Duke's definition of plagiarism? How does this definition compare with what you thought plagiarism is? What is the penalty for plagiarism at your school?

   Students often get confused about what plagiarism actually entails. This website can help students clarify what plagiarism is. You can also incorporate some of this information in your lecture about plagiarism. It is also a good idea to incorporate something about plagiarism and its potential consequences in our syllabi to ensure the utmost clarity for students. Be sure to connect this discussion to the public dialogue and to civility, rather than simply to the ideas of "right or wrong" so students get a larger sense of the implications of plagiarism.

3. **Quoting/Paraphrasing and Works Cited**
   At the end of this chapter you will find a handout that includes information on how to directly quote and paraphrase sources as well as what information to include. Feel free to copy this handout for students as they are preparing for their speeches. An activity on how to directly quote and paraphrase is also included on this handout. Place students into groups of 3-4 and have them practice with the quotes that appear on the handout. You can also do this activity in conjunction with activity #3 of the General Activities section of this chapter.

4. **Practicing Connectives**
   For a quick in-class activity, try the following: Have students write a topic on a piece of scrap paper. Then have students switch their topics around with their peers a few times. Then, have students partner up and work together on creating a connective moving from one topic to the next. Students will be initially confused because their topics may not relate. The object of this activity is to work on connectives, and not necessarily make the topics actually follow one another (part of the success of this activity is in the humor and the student's creativity); however, if students can make the topics directly related through the connective, then they should get "bonus" praise or points. After you have given students a few minutes to work on their connectives, have each pair share their example with

121

the class. This activity works best right after you have defined the different types of connectives, and it also helps divide up a lecture.

A modified version of this assignment is to have students write down topics on a piece of paper and trade them with one another, as above. Then, beginning with a student in one of the end seats (either the front edge of the class or the back), have the first student "preview her or his topic." Then, moving one-by-one around the classroom, have each student use a connective of some kind to connect their topics to the previous person's.

5. **Preparing a Mini-Speech in Small Groups**
To practice general purpose statements, specific purpose and thesis statements, main points and connectives, and source citation, direct students to create mini-speeches in small groups. Begin by placing the students into groups of 3 or 4, and give each group a newspaper or magazine. Tell students that they will develop a mini-speech based on one of the articles they read in the newspaper or magazine. Make sure to emphasize that they need to cite their sources. After you have given students about 20-30 minutes, have each group present their mini-speech. Have other groups critique the speeches focusing on the elements listed at the beginning of the description of this activity. Also emphasize to students that they do not need to choose elaborate or complicated topics for the purposes of this activity. This activity is designed to help students to put all of the different components of the body of the speech together. To prevent the "best" speakers from delivering the speech, ask each member of the group to present a part of the speech.

Quoting and Paraphrasing

Created by
Jennifer Emerling Bone
T. M. Linda Scholz

Citing sources/speaking sources in speeches may be awkward at first; however, it is very important. Citing sources helps speakers establish their credibility by strengthening information and arguments they have to offer. The following are guidelines for citing sources while you are speaking.

Citing Sources While Speaking

You have two options when citing sources while you are speaking: 1) Directly quoting a source; 2) Paraphrasing a source. Regardless of which you choose you always need to give credit where credit is due in order to avoid plagiarism.

Direct Quotes: When you use the source's content word for word.

- ✓ When you directly quote, you should not use a quotation that is more than a few sentences long because of wordiness and confusion.
- ✓ Make sure that **you** are formulating the argument first, and use direct quotes only as support for **your** arguments.
- ✓ Only use direct quotes when someone else's words say it better than you can say it.

Paraphrasing: When you summarize the source's content into your own words, without changing the original intent or meaning.

- ✓ The author and source **still need to be cited.**
- ✓ Diana Hacker in the third edition of her *Pocket Style Manual* recommends that to avoid plagiarism you should "set the source aside, write from memory, and consult the source later to check for accuracy" (112).

Information that must be cited: The following information needs to be stated (cited) while you are speaking.

- ✓ The author of the article, book, magazine, website, etc.
- ✓ The author's title or credentials (for credibility).
- ✓ The date of the publication, when the website/webpage was last updated or accessed.
- ✓ If only two-three authors: state their last names as they appear.
- ✓ If more than three state the first author followed by "et. al."

Samples for Practice

The following are some quotes with which to practice. Decide to either directly quote or paraphrase. Be sure to follow the guidelines above for effective source citation.

1. *Nine of the dead from the pre-dawn raid on Gaza City were children, including one two-month old baby who was borne aloft by angry mourners Tuesday in a funeral procession that brought out tens of thousands of Palestinians to the dusty streets of Gaza.*

   On Wednesday, Palestinians pulled the bodies of three children from the rubble. Palestinians said the names of the children were on the list of dead from Tuesday, and relatives thought their bodies could not be recovered.

   Source:

   Associated Press. "Some Troops May Withdraw, Israeli Foreign Minister Says." *New York Times.*

   July 24, 2002 http://www.nytimes.com

2. *Toronto is the site this year of World Youth Day, a recurring Roman Catholic gathering that the pope began in the mid-1980's and makes a point of attending. His journey here brought him within a few dozen miles of the United States, where revelations of the sexual abuse of young people by Catholic priests have thrown the church into crisis.*

   But the pope made no mention of this, and Vatican officials did not offer any predictions about whether he would do so at the events that he planned to attend between today and Monday, when he departs for Guatemala and then Mexico.

   The officials said the pope was carrying a broader message of hope, and his brief appearance early this afternoon was perhaps most striking as a testament both to his will and to the physical forces that frustrate it.

   Source:

   Bruni, Frank. "Resolute Pope, In Canada, Addresses Young People." *New York Times*. July 24,

   2002 http://www.nytimes.com

3. *Already this summer, in addition to felling a crow in Oklahoma and a blue jay in Nebraska, West Nile has infected more than 50 birds and eight horses in Texas. Health officials in Houston on Tuesday confirmed that a 50-year-old man who went to the emergency room complaining of a stiff neck, nausea, a low-grade fever and slight confusion, was infected with West Nile, that state's first human exposure.*

   "The patient is making a nice recovery. He'll definitely survive," said Dr. Daniel Musher, head of infectious disease at the Houston Veterans' Affairs Medical Center. Factoring in bird migration patterns, temperature, humidity, vegetation, and mosquito abundance, experts are projecting West Nile cases could appear in Colorado, Kansas, and New Mexico before the outbreak season tapers off with fall's chillier weather.

   Source:
   Henderson, Diedtra. "W. Nile Virus on the Way to Colorado." *Denver Post*. July 24, 2002
   http://www.denverpost.com

Sample Connectives for Speeches about Nonprofit Agencies

The following are a few examples of the different connectives that can be used for a speech focusing on a nonprofit agency. Included are the topic, general purpose, specific purpose, thesis statement, and main points. In Chapter 15 of this manual you will also find examples for the different types of informative speeches focusing on nonprofit organizations.

Topic: Neighbor to Neighbor

General Purpose: To inform

Specific Purpose: To inform my audience about the programs offered by Neighbor to Neighbor.

Thesis Statement: Programs offered by Neighbor to Neighbor include mortgage counseling, rental assistance and transitional housing.

Main points:
> I. Mortgage counseling.
> II. Rental assistance.
> III. Transitional housing.

Connectives

Transition

> *"Now that I have told you about mortgage counseling at Neighbor to Neighbor, I will talk about rental assistance."*

Internal Preview

> *"Rental assisting will provide clients with lists of housing availability as well as counseling to find the right house and keep it."*

Internal Summary

> *"To summarize rental assistance, clients are provided with lists of available housing, and are provided with counseling to help keep the rental."*

Signposts and Preview

> *"I will first tell you about mortgage counseling. Secondly, I will tell you about rental assistance. And lastly, I will tell you about transitional housing."*

Supplemental Bibliography

Brake, Mike. "9 Steps to Effective Speech-Writing." *Writer's Digest,* 79 (Jul 1999): 40-43.

> Tips are presented for creating an effective speech. The nine tips include how to structure and organize your speech. If you have a class that likes lists, this is a great resource to use.

Cohen, Jodi R., Communication Criticism: Developing Your Critical Powers. Thousand Oaks, Calif.: Sage Publications, 1998.

> In Chapter 6, "Structure as Organization," Cohen addresses the overall concept of ordering or organizing in communication. The canon of disposition or arrangement is discussed, as well as order in editing, narrative, and drama. This is an interesting chapter about the theory and necessity of ordering communication messages.

Donahue, Elinor. "The Eight Fold Path to Better Speeches: Clarity, Power and Purpose." *Vital Speeches of the Day,* 61 (1995): 669.

> Similar to the nine steps asserted by Brake, these tips come in the form of a speech given about giving speeches. These are great practical tips from a real speech writer and a fun speech to hand out to the class and evaluate together.

Dowis, Richard. The Lost Art of the Great Speech: How to Write It, How to Deliver It. New York: AMACOM, 2000.

> Chapter four, "Outlining and Organization," includes suggestions for how to translate your ideas and research into a structured outline. The speech "A Celebration of Freedom" by John F. Kennedy is included as an example of a particularly well-ordered speech and could be used in classroom discussion.

Meriwether, Nell. 12 Easy Steps to Successful Research Papers. Lincolnwood, IL: NTC Publishing Group, 1997.

> Included in this book are an abundance of tips on how to put together a research assignment, which could be easily adapted to speech class. Chapter eight covers the formulation of the first draft—how to order your thoughts, while Chapter nine has a helpful section on how and when to use citations for outside information.

Winkler, Anthony C. and McCuen, Jo Ray., Writing the Research Paper: A Handbook with Both the MLA and APA Documentation Styles. Fort Worth, TX : Harcourt Brace College Publishers, 1999.

> This is a helpful manual for source citation, showing how to execute the common types of citations your students will be using.

Chapter Nine: Introductions and Conclusions

Chapter Goals

Chapter nine introduces students to the different objectives a speaker should accomplish in the introduction and conclusion of a speech. Students should have an understanding of the following goals as they reach the end of this chapter:

- To describe the four functions of an effective introduction
- To prepare a compelling introduction
- To describe the two functions of an effective conclusion
- To prepare a compelling conclusion
- To identify at least four tips for preparing an introduction and a conclusion

Chapter Outline

I. **The introduction** (pg. 186).
    a. There are **four functions to any introduction**.
        i. **Catch the audience's attention** (pg. 187).
            1. The most important task is to get the audience to listen to you, to be intrigued, curious, and eager to hear more about your topic.
            2. Pique your audience's curiosity and show them how the topic relates to them.
        ii. **Reveal the topic of your speech** (pg. 187).
            1. In revealing your topic, you let the audience know the subject of the speech.
            2. Keeping an audience in suspense is fine for a moment or two, but the introduction should reveal the topic before the first main point.
        iii. **Establish your credibility** (pg. 187).
            1. In your introduction, communicate that you have considerable knowledge about the topic.
            2. Do not lie or mislead the audience about your qualifications, however.
        iv. **Preview your speech** (pg. 187).
            1. A preview is a brief overview of each of the main points in the speech.
            2. In a **preview** you share with your audience a brief overview of each of the main points in your speech.

II. **Preparing a compelling introduction** (pg. 188).
    a. There are several creative ways to writing a compelling introduction.
        i. **Ask a question**.
            1. Questions can arouse curiosity and capture an audience's attention.
            2. Speakers can use a **rhetorical question,** *or a question that the audience is not supposed to answer out loud.*
            3. Speakers also can solicit answers to their opening questions directly from their audience.
        ii. **Tell a story** (pg. 189).
            1. Stories draw an audience into a speech by offering characters and dramas they can relate to.

   2. Stories personalize topics that might seem remote or disconnected to some members of the audience.

  iii. **Recite a quotation or a poem** (pg. 189).

   1. Quotations bring someone else's words into your speech and lend it the credibility of someone more famous or knowledgeable than you are.

   2. Quotations and poems teach lessons or illustrate perspectives that are relevant to a speech.

   3. Quotes can be simple or complex.

   4. Make sure the quote relates directly to the topic or illustrates the importance of the subject.

   5. Cite the source of the quote or poem, and deliver it so the audience knows it is not your own words.

  iv. **Give a demonstration** (pg. 190).

   1. Speeches about activities, sports, arts, and crafts are good possibilities for demonstrations.

   2. The demonstrations should be only a few minutes or even seconds.

  v. **Make an intriguing or startling statement** (pg. 192).

   1. Startling statements catch the audience's attention, but use caution so as not to offend an audience.

   2. The statement should invite an audience to listen, not shut down communication.

  vi. **State the importance of the topic** (pg. 193).

   1. When you state the importance of the topic, you tell the audience why they should listen.

   2. Speakers can show that a significant amount of people is affected by the topic.

   3. Speakers can show that most people engage in a certain type of behavior.

   4. Speakers can show that although a certain practice or phenomenon is uncommon, it has a significant impact.

  vii. **Share your expertise** (pg. 194).

   1. Sharing your expertise does not mean boasting and bragging.

   2. Establishing your credibility often is a subtle process.

  viii. **State what's to come** (pg. 194).

   1. When a speaker previews a speech, they give their audience an overview of the main points.

   2. This helps the audience follow the ideas in the speech.

  ix. There are several **tips to preparing an introduction** (pg. 196).

   1. *Look for introductory materials as you do your research.*

   2. *Prepare and practice the full introduction in detail.*

   3. *Be brief.*

   4. *Be creative.*

III. **The conclusion** *is the final contact a speaker has with his or her audience and thus the last impression the audience has of the speaker* (pg. 196).

 a. **There are two goals in a conclusion.**

  i. **End your speech.**

   1. When you have concluded your final main point, use a shift in delivery to signal to your audience that you are about to wrap up.

   2. Use a clear transition.

  ii. **Reinforce your thesis statement** (pg. 197).
    1. A speaker reminds the audience of the core idea behind the descriptions and assertions made in the speech.
    2. This step can either be a succinct summary or a more elaborate one.
 b. There are several **ways to prepare compelling conclusion** (pg. 198).
  i. **Summarize your main points.**
    1. A **summary** *is a concise restatement of the main points at the end of a speech.*
      a. The summary can be used to review ideas and remind the audience about what's important in the speech.
      b. Three things should be done during a summary.
        i. Offer only a summary, and do not restate too much from the speech.
        ii. Do not introduce new ideas in the summary.
        iii. Try to use the same kind of language in the conclusion as was used in the body of the speech.
  ii. **Answer your introductory question** (pg. 198).
    1. If a speaker begins the speech with a question, they can answer that question in the conclusion.
    2. This technique reminds an audience of what they have learned and the importance of understanding more about a particular issue.
  iii. **Refer back to the introduction** (pg. 199).
    1. If a speaker opens with a word, phrase, or idea, they can return to it in the conclusion.
    2. This technique is usually combined with other techniques for conclusions, such as summarizing the main points.
  iv. **Recite a quotation** (pg. 199).
    1. A concluding quotation can come from someone cited in the speech.
    2. A concluding quotation can come from someone famous the audience may recognize.
 c. **Tips for a conclusion** (pg. 199).
  i. *Look for concluding materials.*
  ii. *Be creative.*
  iii. *Be brief.*
  iv. *Don't leave the conclusion to chance.*

End of the Chapter Activities and Discussion Questions

The following questions can be found at the end of Chapter Nine.

Review Questions and Activities

1. Name eight different techniques for catching the attention of the audience and revealing the topic of a speech. Identify the strengths of each technique.

 This can be a good exam review question for students to respond to. Also, have students consider this question if they are facing challenges when preparing their introductions.

2. Why should speakers establish their credibility and preview the main points of a speech? Are these components of an introduction important?

   This is great question to ask students as you present your lecture material. It also is a good exam review question for students. You can also have students respond to this question during a lecture about credibility.

3. Suppose you have been asked to give a speech on the history of bubble gum. How would you establish your credibility on this topic? How creative do you think you could be in introducing this topic? Give examples of how you would establish credibility and your creativity.

   You can posit this question to students in small groups or ask them to consider their options individually. If you place students in small groups, students can also see that different speakers will approach the same topic in different ways. If you ask them to respond individually, have students share their ideas so that they can see the different ways people can approach establishing credibility in a speech.

4. Name the four different techniques for concluding a speech. Identify the strengths and weaknesses of each one.

   Students may be able to identify the four techniques, but they may not be able to remember the strengths and weakness of each. Place students into groups, ask them to name the four techniques and to discuss the strengths and weaknesses of each, (using their books as a reference if they have them in class is fine). This is a great way to review conclusions before a round of speeches begins or before an exam.

5. In class, write a possible speech topic on a slip of paper and trade that paper with another student. Now write an introduction and a conclusion for a speech on that topic using the techniques discussed in this chapter. Present your introduction and conclusion to the class for feedback on each of their components.

   You can easily conduct this activity in small groups. This can be a fun way to reinforce for students the importance of developing sound introductions and conclusions.

6. Check out Speech Studio to see how other students handled their speech introductions and conclusions. Do the techniques they used give you ideas for your own introductions and conclusions? Or record a speech you're working on, upload it to Speech Studio, and ask your peers for their feedback. What feedback could you use to fine tune your introduction and conclusion before you give your speech in class?

Web Activities

1. **Starting with a Quotation**
    Purpose: To identify quotations that could be used in the introduction to a speech.
    Directions: The Quotations Page is the oldest quotation site on the internet with 26,000. quotations from over 31,000. authors and a forum section to answer questions about quotations. Go to http://Quotationspage.com/ to explore find a quotation you might use in your next speech. What tone would the quotation set for the speech? Is the quotation humorous or serious? Assess the credibility of the speaker of the quotation. Is this someone you would be wise to use in your speech? How does the quotation relate to your topic?

    Students will be interested in accessing this website for ideas for their own speeches so encourage them to use the website. If you have access to the internet in your classroom, you may also want to bring this website up during lecture to show students what is on it. You can also ask students to log on, bring several options to class with them, and then share some of the selections students made during your lecture.

2. **Amusing Facts.com**
    Access this website at http://www.amusingfacts.com and select a category "for amusement." As you browse through the site, what facts might you use to help in the introduction of your speech? Which facts might be helpful to conclude your speech?

    Students are consistently challenged by creating effective attention getters in their introduction. Additionally, they are challenged by concluding their speeches on a strong note. Have them access this website, and in small groups of 3 have them create an introduction and conclusion utilizing an amusing fact from the website.

InfoTrac College Edition Activities

1. **InfoTrac College Edition Activity 9.1: Establishing Significance**
    Purpose: To understand how speakers establish the importance of their speech.
    Directions: Use InfoTrac College Edition to locate President Bush's stem cell speech in *Vital Speeches,* September 1, 2001. Read the opening lines. To what degree does Bush effectively communicate the significance of his speech topic? Does he adequately convey the magnitude of the issue of stem cell research? What might he have done differently?

    Instruct students to read this speech before class so they are prepared to discuss it. Ask students to bring their copies of the speech to class with them and, either as a full class or in group, ask students to identify the specific phrases and words Bush uses to communicate the significance of his topic. Consider the structure of his argument and his language choices as you discuss this speech.

2. **InfoTrac College Edition Activity 9.2: Establishing Credibility**
   Purpose: To explore how speakers establish credibility in their introductions.
   Directions: Use InfoTrac College Edition's PowerTrac feature to locate two speeches in *Vital Speeches*. How did each speaker establish credibility? Who was most effective? Why?

   Ask students to locate speeches by one individual they know nothing about and another whom they are familiar with. Or, have them locate two speeches on the same issue by different speakers. Ask them to compare the strategies each speaker used in their speeches to establish credibility. You can also place students with partners and have them work on this assignment during a library day. Discuss the specific strategies each speaker used, including arguments and language.

3. **InfoTrac College Edition Activity 9.3: Concluding Remarks**
   Purpose: To understand how speakers conclude their speeches.
   Directions: Use InfoTrac College Edition's PowerTrac feature to locate three speeches in *Vital Speeches*. Read the conclusion of each speech. What technique did each speaker use to conclude? How effective was each conclusion? Were there any of the three speeches that lacked a conclusion? How might the audience have perceived that speech? Which of the three conclusions was the most effective?

   Use the same guidelines for question #2, above, discussing conclusions rather than credibility. Ask students, either individually or in groups, to share the specific steps they identified in the conclusions of the speech. If they can't find the specific steps, discuss the effectiveness of the speeches without explicit conclusions as compared to those that have strong conclusions.

Interactive Student and Professional Speech Videos Website

1. **Video Clip 1: Student Speech: Brandi's Introduction**
   As you watch Brandi's story about feeding wildlife, notice at what point you realize the topic of the speech. At what point do you realize Brandi's position on this topic? Does her story motivate you to listen to the rest of her speech? Why or why not?

   Show this video in class as a sample speech. Have students respond to the questions listed here during class discussion, identifying the specific components of an introduction as Brandi speaks. Be sure to emphasize to students what you are specifically looking for in their speeches, and how you are going to grade them on these different components.

2. **Video Clip 2: Student Speech, Mike Piel, Preview**
   Watch Mike's preview of his speech. Based on his preview, do you think his speech will be easy to follow? What are the topics he will cover? Are there times when a speaker may not want to use a preview?

   Show this video in class as a sample speech. Have students respond to the questions listed here during class discussion, identifying the specific components of the introduction as Mike speaks. Be sure to emphasize to students what you are specifically looking for in their speeches, and how you are going to grade them on these different components.

3. **Video Clip 3: Student Speech, Mike Piel, Conclusion**
   Watch Mike's conclusion of his speech. Based on his conclusion, do you think his speech was easy to

132

follow? What are the topics he covered, did they coincide with the ones he previewed in his introduction? Are there times when a speaker may not want to use a summary?

Show this video in class as a sample speech. Have students respond to the questions listed here during class discussion, identifying the specific components of the conclusion as Mike speaks. Be sure to emphasize to students what you are specifically looking for in their speeches, and how you are going to grade them on these different components.

4. **Video Clip 4: Student Speech, Chelsey, Conclusion**
   As you watch Chelsey's conclusion, pay particular attention to how she transitions into her conclusion with startling statistics. Is her use of statistics effective for her conclusion? How does she also appeal to her audience as she concludes? Is this effective for her conclusion?

   Show this video in class. Facilitate a discussion centered on the questions listed here. Discuss the effectiveness of her use of statistics at the end of her speech, in addition to her use of emotional appeals.

Additional Exercises and Resources

1. **The Speech Introduction**
   Go to http://www.nvcc.edu/home/npeck/spd100/blueprintfiles/intro.htm to read tips about speech introductions. Compare the tips on the website with the advice given in this book. What additional tips does the author of the article suggest? Which of these tips do you think reflects the goals of public speaking that have been discussed in the text? Is there any advice on this page you believe would hinder your dialogue with an audience?

   You can have students access this website, and be prepared to discuss it during class, or pull it up during your lecture if you have internet access in the classroom. Students like it when instructors adapt in-class content to real world examples, so this is a great site to use. Ask the students if they agree or disagree with the author. When students respond, encourage them to support their "claims" fully and logically. These questions can also be addressed after the first round of speeches so that students can discuss what made introductions effective.

2. **A Mini Group Speech**
   Usually, introductions and conclusions are covered last when preparing students for their first speech. So, this is an activity you can use after lecturing about introductions and conclusions that asks students to pull all the parts of a speech together. Place students in groups and have students create a mini-speech on a topic of their choice. Direct them to consider the following: a clear and compelling introduction, a well-organized body, and a clear and compelling conclusion. Have the groups designate a "speaker" who will deliver the speech. After about 20 minutes, have each group's "speaker" actually give the speech written by the group. After each speaker has spoken, have the class "critique" the speech. Did the "speaker" accomplish every goal in the introduction and conclusion? Was the body of the speech well organized? Did the conclusion incorporate the two components of a strong conclusion?

3. **Writing an Introduction in Different Ways**
   Divide the class into groups of 4 students each. Give all the groups the same topic, or give half of the groups one topic and the other half another topic. Then, give each group different "techniques for

133

preparing compelling introductions." For instance, one group might get "Demonstration" another group might get "Tell a story" and so on. Give the groups some time to prepare an introduction to their topic using their assigned technique. Remind them of the four goals they also should accomplish in their introductions. After they have prepared, have a designated speaker from each present the introduction to the full class. Have the class give a critique of the introduction. Was it effective? How so? What could have been done differently in order to make the introduction more effective? This is a great way to illustrate how a single topic can be introduced in many different ways.

4. **Writing a Conclusion in Different Ways**
   Do the same as in number 2 above, but this time have the different groups focus on a conclusion.

Supplemental Bibliography

Brake, Mike. "9 Steps to Effective Speech-Writing." *Writer's Digest*, 79 (Jul 1999): 40-43.

> Emphasizes the need to close the speech "with a bang." A great handout or resource for lecture and discussion.

Detz, Joan. *How to Write and Give a Speech: A Practical Guide for Executives, PR People, Managers, Fund-Raisers, Politicians, Educators, and Anyone Who Has to Make Every Word Count.* New York: St. Martin's Press, 1984.

> Chapter five includes information on writing speech introductions and conclusions. For both, several "rules" are offered for crafting introductions and conclusions. These rules could be used in classroom discussion or lecture to help students write more engaging beginnings and endings.

Donahue, Elinor "The Eight Fold Path to Better Speeches." *Vital Speeches of the Day.* 61 (1995): 669.

> Donahue offers tips on writing better speeches, including the importance of strong introductions and conclusions.

Dowis, Richard. The Lost Art of the Great Speech: How to Write It, How to Deliver It. New York: AMACOM, 2000.

> Chapter five, "Beginning Well," and chapter thirteen, "Closing the Speech," are both valuable tools in that they offer suggestions for writing better introductions and conclusion and then go on to show examples of each from famous American speeches. A nice resource for lecture or even a homework assignment.

Ehrlich, Henry. Writing Effective Speeches. New York: Paragon House, 1992.

> Section four "Parts of a Speech" offers suggestions for different types of attention-getters to use in the introduction of a speech. This material is useful for lecture material, examples, or as a resource to share with students.

George L. Morrisey, Thomas L. Sechrest, and Wendy B. Warman. Loud and Clear: How to Prepare and Deliver Effective Business and Technical Presentations. Reading, Mass.: Addison-Wesley, 1997. 4th ed.

> This text offers brief but helpful information. Chapter five explains the importance of both introductions and conclusions and provides examples and exercises for each. A great resource for lecture and ideas for in-class activities.

http://davelawrence.org/speaking_center/handouts/011_introductions_conclusions.html

> A nice handout source for introductions and conclusions

Chapter Ten: Language

Chapter Goals

Chapter Ten introduces students to the effective use of language in public speaking. As students reach the end of this chapter they should have an understanding of the following goals:

- To use clear and accurate language in speeches
- To use language that is culturally inclusive and gender inclusive
- To explain the difference between spoken and written language
- To describe at least two ways to use language to create memorable images
- To describe at least four ways to use language to create a pleasing rhythm

Chapter Outline

I. **Language** *is the system of verbal or gestural symbols a community uses to, and is central to, the speechmaking process* (pg. 203).
   a. In the public dialogue, language allows us to share our thoughts, question the ideas of others, and invite our audiences to consider our positions.
   b. **Language is ambiguous** (pg. 204).
      i. The three components of the **semantic triangle** help us in understanding the ambiguity of language.
         1. **The symbol,** appearing at the left corner of the triangle, *is the word or phrase spoken by the speaker.*
         2. **The referent**, appearing at the right corner of the triangle, *is the object, concept, or event the symbol represents.*
         3. **The thought or reference**, appearing at the top of the triangle, *is the memory and past experience audience members have with an object, concept or event.*
      ii. When speakers forget that words do not mean the same thing for everyone, they unintentionally create ambiguity for their audience.
         1. They can alienate their audience when they forget that people may share symbols, but not the same experiences.
   c. One way to clear up ambiguity is to use **concrete words** or *words that refer to a tangible object (a person, place or thing).* (pg. 206).
   d. Concrete words will help you avoid **abstract words** or *words that refer to ideas or concepts, but not to specific objects.*
II. **Language and culture** (pg. 206).
   a. People in different cultures name and define the world differently.
      i. In American Sign Language, signs are subtly altered to reflect the visual aspects of objects and events.
      ii. In spoken English, words are only occasionally modified to emphasize some aspect of appearance.
         1. To emphasize a visual aspect we add more words to the description.
         2. To emphasize a visual aspect we also may choose a different word all together.

136

      iii. Subcultures, or groups within a larger culture that share its language, may also use the language differently.
         1. The language of rap music has roots in the African American tradition of signifying.
  b. Signifying is governed by its own rules of grammar, semantics, and syntax.
  c. It allows people to make statements that have double, and often multiple, meanings that are not understood by people outside that group.
      i. Speakers can identify words the audience might not understand because of cultural or regional differences in order to offer clarification rather than confusion.
      ii. Speakers should "unpack" the meanings of **idioms** which are *fixed distinctive expressions whose meaning is not indicated by its individual words* (pg. 207).
      iii. Speakers familiarizing themselves with how cultural groups prefer to identify can prevent potential offense.
  d. This manner of speaking is not about "political correctness" but about respecting others.
  e. Groups name themselves because they wish to emphasize aspects of their lives that are important to them. **(See Table 10.1 for Appropriate Labels for People of Different Cultures)** (pg. 207).

III. **Language and gender** (pg. 209).
  a. It is important to use gender-neutral language so that speeches address both women and men.
      i. The American Psychological Association offers guidelines for gender-inclusive language.
      ii. Increasingly, speakers (including politicians) are using gender-inclusive words and phrases in their speaking.
        (See Table 10.2 for Guidelines for Gender-Inclusive Language) (pg. 209).
      iii. **Language and accuracy** (pg. 210).
  b. Speakers sometimes use words incorrectly (ex. persecuted vs. prosecuted).
  c. Using language accurately is important because errors can affect a speaker's meaning and credibility.
  d. Three tips can help speakers improve the accuracy of language.
      i. Check the definitions of words you are using.
         1. When a word is central to the meaning of a sentence, double check the definition in the dictionary.
         2. Looking up words can save a speaker considerable embarrassment.
      ii. Work with someone who has strong language skills if your use of language is not as strong as you would like.
      iii. Study the language.
         1. Speakers can read more books, magazines and newspapers.
         2. Speakers can take courses that focus on language skills.
         3. Speakers can practice with language and vocabulary workbooks from the library, bookstores, and teaching supply stores.

IV. **Language and public speaking** (pg. 211).
  a. Speakers should use language meant to be spoken and not read.
  b. The most effective speakers use an **oral style**, or a style that reflects the spoken rather than the written word.
  c. There are three differences between the spoken word and the written word.
      i. **Spoken language is more interactive** (pg. 211).
         1. Speakers make adjustment as they speak.
         2. Speakers ask or respond to questions.

3. When speaking in public, language reflects the shifts, pauses, and adjustments made for the audience.
4. Speakers carry on conversations with their audience in ways that are not reflected in the written word.
5. Nonverbal communication also reflects this interactive mode.

ii. **Spoken language is more casual** (pg. 212).
1. Written language tends to be more formal than spoken language.
2. When speaking, more contractions are used.
3. We run words together during speaking.
4. Speakers who speak in a written style sound more distant than speakers who talk to the audience.

iii. **Spoken language is more repetitive** (pg. 213).
1. Repetition is necessary in oral cultures to help audiences remember stories and information.
2. Public speakers also use more repetitive language to help audiences remember what they hear.
   i. Public speakers repeat main ideas.
   ii. Public speakers repeat main arguments.
   iii. Public speakers use repetitive tools.

V. **Language, imagery, and rhythm** (pg. 213).
a. There are several verbal techniques speakers can use to draw listeners into ideas.
   i. **Language that creates memorable imagery** (pg. 213).
   1. **Similes** *make an explicit comparison of two things that uses the words 'like' or 'as'* (pg. 213).
   2. A **metaphor** *makes a comparison between two things that describes one thing as being something else.*
      i. A **mixed metaphor** *is a metaphor that makes illogical comparisons between two or more things.*
      ii. Mixed metaphors should be avoided because they create confusion or humor at the expense of the speaker.
   3. **Personification** occurs *when we attribute human characteristics to animals, objects, or concepts* (pg. 214).
   ii. Speakers also can use **language that creates a pleasing rhythm** (pg. 214).
   1. **Parallelism** occurs *when we arrange related words so they are balanced, or related sentences have identical structures* (pg. 216).
   2. **Repetition** occurs *when we repeat keywords or phrases at the beginnings or endings of sentences or clauses* (pg. 216).
   3. **Alliteration** is *the repetition of a particular sound in a sentence or a phrase* (pg. 217).
      i. Alliteration can be used to create a mnemonic device.
      ii. A **mnemonic device** is *a rhyme, phrase, or other verbal device that makes information easier to remember.*
   4. **Antithesis** *places words and phrases in contrast or opposition to one another* (pg. 217).

138

End of the Chapter Activities and Discussion Questions

The following questions can also be found at the end of Chapter Ten.

Review Questions and Activities

1. Look up the dictionary definitions of five to seven keywords you will use in your next speech. Do they mean what you thought they meant? Have you been pronouncing them correctly? If you were using an incorrect word, replace it with a correct one.

    Students often mispronounce and misuse words in their speeches. Encourage them to look up words to ensure clarity and to avoid mistakes. They will also want to avoid embarrassment. Reminding students of this during your lecture can be very helpful. Also, after their speeches, if they do misuse a word, gently correct the word and say something to the effect of "a lot of people make this mistake" or "this has happened to me, too." Students will be open to this as long as you establish an environment that is appropriate and gentle under these circumstances.

2. Bring a newspaper or magazine to class and look for language that is sensitive or insensitive to culture and gender. In what ways is the language appropriate or inappropriate? What mistakes do you think the authors of the articles make, if any? What are the implications of these mistakes? What are the implications of the appropriate choices the author made?

    If you have time before class, look at a current issue of the school paper and identify some examples of labels there, then direct them to look for these labels in the papers they are using. They can look at cartoons as examples, as well as advertisements and the written text. Encourage students to find examples of both appropriate and inappropriate labels.

3. Bring a dictionary to class. Look up the following commonly confused pairs of words:

    accept/except, compose/comprise, nauseated/nauseous, adverse/averse, explicit/implicit, principal/principle, affect/effect, poured/pored, anxious/eager, fewer/less, reign/rein, appraise/apprise, healthy/healthful, stationery/stationary, between/among, imply/infer, uninterested/disinterested, compliment/complement, lay/lie, who/whom

    How many of these words did you have confused before you began this exercise?

    This is a very insightful activity for students. During lecture when you discuss how speakers may confuse words, students will nod in understanding; however, showing them actual examples can really drive the point home. And, when they do the work of looking up these commonly confused words, they see that they make mistakes they did not realize they were making. A variation of this activity can be for you to have students write down these words after you say them. After they have spelled the words, let them know the correct spelling, and discuss the proper meaning. Students do not have to reveal their own spelling or understanding of the words; they can keep these mistakes anonymous. Even doing this as a full class can really emphasize the importance of double-checking word usage.

6. Select a topic for an imaginary speech. Write out your introduction or first main point for that speech.

139

Now read that to a small audience. Put the paper aside and talk that part of your speech in an oral style. What differences do you notice? Is the oral style interactive, casual, and repetitive?

This activity can be done during class in small groups Ask students to follow the directions here, than have the other students respond to the questions. At the end of the activity, have students report back to the class. As they share their observations, emphasize and review the differences between the written and spoken word. This will also be a good place to remind students not to recycle their composition papers as their speeches because their speeches will sound like papers.

7. Divide into groups and select one of the following terms:

    smoking   greyhound racing   the draft   Halloween   gasoline

    Using the seven devices for creating imagery (simile, metaphor, personification, parallelism, repetition, alliteration, antithesis), write statements about this topic. Share your results with the class. Which devices helped you do a particularly good job conveying your ideas? Why do you think so?

    This activity can be done quite easily during class and is a fun way to get students thinking creatively about language and practicing devices they then can use in their speeches. After giving each group about 10 to 15 minutes to work, have them share their examples with the class.

6. Check out Speech Studio to see how other students use language in their speeches. In what ways do they use language accurately, to create memorable images, and to create pleasing rhythms? Or record a speech you're working on, upload it to Speech Studio, and ask your peers for their feedback. What feedback could you use to fine tune your language before you give your speech in class?

Web Activities

1. **CourseMate 10.3: Merriam-Webster Online**
    Merriam-Webster is one of the most well-respected dictionary publishers in the United States. Explore their site at http://www.m-w.com/ to learn how to use words more effectively. For example, click on the "Word of the Day" and use that word in a sentence during the day. Or click on the pronunciation guide to learn how to say words correctly. What other features of the site do you find useful?

    Encourage students to access this website to help them to use words more effectively in their speeches. You can even turn the "Word for a Day" into an activity in class or when you have a few minutes at the end of the period. For example, you can place the word for a day on your role sheet, and give students extra credit points for using the word correctly in an impromptu speech. Or, you can use the "Word for a Day" specifically as an impromptu topic at the end of a class period.

2. **American Rhetoric**

   Access http://www.americanrhetoric.com/to find multiple examples of political speeches. Look through some of the texts that are available in this website and pay close attention to how language is used throughout these texts. Does the language reflect written or oral style?

   This resource and discussion about the texts accessed by students can yield an interesting discussion in class about the differences between oral and written styles.

3. **Hip Hop Summit**

   Access www.hsan.org to learn more about the Hip Hop Summit.

   Currently, hip hop culture is a big part of students' lives. Have them access this web resource to find out more about this summit and the activism connected to it.

InfoTrac College Edition Activities

1. **InfoTrac College Edition Activity 10.1: Learning New Words**
   Purpose: To explore the meanings of new words.
   Directions: Use InfoTrac College Edition to look up and read an article that interests you. Make note of any new words you encounter in the article. Look up these words at Merriam-Webster Online (http://www.m-w.com/) or use a traditional dictionary. To what degree did learning the meaning of the word help you better understand the article? Why did the author of the article use complicated words?

   Assign this as a homework activity or extra credit activity. Once students have located their article, have them respond to the questions listed here. Ask them to bring their lists to class and share some of the words that they looked up in the dictionary.

2. **InfoTrac College Edition Activity 10.2: Comparing Written and Spoken Language**
   Purpose: To compare and contrast written and spoken language.
   Directions: Use InfoTrac College Edition to locate the article you read in InfoTrac College Edition Activity 12.1, or locate and read another article that interests you. Next, use InfoTrac College Edition's PowerTrac to search for a speech in *Vital Speeches*. Choose a speech that interests you and read it carefully. Then, compare and contrast the language used in the article and in the speech. How is the language in the speech interactive? What type of nonverbal communication do you imagine the speaker used? To what degree is the speech more casual than the article? To what degree is the language repetitive in the speech?

   Students can use the article they used in #1, or select a new article. Once students have decided on the speech, have them respond to the questions listed here. Have students identify the interactive qualities of language. Also, have them identify casual words used in the speech, and compare word usage between the speech and the article. This activity can be assigned as homework for students to work individually, or with partners.

Interactive Student and Professional Speech Videos Website

1. **Video Clip 1: George Bush, Inaugural Speech**
   Watch George Bush's inaugural speech and pay close attention to his use of language. How does he use language? Does he follow the guidelines provided in this chapter? Does he use imagery and rhythm to help make his speech more audience centered?

   Show this video clip in class, and facilitate a discussion centered on the questions listed here. Students often times feel that using "eloquent" language is beyond their means. Emphasize to students that with practice, they too can use language in creative ways so as to remain audience centered.

2. **Video Clip 2: Student Speech: Casual Style of Speaking**
   As you watch Brandi speak, pay attention to the casual style of language she uses. When would a more formal style of speaking be necessary? When is it appropriate for a speaker to be more casual?

   Show this video clip in class and have students address the questions listed here.

3. **Video Clip 3: Student Speech, Stacey Newman, Imagery and Rhythm**
   As you watch Stacey's speech, pay close attention to her use of imagery and rhythm. What makes her speech effective? Can you pick out the specific forms of imagery and rhythm?

   Show this clip in class, and have students respond to the questions listed here. It is often very useful to show students clips with good examples of the stylistic devices addressed in the chapter. A refresher of the different forms of rhythm and imagery can be very useful to students, and they appreciate it as they move into writing their speeches.

Additional Exercises and Resources

1. **Exploring Idioms**

   Purpose: To understand how we use idioms in our everyday communication.

   Directions: Read the meanings of several of the idioms listed at http://www.eslcafe.com/idioms/. Which of these idioms do you use? How widely shared do you think the meanings of these idioms are? How might they confuse someone who doesn't share your culture?

   If you have access to the internet in your classroom, access this website during class to help supplement your lecture. Or, simply access this website to incorporate examples into overheads or PowerPoint slides. This great website also has quizzes and other resources you can incorporate into your speech classroom. This site may also be helpful for international students.

2. **Choosing Gender-Neutral Language**

   Purpose: To learn how to use gender-neutral language.

   Directions: Take the quiz located at http://grammar.ccc.commnet.edu/grammar/quizzes/nova/nova6.htm to practice using gender-neutral language. Did you think the quiz was difficult? What uses of gender biased language were especially difficult to correct? To what extent do you think gender-neutral language reflects the needs and experiences of your audience members?

   Students often think that gender-neutral language is an extreme request or just angry people trying to force others to be "politically correct." As instructors in the field of communication, we know that this is not the case, but our students aren't always so sure. If you have access to the internet in your classroom, access this site during your lecture. You can also place some of the examples on an overhead or PowerPoint slide. There are quizzes on this website that your students might enjoy taking as a class and that will help you as you provide evidence of the harms of using language that isn't gender inclusive.

3. **Using Similes and Metaphors**

   Purpose: To appreciate how similes and metaphors can create meaning for audiences.

   Directions: Go to http://www.americanrhetoric.com/speeches/gwbushsecondinaugural.htm and watch George W. Bush's second inaugural address. Look for the similes and metaphors he used in his speech.

   You can have students access this website and speech, and approach the activity as you might activity #4 in the "Additional Exercises" section of this chapter. This can be very helpful for students to identify the different uses of imagery in every day speeches.

4. **The Semantic Triangle of Meaning**

   A variation of question #1 is to ask students to bring in rough drafts of the body of their outlines. Have them switch outlines, and select 3 or 4 words from someone else's outline they find ambiguous. Direct students to draw the semantic triangle for these words. After each student has had time to fill out the semantic triangle, return the outline to its original owner and a have students address the confusion their words might cause. As a class or working in pairs, clear up the ambiguities by using the suggestions in this chapter. A handout is included at the end of this chapter to go along with this activity.

143

5. **Language and Culture**

Have students access, or bring to class yourself, a copy of the article "Lauren Booth—Racial Slurs" *New Statesman*, 2 July 2001, p. 63 by Lauren Booth. Using the article as a springboard, discuss the concept of language and culture and the importance of appropriate labels for different groups. Validate students by telling them that oftentimes people feel very uncomfortable addressing these issues in public for fear of "offending someone." Some students also believe that no matter what they say or do, someone will always be offended. Tell students that if they follow the guidelines provided in this book, and genuinely approach their audiences with the intent of contributing to the public dialogue and staying audience centered, that they will be more successful. Let students know that sometimes speakers do say something that is not meant to be offensive or exclusive, but is. A good tip to also share with students is: The more speakers are open to questions and answers, to criticism and asking audience members for their own perspective to assist in clarification, then the more successful they will be as speakers. And, it never hurts to apologize if a speaker says something a member of the audience is offended by. This is also a good lesson for instructors!

6. **Imagery and Rhythm**

As a homework assignment, have students list and define each of the imagery and rhythmic devices defined on this chapter. Then, have them provide an example of each, other than what is in the textbook. Encourage them to use their speech topics as resources for creating their own examples. On the due date of the assignment, place students into small groups. Each group will be responsible for defining one or two of the stylistic devices, and sharing with the class the best example from the group. Students will not only be able to review this material and will be held responsible for reading the textbook, but they will be the ones to present the material to the class. Make sure to assign the reading ahead of time, and give them a specific due date for the assignment.

7. **"I Have a Dream" The Written and Spoken Work**
   Part One: The Written Speech

   Provide a copy of Martin Luther King, Jr.'s "I Have a Dream" speech to your students (full text of the speech can be found at the following website: http://www.americanrhetoric.com/speeches/Ihaveadream.htm). In small groups, have them read through the speech and respond to the following questions:
   1)   Can you find examples of denotative and connotative meaning in this speech (Chapter 10) and what role does culture play in these meanings?

   Issues related to master statuses and culture usually become apparent in this discussion. For example, African American students often describe the connotative definitions different from the white, European Americas students, although all students are profoundly affected by the speech. Prompt students to discuss these potential differences in light of master statuses and experiences and how this is reflected in how some audience members may respond to the language in their own speeches.

   2)   Can you identify the different types of imagery (simile, metaphor, and personification)? Why are those images powerful?

   Prompt students to pick out specific examples from the speech to illustrate each of these types of imagery. This serves also as a good review.

3)   Can you identify the different types of rhythm (parallelism, repetition, alliteration, and antithesis)? Can you get a good sense of the rhythm while reading the speech? At which points in the speech can you get a sense of the rhythm?

Prompt students to pick out specific examples from the speech to illustrate each of these types of rhythm. This serves also as a good review.

4)   Can you locate casual words in this speech? How effective might those words have been for the audience? Why would it have been important to use those words?

Prompt students to pick out specific examples from the speech.

5)   How might the spoken version of this speech be different from the written version of this speech?

Obviously, this speech was meant to be spoken, however, have students discuss the potential differences between reading the speech and actually hearing the speech. Some students in the class may have not ever seen the speech in its entirety. Encourage those students to lead this part of the discussion in their small groups. It will be interesting to get their perspectives before they actually view the speech and after.

Part Two: The Spoken Speech

After students have worked in small groups, have them share some of their responses with the class as a whole. Once they have shared their responses to the above questions, show the actual speech. After they have seen the speech, have students discuss the differences between the written version for the speech and the spoken version of the speech. Ask them what makes the spoken version more powerful for them. An important element to also address is how well Dr. King delivers the repetitive phrases. Also, talk about his vocal variety, including nonverbal signals such as gesturing, facial expressions, etc. This part of the activity can be conducted as a full class discussion. This speech is great to illustrate imagery and rhythm as well as the elements of delivery. This activity can easily take the whole class period, perhaps even moving on to the next class depending on how in-depth students go with the first part of the activity.

The Semantic Triangle

Select three or four especially complex or ambiguous words from a newspaper article, or from one of your own speeches. Using the semantic triangle of meaning, identify the symbol, referent, and thought or reference you have for these words. Are your thought and references the same? Find a way to explain the ambiguous words more clearly.

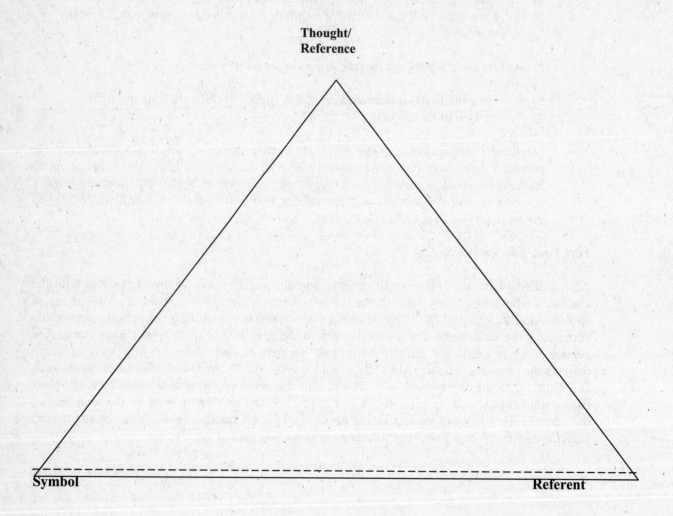

**Thought/
Reference**

Symbol

Referent

Supplemental Bibliography

Benoit, William L., "Framing Through Temporal Metaphor: The 'Bridges' of Bob Dole and Bill Clinton in their 1996 Acceptance Addresses." *Communication Studies,* 52 (Spring 2001): 70-84.

Benoit examines the use of the "bridge" metaphor in the two speeches. This essay is a nice resource because it shows the skillful use of metaphor and its power in public speaking. Great for lecture material.

Hayakawa. S.I., Language in Thought and Action. New York: Harcourt Brace Jovanovich, 1990, 6th ed.

An excellent investigation of the study of the functions of language, and the relationship of language and thought. Great lecture resource.

Ivy, Diana K., and Backlund, Phil., Exploring GenderSpeak: Personal Effectiveness in Gender Communication. New York: McGraw-Hill, 1994.

Ivy and Backlund offer a comprehensive textbook about gender and communication including an exploration of sexist language, gendered communication in the workplace, and gendered communication in educational settings. Valuable for an understanding of how language can differ between the genders. Great examples and full of humorous anecdotes.

Leap, William. American Indian English. Salt Lake City: University of Utah Press, 1993.

For an example of the relationship between language and culture see this book which covers the structures, tradition and history of American Indian English.

Maggio, Rosalie., Talking About People: A Guide to Fair and Accurate Language. Phoenix, Az: Oryx Press, 1997.

Maggio offers guidelines for bias free, non-sexist, and inclusive language. The book also includes a dictionary of terms which could be used in class discussion as to why or why not the words are fair or unfair.

Montgomery, Martin., An Introduction to Language and Society. New York: Routledge, 1995. 2nd ed.

Montgomery covers language development and linguistic diversity among cultures, classes, and genders. He also explores how the representation of the world can differ between languages. A great resource for lectures and discussion.

Rickford, John Russell, and Rickford, Russell John., Spoken Soul: The Story of Black English. New York: John Wiley and Sons, 2000.

The term "spoken soul" refers to what Rickford and Rickford term "black talk" or African American dialect and is examined here using examples including African American writers, preachers, comedians, and rappers. This volume also touches on Ebonics and examines the relationship of spoken soul and African American identity. Useful in understanding language and culture in a specific context.

Sommer, Elyse, and Weiss, Dorrie (Eds)., <u>Metaphors Dictionary</u>. New York: Gale, 1995.

For examples of metaphors to use in your classroom discussion, this is a great volume.

Sommer, Elyse, and Sommer, Mike, (Eds). <u>Similes Dictionary</u>. Detroit: Gale, 1988.

For examples of similes to use in your classroom discussion, this is a great volume.

Williams, Joseph M. <u>Style: Ten Lessons in Clarity and Grace.</u>, Glenview, IL: Scott, Foresman, 1985. 2nd ed.

A handbook on how to write clearly and accurately to communicate the actual meaning intended.

Wilson, Paula. "The Rhythm of Rhetoric: Jesse Jackson at the 1988 Democratic National Convention." *Southern Communication Journal* 61(Spring 1996): 253-264.

Wilson's essay is an exploration of the use and importance of rhythm in Jackson's speech. Wilson suggests that a new method of rhetorical criticism, with rhythm as a key construct, should be devised for the study of African American oratory. The article is easy to read and a great resource for lectures and discussions of style and language.

Chapter Eleven: Delivering Your Speech

Chapter Goals

Chapter eleven introduces students to the different methods of delivery, the verbal and nonverbal components of delivery, and tips to effectively deliver a speech. As students reach the end of this chapter, they should have an understanding of the following goals:

- To identify and describe four different methods of delivering a speech
- To list and demonstrate the verbal components of delivery
- To list and demonstrate the nonverbal components of delivery
- To identify effective strategies for rehearsing your speech

Chapter Outline

I. **Delivery** *is the action and manner of speaking to an audience* (pg. 221)
   a. When we delivering our speeches, we carry our message to others.
   b. Our delivery gives birth to our ideas as we bring our hard work and thoughts to life for our audiences.
   c. Delivery is a way of connecting with the audience and sharing ideas with them.
II. Speakers can use **four methods of delivery** (pg. 222).
   a. **Extemporaneous delivery** is when you present a carefully prepared and practiced speech from brief notes rather than from memory or manuscript.
      i. It is one of the most common methods because it tends to be more natural than other methods of delivery.
      ii. Speakers use a speaking outline to deliver a speech extemporaneously.
      iii. There are several advantages to extemporaneous delivery.
         1. The speaking outline or speaking notes prompt ideas but do not allow a speaker to read every word to an audience.
         2. Eye contact and gestures are natural.
         3. The tone is conversational.
         4. A speaker stays audience centered because extemporaneous deliveries encourage direct communication between the speaker and audience.
      iv. There are several *delivery tips* for extemporaneous speaking.
         1. Add more keywords and phrases (not full sentences) to the outline.
         2. Practice the speech often before it is given for more confidence.
      v. "Talk" your speech rather than reading it.
      vi. An extemporaneous speech follows a **conversational style**, which is more formal than everyday conversation but remains spontaneous and relaxed.
   b. **Impromptu Delivery** is when you present a speech that you have not planned or prepared in advance (pg. 224).
      i. This delivery commonly occurs in meetings or public gatherings when someone is asked to speak or feels the need to share her or his perspective.
      ii. Deciding to speak gives the speaker a few moments to organize his or her ideas.

   iii. If asked to speak, a speaker may not be able to jot down ideas, but a speaker can still organize their thoughts.

   iv. There are several *delivery tips* a speaker can follow for effective impromptu speaking.

     1. Quickly and calmly decide on the main points you want to make.

     2. Introduce those main points as you would if you had prepared in advance.

     3. Support your main points with sub and subpoints and Sub-subpoints.

     4. Summarize your main points in a brief conclusion.

  c. **Manuscript delivery** is when you read to an audience from a written text (pg. 225).

   i. There may be different reasons a speech might require manuscript delivery.

     1. A manuscript can be used when detailed and exact information must be reported carefully.

     2. A manuscript can be used when your speech will be scrutinized word by word, archived, and referred to later.

     3. A manuscript can be used when your speech text will be used later for some other purpose.

     4. Manuscript speaking requires more preparation and skill than extemporaneous or impromptu speaking.

       a. Manuscript speeches can sound like a written rather than an oral text.

       b. The speaker may be inclined to read to the audience and talk with them.

   ii. There are several delivery tips a speaker can use when delivering from manuscript.

     1. Working from your preparation outline, speak the words aloud as you write them on your computer or paper.

     2. If you find yourself thinking the speech rather than saying it aloud, go back and speak the part you have just written (a way to notice you have slipped into a writer's style instead of a speaker's style.

     3. Change the language to reflect spoken ideas rather than written ideas (goal is to write a speech not an essay).

  d. **Memorized Delivery** is when you present a speech that has been written out, committed to memory, and given word for word (pg. 226).

   i. You give this type of speech without any notes.

   ii. Speakers can use memorized speeches in a few situations.

     1. Deliver a memorized speech when the speech is very short.

     2. Deliver a memorized speech when the speaker wants to say things in a very specific way.

     3. Deliver a memorized speech when notes would be awkward and disruptive.

   iii. There are several tips speakers you can follow when delivering a speech from memory.

     1. Write a manuscript of the speech using oral style, not a written style.

     2. Commit each line of the speech to memory.

     3. Every few lines, set the manuscript aside and practice delivering them to an imaginary audience without reading them. Repeat until you can deliver the entire speech naturally and with confidence.

     4. Once you've learned the full speech, practice it over and over, reminding yourself to listen to the meaning of your words (bring the words to life and connect with your audience).

  e. **See Table 11.1 Advantages and Disadvantages of the Four Delivery Methods** (pg 227).

III. **Verbal components of delivery** (pg. 227).
   a. Verbal components of delivery are reflected through our use of **vocal variety,** which are changes in volume, rate, pitch, inflection, and pauses that affect the meaning of the words delivered.
   b. There are different components of delivery speakers can use.
      i. **Volume** is the loudness of the speaker's voice (pg. 269).
         1. Culture affects the meaning of loudness.
            a. In some Mediterranean cultures, a loud voice signals sincerity and strength.
            b. In the United States, loudness may signal aggression or anger.
            c. In some Native American and Asian cultures, a soft voice signals education and good manners.
            d. In some European cultures, a soft voice may signal femininity, secrecy, or even fear.
         2. There are some tips speakers can follow when considering volume.
            a. Pay attention to the nonverbal cues given by the audience.
            b. If using a microphone, before beginning the speech test your voice with the microphone.
      ii. **Rate** is the speed at which we speak (pg. 228).
         1. The rate at which we speak can convey different feelings.
            a. When we speak quickly we project a sense of urgency or excitement, or even haste.
            b. When we speak slowly, we convey seriousness, heaviness, or uncertainty.
         2. You can check your rate by taping yourself for several minutes.
      iii. **Pitch and inflection** (pg. 228).
         1. **Pitch** *refers to the position of tones on the musical scale, and in public speaking, it reveals itself in the highness or lowness of a speaker's voice.*
         2. **Inflection** is the manipulation of pitch to create certain meanings or moods (pg. 228).
            a. Pitch and inflection help us communicate emotions.
            b. Both men and women manipulate pitch to create meaning during their speeches.
            c. Variations in pitch can clarify meaning and help catch and keep an audience's attention.
            d. Speakers who do not alter their pitch speak in a monotone.
               i. An audience will lose interest when there is no inflection or vocal variety.
               ii. When a speaker uses only a high pitch, an audience does not know which points are the most important.
            e. There are some tips speakers can follow when considering pitch and inflection.
               i. A speaker can tape her or himself and hear their pitch.
               ii. Practice breathing more deeply if you speak with too high a pitch.
               iii. Speak from the diaphragm rather than the throat.
      iv. **Pauses** are hesitations and brief silences in speech conversation (pg. 229 - 230).
         1. Pauses serve several functions.
            a. They give us time to breathe and collect our thoughts.

151

      b.   They give the audience time to absorb or process information.

      c.   They can reinforce a word or point.

2.   Pauses can add clarity.

3.   Avoid **vocalized pauses** or pauses that speaker fills with words or sounds like 'um,' 'er,' 'uh.'

4.   If you have a habit of vocalized pause, try the following process to eliminate them

      a.   Listen for vocalized pauses in your daily speech.

      b.   When you hear one, anticipate the next one.

      c.   When you feel the urge to say "um" or "er" to fill space, gently bite your tongue and don't let the word escape.

      d.   Wait until your next word of substance is ready to come out and say it instead.

v. **Articulation** is the physical process of producing specific speech sounds in order to make language intelligible to our audience (pg. 230).

   1.   Articulation depends on the accuracy of movement of our tongue, lips, jaws, and teeth.

   2.   Public speaking audiences expect public speaking to be more articulate than private conversation.

   3.   To improve articulation, try the following exercise.

      a.   Several days before the speech, select a part of the speech text to read aloud.

      b.   Practice saying each selection as slowly and clearly as possible.

      c.   Repeat the exercise once or twice a day before you give the speech.

vi. **Pronunciation** is the act of saying words correctly according to the accepted standards of a language (pg. 231).

   1.   Pronunciation refers to how *correctly* a word is said.

   2.   Articulation refers to how *clearly* a word is said.

   3.   Pronouncing words correctly communicates to your audience that you have listened carefully to the public dialogue going on around you.

   4.   Correct pronunciation of terms and names communicates your respect for others, especially if they are from a different culture.

vii. **Dialect** is a pattern of speech shared among ethnic groups or people from specific geographical locations (pg. 231).

   1.   Dialects can include specific vocabulary that is unique to a group.

   2.   Dialects can include styles of pronunciation shared by members of a group.

   3.   Everyone has a dialect but we sometimes view the dialect of others as inferior.

   4.   If you know your dialect will be unfamiliar, try the following.

      a.   Acknowledge your region of birth or ethnic heritage.

      b.   Talk about how that shapes your use of language by giving examples of some of the differences you've encountered between your dialect and those of your audience.

      c.   Define terms that are unfamiliar to your audience.

      d.   Soften your accent associated with your dialect if that accent is fairly strong and might hinder understanding.

IV. **Nonverbal components of delivery** are those aspects communicated through our bodies and faces (pg. 232).

    a. Nonverbal communication has a powerful impact on the meanings exchanged between people.

    b. There are several components of nonverbal delivery a speaker should consider.

        i. **Personal appearance** is the way you dress, groom, and present yourself physically (pg. 233).

            1. The standard for public speaking is that a speaker's dress should be appropriate to the occasion.

            2. A second standard is to wear attire that is neither too revealing nor too restricting.

        ii. **Eye contact** is the visual contact with another person's eyes (pg. 233).

            1. Appropriate eye contact is influenced by culture and gender.

                a. Most North Americans and western Europeans expect a speaker to make extensive eye contact.

                b. Native American cultures and in parts of Japan and Africa extensive eye contact is considered invasive and disrespectful.

                c. For men, direct eye contact with another man may be perceived as a challenge or threat.

                d. For women, direct eye contact with a man may be interpreted as an invitation to flirt.

            2. Eye contact has three functions.

                a. It is a way to greet and acknowledge the audience before the speech begins.

                b. It is a way to gauge and keep our audience's interest.

                c. It is a way to communicate sincerity and honesty.

        iii. **Facial expression** is the movement of your eyes, eyebrows, and mouth to convey reactions and emotions (pg. 234).

            1. With facial expressions, you can express your own interest in the topic.

            2. You can express your own agreement or disagreement with a point.

            3. You can express your openness to an idea or an emotion surrounding an issue.

        iv. **Posture** is the way we position and carry our bodies (pg. 234).

            1. Posture affects whether or not we are perceived as confident and relaxed.

            2. Posture affects the audience's perceptions of whether we are tense and insecure.

            3. Become aware of your body posture when you practice your speech.

        v. **Gestures** are movements, usually of the hands but sometimes of the full body, that express meaning an emotion or offer clarity to a message (pg. 235).

            1. Gestures should be as natural as possible rather than memorized.

            2. Gestures make our delivery lively, offer emphasis and clarity, and convey our passion and interest.

                a. Vary your gestures.

                b. Use gestures that fit your message.

                c. Stay relaxed.

        vi. **Proxemics** is the way we use space to communication (pg. 236).

            1. The farther a speaker is away from an audience, the stronger the idea of separation.

            2. The higher up a speaker is (on a platform) the more idea of power is communicated.

V. **Rehearsing your speech** (pg. 236).
    a. The more practice a speaker has, the more natural they will sound.
        i. Practice helps a speaker know their speech much better.
        ii. Speakers will also feel more comfortable with verbal and nonverbal components of delivery if they rehearse their speech.
    b. Speakers will feel more confident as they practice their speech.
    c. Here are some guideline for rehearsing speech delivery:
        i. Practice giving your speech aloud using your speaking outline (Chapter 8).
        ii. Practice all stories, quotations, statistics, and other evidence until you can deliver them exactly as you want.
        iii. When you are comfortable with your material, practice your speech in front of a mirror. Monitor your nonverbal communication and make adjustments as needed so you communicate your message clearly.
        iv. Now tape your speech and listen for vocal variety. Check your volume, rate, pitch and inflection, pauses, and how you articulate and pronounce words. If you think your dialect will hinder your delivery, make adjustments.
        v. Practice your speech again, incorporating the verbal and nonverbal changes you worked out in steps 1 through 4.
        vi. Now practice a few times in front of a friend. Have the person ask you questions at the end of the speech and practice answering them. Incorporate any useful feedback your friend may offer.
        vii. Stage a dress rehearsal. Consider your personal appearance by wearing the clothing you will wear on the day you speak. Set up your practice area so it resembles the actual speaking situation as closely as possible. Consider proxemics and the space you want between you and the audience.

End of the Chapter Activities and Discussion Questions

The following questions can be found at the end of Chapter Eleven.

Review Questions

1. Identify speakers you would consider as having good delivery. What characteristics make their delivery strong? How many of these characteristics might you incorporate into your style of delivery?

    This is a question that can be easily addressed in class as you lecture about delivery. It is also a good question with which to begin the semester because students generally notice delivery before they notice structure. Ask students to describe some of the speakers they have heard, and what made the speaker's delivery effective. Make sure to encourage students to point out specific examples. For instance they may say: they were "dynamic" speakers; they were "lively" speakers; they used humor; etc. Explore what they mean by these types of adjectives. This will get students in the practice of identifying "tangible" examples of delivery.

2. Which method of delivery will you choose (or have you been assigned) for your next speech? Why? How will you make that method the most audience centered possible? Now identify the method of delivery that you actually prefer. If the two don't match, what will you do to feel more comfortable with the type of delivery you will use for your next speech?

Often, instructors will assign a specific method of delivery for each speech. However, if you are giving students the freedom to choose the method of delivery, then have them address this question, identifying the specific reasons they chose that method of delivery and the specific ways they will stay audience centered. You can also modify this question by asking students which method of delivery is required, and how might it differ from the other forms of delivery. Hint: To simplify grading, you may want to require a specific method of delivery for each speech. Some students may find memorization easier than extemporaneous speaking and so choose only this method. When compared to an extemporaneous delivery, the two are hard to grade consistently.

3. Review the discussion in Chapter 1 about nervousness. Are there any tips in Chapter 1 that you can incorporate into your delivery? Which ones? Why do you think they are useful?

Ask students to review Chapter 1 and respond to the questions here during an in-class discussion about nervousness and the different methods of delivery. As you discuss these two topics, make specific suggestions about how the tips for reducing nervousness can help students with their delivery, regardless of the style they are using for their next speech. You can also place students into groups, place the tips for reducing nervousness on the board, on a power point slide, (or have students bring their books to class), and assign each group the task of connecting a specific tip to each of the four methods of delivery.

4. Identify the differences among extemporaneous, impromptu, manuscript, and memorized deliveries. What are the strengths and weaknesses of each type of delivery?

This can be a very good review question for students to address after they have done the reading about different methods of delivery. This question can also be incorporated into an exam (see the Test Bank that accompanies Invitation to Public Speaking). If you want to take class time, place students into groups, have them identify the differences as well as the strengths and weaknesses, and then share their responses with the full class.

5. Write a quick speech and exchange speeches among classmates. In groups, give that speech as though it was a tragedy, a surprise, or a hilarious story. Or choose some other approach that will allow you to work on vocal variety. How well are you able to match the verbal components of your speech to the mood you have selected?

This activity will take a bit of time in class, so be sure to set aside most of the class period. You can also have students write a speech with partners to make the process a bit easier and a bit quicker or ask them to write their speeches and bring them to class at the next meeting. When students perform these speeches, be sure to have students provide specific examples of what made their delivery clear. For example, when students were delivering their speech as a tragedy, was their use of volume effective? Was their use of gestures effective? Was their use of eye contact effective? By encouraging students to specify components of delivery, they can better put these concepts into practice in their own speeches.

6. Check out Speech Studio to see how other students deliver their speeches. Or record a speech you're working on, upload it to Speech Studio, and ask your peers for their feedback. What feedback could you use to fine tune your delivery before you give your speech in class?

Web Resources

1. **How to Give a Successful Impromptu Speech**
Go to http://www.creativekeys.net/PowerfulPresentations/article1015.html. Chris King offers insight into giving an impromptu speech. Read his advice and then consider occasions in which you have been called on to give an impromptu speech. How prepared did you feel for these occasions? Was the speech effective? How might you have improved your performance?

Many instructors require impromptu speaking in their speech courses. Most students get quite nervous at the prospect of having to give an impromptu speech so accessing this web page can help put students' minds more at ease before they give an impromptu speech. You can also assign this web link after a round of impromptu speeches, so that students have a recent experience to consider as they read the article.

2. **Memorize, Read or Extemporize?**
Purpose: To consider delivery options.
Directions: Go to http://www.sas.upenn.edu/cwic/resources/dl2.html and read what the University of Pennsylvania's Communication within the Curriculum website has to say about extemporaneous speaking. Think about a speech you have recently attended, such as a lecture, a sermon, a political speech, or a sales pitch. Was the speech delivered extemporaneously? Was it effective? How could it have been more effective? What can you do to improve your effectiveness as an extemporaneous speaker?

Most speech instructors require students to use an extemporaneous style of delivery. Some students are quite challenged by this style of deliver so encourage students to access the website given here, and respond to the questions listed. Then, if you have time, have students give a sales pitch as an impromptu speech during class to reduce their anxiety about this style of delivery.

3. **Improving Vocal Variety**
Purpose: To improve your vocal variety.
Directions: Read Candice M. Coleman's web article "Improving Vocal Variety" here http://www.sayitwell.com/Improving_Vocal_Variety.html. Use her advice to practice your next speech, paying particular attention to your vocal variety. Use a video camera or tape recorder to hear your presentation. To what degree do you achieve vocal variety? What aspects of your delivery could be more varied?

This activity can assist students with incorporating vocal variety in their speeches. Direct students to access this website at home as homework, then have them come to class prepared to discuss the advice given by Coleman and ways they can use the advice she offers. If you require that students tape their speeches and review them after each speech, you can assign this article in conjunction with one of their reviews. See also "Additional Exercises and Activities" in this chapter for additional activities.

156

4. **Dress for Success**
   Go to http://jobsearch.about.com/od/interviewsnetworking/a/dressforsuccess.htm. Read the advice on this page about personal appearance in the job interview. How is this advice audience centered? Are there times when you might disregard this advice? Why or why not? How will you dress for your next speech?

   This web page can be very helpful for students to consider the importance of dressing for success. Students often ask speech instructors about what is considered appropriate dress for interviews. Send them to this web page for some ideas.

InfoTrac College Edition Activities

1. **InfoTrac College Edition Activity 11.1: Using Nonverbal Communication**
   Purpose: To understand the importance of nonverbal communication.
   Directions: Use your InfoTrac College Edition account to read Anne Warfield's article, "Do You Speak Body Language?" *Training and Development* (April 2001), p. 60. According to the article, how important is nonverbal communication? If possible, review a videotape of your last speech or last rehearsal. How effectively do you use nonverbal communication, according to what you have read in your book and the article? Read the accompanying article, "Read the Signs," and describe ways you can use inclusive nonverbal communication. How can you communicate honestly?

   This can be a great activity for students to do as a homework assignment. Have students access the article via their InfoTrac account. Then, have them respond to the questions asked here. It is important that students have a discussion about nonverbal communication because of the huge role it plays in everyday communication, and in public speaking. Asking them for the kinds of specific information the questions in this activity ask for is an excellent way to get them to explore their own nonverbal communication.

2. **InfoTrac College Edition Activity 11.2: Communicating Sincerity**
   Purpose: To understand how speakers communicate sincerity.
   Directions: Use your InfoTrac College Edition account to access Bill Crounse's article, "Talking the Talk: Helpful Tips on Giving Political Speeches," *Campaigns and Elections* (July 2000), p. 64. Read the article to learn the importance of appearing genuine when you communicate. How important is communicating sincerity, according to the article? How do speakers achieve sincerity?

   This activity can be very valuable for students as they are entering the persuasive and invitational speeches. Both of these speeches require students to be sincere when they are giving their speeches and when they are engaging their audience in a dialogue. On the due date of the assignment, have students report to the class their perspectives about communicating sincerity and the specific strategies for doing so.

Interactive Student and Professional Speech Videos

1. **Video Clip 1: Barack Obama, Delivery**
   Watch this video clip of Barack Obama speaking. How does his delivery help him to remain audience centered? What does he do effectively? Consider all elements of delivery, including the verbal and nonverbal aspects.

   Show this video clip in class, and have students consider the questions listed here. Facilitate a discussion about the effectiveness of Barack Obama's speaking style and delivery.

2. **Video Clip 2: Student Speeches: Shelley and Eric**
   Compare the delivery styles of two student speakers, Shelley and Eric. How can you tell that Shelley is using an extemporaneous style? What makes Eric's delivery look like he is reading from a manuscript? Which style do you think is more effective? Why? Are there times when an extemporaneous style is more appropriate than a manuscript style? Are there times when reading from a manuscript would be more effective than using an extemporaneous style?

   Show this video clip in class, and have students respond to the questions listed here. As students respond, be sure to point out your own expectations for each given method of delivery.

3. **Video Clip 3: Student Speech, Brandi, Amy, Carol, and Hans, Delivery**
   Watch this clip and compare the different speaking styles of each speaker. What makes each unique? How are they similar? How do their speaking styles differ from your own? What adjustment will you make to your own delivery after having seen these four speakers?

   Show this clip in class, and facilitate a discussion with students centered on the questions listed here. Emphasize to students that each speaker, including your students, will have different speaking styles which can all be very effective. As well, clarify for students what your expectations are regarding their delivery.

Additional Exercises and Resources

1. **Practicing Articulation**
   Purpose: To learn and practice proper articulation.
   Directions: For a technical explanation of articulation, read this web page created by Kevin Russell of the University of Manitoba (http://www.umanitoba.ca/faculties/arts/linguistics/russell/138/sec5/s5-poa.htm). Which words do you have difficulties articulating? Why? How can you improve your articulation of those words using the information on this page?

   Share the topic and specific purpose of your next speech with the class. Let them ask you questions about that topic and purpose, and practice answering those questions as though you were in a question-and-answer session.

   Many students have a lot of difficulty with articulating certain words correctly (and don't realize that they do). Encourage students to access the websites listed here, and practice working on their articulation. Remind students that not articulating words correctly can affect not only their credibility but also their audience's ability to understand their ideas.

2. **Practicing Your Gestures**

   Purpose: To practice effective gestures.

   Directions: Go to http://www.soyouwanna.com/site/syws/speaking/speaking4.html and use the tips it provides to practice your next speech, paying particular attention to your gestures. Record your rehearsal with a video camera and then review the tape. Is it difficult for you to gesture effectively? Why or why not? Do you gesture too much? Not enough? Are your gestures appropriately timed?

   Students are regularly challenged by the subject of gestures. In fact, you will find that many students have horror stories about a past speech teacher who told them "do not ever use gestures" or "if you do not use gestures, I will reduce your grade." Each instructor's approach is different so be sure to give students a clear idea of your own expectations about gesturing. Remember, gestures come very naturally to some students, have them access the website listed here and respond to the questions. Or, assign this website in combination with a review of one of their speeches.

3. **Different Methods of Delivery**

   It is a good idea to vary the different methods of delivery for certain speeches. While the most common method of delivery is extemporaneous, you do not have to require only that method. Varying assignments can help students use different methods of delivery. For example, special occasion speeches or speeches of introduction might be given from memory or from manuscript. Informative, persuasive and invitational speeches can be given extemporaneously. You also can require at least one impromptu speech during the course of the semester, or use impromptu activities to fill the time when a lecture, discussion, or round of speeches finishes early.

4. **Impromptu Speech Assignments**

   There are different ways to handle impromptu speech assignments.

   A) ***As a graded speech, worth significant points***

   Some instructors assign an impromptu speech as a significant speech assignment. If this is your approach, you will want to make sure you spend quite a bit of time discussing guidelines on how to prepare effective impromptu speeches. If you have a Forensics Team (speech and debate team) on campus, you might want to bring in their top impromptu speakers to illustrate for your students what impromptu speeches can sound like. Ask them to discuss with the class the strategies they use to give their impromptu speeches. In competition, these speakers usually are given 7 minutes total: 1-2 minutes to prepare, and 5 minutes to speak. Vary the time as you see appropriate for your beginning public speaking students recognizing that beginning public speaking students might need more time to prepare their speeches.

   B) ***As a smaller assignment***

   Another option is to require an impromptu speech as a smaller assignment. For instance, you can fill any extra time during class with impromptu speeches or shorten a lecture to make time for these speeches. The time for this impromptu can be quite short: three minutes to prepare, two minutes to speak. You can either assign points for these speeches (some instructors work their way through the class roster throughout the semester so that each student gives one graded impromptu speech) or simply use this activity as ungraded speech practice. Topics for impromptu assignments can be entirely up to your discretion. Quotes usually work very well. For shorter impromptus, objects can work quite well, or keep a stack of note cards with you with topics on them to use as impromptu topics. At the end of this chapter, you will find an example of an impromptu description sheet and critique sheet that you can use as a model for your own classes.

5. **Manuscripts**

There are several different options for effective manuscripts. Each instructor's perspective will vary and you can encourage students to go beyond the "staple my pages together" manuscript. Here are some options that might be helpful.

A) *Plastic Page Protectors*

The plastic page protectors will help students turn each page. They also minimize paper "noise." They are fairly affordable at book stores. Students can use just the pages as their manuscript, or they can place them into a binder.

B) *Binders*

Students can place their plastic page protectors in binders. The binder provides a nice solid foundation, and the page protectors, again, help students turn pages without the paper sticking together. Sometimes students will select binders that are too big for their hands. You might want to suggest that students use smaller binders that can fit more easily in their hands.

C) *Construction Paper*

Some students might like the construction paper option. They can choose a color of construction paper that is appropriate for the speech, and glue their manuscript onto it. This option can also help students turn from page to page with more ease. Some students might even want to tie the pages together with yarn. Remind students that they do not want to use colors that are too "out there" for fear of distracting their audience.

Structuring the Manuscript

An effective way of actually "structuring" the manuscript is to have the introduction of the speech on one page, then the first main point on the next, and so on. The page turns in between parts of the speech and main points can help the timing and rhythm of the speech.

The Student's Manuscript and the Manuscript Given to the Instructor

Encourage students to make the manuscript work for them. For instance, some students will need to use a larger font so they don't lose their place while others are fine with a regular font but more spaces between lines or points. Other students may want to highlight certain parts of their speech to remind themselves to emphasize certain words, or to deliver the line in a certain way. Encourage them to "write" their manuscript in the way that works best for them. The manuscript that students turn into the instructor, however, can be the clean 3-4 pages printed out from their computer.

Impromptu Speaking
10 points

You will be surprised to learn that many of the speeches you give throughout your professional and personal lives will be impromptu speeches. Responding to something a peer or instructor says in a class, responding to a co-worker or supervisor at work, responding to your parents about finances, etc. All of these scenarios can be considered impromptu speeches because you speak with little or no preparation. During the course of the semester, everyone will be required to give an impromptu speech. The speeches will, however, be more structured than perhaps the scenarios listed above. DON'T WORRY! This structure will actually make it easier for you (and improve your future impromptu speeches) and may be familiar to you already. Impromptu speeches are worth 10 points. This is how they work:

Step One

You will choose between three categories:

> ➢ A quote (from a book of quotes)
> ➢ A general topic (i.e. heroes/heroines)
> ➢ An object (Absolutely anything. Students are welcome to bring in any objects—as long as appropriate—to share with peers.)

I will then provide you with a specific item from the category of your choice. Once you have been given the item, you cannot change your mind!

Step Two

You will then have three minutes to prepare a two-minute speech. You can write a speaking outline as your prepare or make any other notes that will be helpful.

Step Three

You will deliver the speech to the class. You can speak from the outline/notes you prepared.

Helpful Hints
Use the critique sheet as you prepare. You might even want to look over the critique sheet at home to practice! Organization is key in impromptu speaking. Accomplish what you need in your introduction. Keep in mind the guidelines for main point organization. Accomplish what you need in your conclusion. As always, keep in mind effective delivery skills. Have fun with this speech!

Impromptu Critique Sheet
3 minutes to prepare a 2 minute speech

Name _____ Time _____ Points _____

Key: + = Excellent; √ = Satisfactory; – = Needs improvement; 0 = Failed to complete

INTRODUCTION

Captured attention and interest/related to the audience _____
Introduced the topic _____
Established credibility _____
Previewed main points _____

BODY

Main points clear _____
Connectives _____
Main points balanced _____
Reasoning sound _____

CONCLUSION

Signaled the finish _____
Summarized main points _____
Closed decisively _____

DELIVERY

Eye contact _____
Volume _____
Avoided distracting mannerisms _____

Additional comments:

Supplemental Bibliography

DeVito, Joseph A., and Michael Hecht (Eds)., <u>The Nonverbal Communication Reader.</u>, Prospect Heights, IL: Waveland Press, 1990.

>An excellent volume of articles with essays on the range of different aspects of nonverbal communication. Addresses such subjects as body paralanguage, for example. Almost any aspect of nonverbal communication you may wish to further explore with your class is discussed in this book.

Jacobi, Jeffrey., <u>The Vocal Advantage</u>. Englewood Cliffs, NJ: Prentice Hall, 1996.

>Jacobi discusses how your voice can help keep your audience interested, help persuade your audience, and enhance your credibility. Also offers practice exercises for improving voice. A great resource for activities and lecture examples.

McCallion, Michael., <u>The Voice Book: For Everyone Who Wants to Make the Most of Their Voice</u>. New York: Theater Arts Books/Routledge, 1999.

>This book is comprised of exercises to improve verbal components of delivery. You can use these helpful exercises during class when discussing verbal components so students can then begin to experience first-hand the elements of delivery before their actual speech.

Mino, Mary., "The Relative Effects of Vocal Delivery During a Simulated Employment Interview." *Communication Research Reports*, 13 (1996), 225-238.

>Mino offers an interesting article that relates good vocal delivery skills to the real-life situation of job interviews. This would be helpful in explaining to your students the real importance of having good delivery. A great resource for those regularly asked "what do I do in an interview?" questions.

Remy, Mark., "Two Stress-Busters You'll Really Love." *Prevention* 50 (Sep 1998): 34-35.

>Remy discusses two ways to relieve stress before impromptu classroom speeches. Many students are extremely apprehensive about these speeches, and these strategies may help improve performance.

Robbins, Jo., <u>High Impact Presentations: A Multimedia Approach</u>. New York: John Wiley and Sons, 1997.

>Chapters eight and nine cover verbal and nonverbal communication. Robbins includes checklists and exercises for students to use to analyze their voices and nonverbal communication. This is practical and easy to implement in the classroom to help students really understand these concepts and relate them to their own performances.

Stuart, Cristina., <u>How to Be an Effective Speaker</u>. Chicago: NTC Publishing Group, 1989.

Stuart's book contains brief but helpful chapters on "finding your voice" which addresses breathing, projection, volume, variety, and pauses. Also offers exercises for practicing articulation.

Woodall, Marian K., <u>Thinking On Your Feet: How to Communicate Under Pressure.</u> Lake Oswego, OR: Professional Business Communications, 1996.

An excellent reference guide for question and answer sessions. This goes in depth about types of questions a speaker may encounter, how to address difficult and negative questions, and how to incorporate good delivery skills into the question and answer period.

http://www.speechdelivery.com/

A Blog on the topics associated with Speech Delivery

Chapter Twelve: Visual Aids

Chapter Goals

Chapter twelve introduces students to the effective use of visual aids in their speeches. As students reach the end of the chapter, they should be able to meet the following goals:

- To discuss the importance of using visual aids
- To identify and describe the different types of visual aids
- To determine what to show on a visual aid
- To format visual aids effectively
- To identify five guidelines for using visual aids

Chapter Outline

I. **Why visual aids are important** (pg. 241).
   a. **Visual aids help gain and maintain audience attention.**
      i. A visual aid gives an audience something to focus on.
      ii. A visual aid reinforces your verbal message.
   b. **Visual aids help audiences recall information.**
      i. Research indicates that audience members do not recall as much information when visual aids are not used in a speech.
         1. When a speech does not include visual aids, the audience recalls 70% of the information three hours after the speech. Three days later, an audience recalls only 10% of the information.
         2. When the same message is delivered with visual aids only, audience members recall 72% of the information three hours after the speech. Audience members recalled 35% after three days.
         3. When the same message is delivered with both words and visual aids, audience members recall 85% of the information three hours after the speech. Audience members recalled 65% after three days.
   c. **Visual aids help explain and clarify information.**
      i. Complex ideas and numbers can be easier to understand when displayed visually.
      ii. Presenting ideas visually makes them more concrete.
      iii. Handouts increase the audience's continuity of thought.
   d. **Visual aids may increase persuasiveness and enhance credibility** (pg. 242).
      i. Visual aids can help you clarify your message, organize information, identify key points, and facilitate the reasoning process.
      ii. Images encourage audiences to make associations.
      iii. They contribute to your credibility by bringing a visual dimension to your speech.
      iv. Professional-looking visual aids can energize a speech, causing you to seem more prepared, engaging, and lively.
      v. By helping you organize and clarify information, they communicate an audience centered perspective.

e. **Visual aids may reduce nervousness.**
    i. With a visual aid, you pay more attention to the effectiveness of your speech's organization.
    ii. Being better organized can reduce your nervousness.
    iii. Visual aids can direct attention away from you and give you something else to focus on.
    iv. They also give you something to do with your hands.

II. **Types of visual aids** (pg. 242 - 243).
    a. **Objects, models and demonstrations**.
        i. **An object** *is something than can be seen or touched.*
            1. Objects can help your audience understand certain ideas better.
            2. Sometimes they can be impossible or impractical to bring to a speaking situation, so consider the object carefully.
        ii. **A model** *is a copy of an object, usually built to scale, that represents that object in detail.*
            1. Models can be smaller than the objects they represent.
            2. Models can be larger than the objects they represent.
            3. Models can also be life size.
        iii. **A demonstration** *is a display of how something is done or how it works.*
            1. There are several guidelines to follow when using an object, model or demonstration.
                a. *Make sure your visual aids and demonstration enhance understanding.*
                    i. Try to avoid demonstrations that are too complex, require a lot of equipment, or might make you look awkward or unprofessional.
                    ii. If your process is complex, simplify it for your demonstration or show only a part of the process.
                    iii. If you can't demonstrate the process yourself, you can show a process from a YouTube (or other) video clip.
                b. *Choose objects that are legal and nonthreatening.*
                    i. Avoid displaying weapons, chemicals, drugs or animals.
                    ii. You cannot always predict what can happen when attempting to display any of these objects.
                c. *Practice your demonstration before your speech.*
        iv. **Handouts** (pg. 245).
            1. Business speakers use different types of handouts.
                a. They use bound copies of business plans or year-end summaries.
                b. They use agency or product brochures.
                c. They use maps and photographs.
                d. They use photocopies of graphs, charts, or articles.
            2. Handouts can provide detailed information that the audience can refer to during a speech or read later and pass along to others.
            3. Many handouts can be displayed on a PowerPoint slide or distributed to your audience electronically before hand.
            4. There are several guidelines you can follow if you use handouts during a speech.
                a. *Mark the point you want to emphasize.*

        i.   Use letters, symbols, or colors to point out key information to your audience.

       ii.   You can also show the page, chart, or map on an overhead projector or PowerPoint slide.

    b.   ***Distribute the handout before or after a meeting.***

        i.   This can be less disruptive than distributing them during your speech.

       ii.   Your handout can include information you want the audience to review later.

    c.   ***Remember that the handout supplements the message.***

        i.   The handout should add information and not become the text of the speech.

       ii.   Refer to key points on the handout, do not read lengthy passages from it.

  v. **Whiteboards and SmartBoards** (pg. 246).

    1.   These can be convenient when you need to create a visual aide as you speak.

    2.   They come in handy when you need to respond immediately to your audience.

    3.   They can help you keep information in front of an audience without having to remove it.

    4.   There are several guidelines you can follow when using a chalkboard or whiteboard.

       a.   ***Write neatly and legibly.***

       b.   ***Speak to the audience, not the board.***

  vi. **Poster Boards and Flip Charts** (pg. 246 - 247).

    1.   Poster boards and flip charts are good for speeches you need to deliver more than once because they are durable and reusable.

    2.   You can use them like chalkboards and whiteboards to record information during a speech.

    3.   There are several guidelines to follow when using a poster board or flip chart.

       a.   ***Make the design as professional as possible.***

       b.   ***Speak to the audience, not the poster board or flip chart.***

  vii. **DVDs and internet pages** (pg. 247).

    1.   These visual aids allow you to show the audience images and to hear the sounds of what you are describing.

    2.   They can bring a place or event to life.

    3.   There are several guidelines to follow when using video or audiotapes.

       a.   ***Keep your clip brief.***

       b.   ***Cue and edit your segment.***

       c.   ***Don't compete with your visual or audio clip.***

  viii. **PowerPoint Presentations** (pg. 248).

    1.   PowerPoint technology allows speakers to create slides containing text, diagrams and images which can be arranged in any sequence, edited to include audio and video clips, printed on paper (for use as handouts) and projected onto screens or a monitor for viewing during presentations.

    2.   There are several guidelines you can follow when using PowerPoint slides.

       a.   ***Understand the purpose of a visual aid.***

       b.   ***Prepare and practice in advance.***

III. **What to show on a visual aid** (pg. 248).

  a. **Lists** *are a series of words or phrases that organize ideas one after the other.*

   i. They are text-based in that they rely on the written word rather than on images to convey meaning.

   ii. Use lists when your material lends itself to itemizing a group or series, such as names, key features or procedures.

   iii. There are several guidelines you can follow when using lists.

     1. *Make your list brief and balanced.*

      a. Use key phrases or words rather than full sentences.

      b. Your goal is to prompt your audience members, not to have them read your full text.

     2. *Include a heading.*

  b. **Charts** *can help you show steps in a process or parts of a concept* (pg. 250).

   i. A ***flow chart*** illustrates direction or motion.

   ii. An ***organizational chart*** illustrates the structure of groups such as organizations, business, or departments.

   iii. There are several guidelines you can follow when using a chart.

     1. *Emphasize the visual image.*

      a. Make the visual element primary and the text secondary.

      b. Use single words or short labels for titles and positions.

      c. Use as few words as possible to describe the steps of a process.

     2. *Use lines, arrows, shading, and color to show relationships and direction.*

  c. **Graphs** *are visual comparisons of amounts or quantities and they help audiences see growth, size, proportions, or relationships* (pg. 251).

   i. Use graphs when you are presenting numbers and statistics and want your audience to see the relationship between them.

   ii. There are different kinds of graphs.

     1. *Bar graphs* compare quantities at a specific moment in time.

     2. *Line graphs* show trends over time.

     3. *Pie graphs* show the relative proportions of parts of a whole.

     4. *Picture graphs* present information in pictures or images.

   iii. There are several guidelines you can follow when using graphs.

     1. *Use clear and consistent labels.*

     2. *Use a computer to design your graph.*

  d. **Drawings** *are diagrams and sketches of someone or something* (pg. 253).

   i. Diagrams add clarity to your presentation because they help you show your audience what something looks like.

   ii. You can draw your own images; photocopy, photograph, or scan images from books and magazines, or use computer clip art.

   iii. There are several guidelines you can follow when using drawings.

     1. *Simple is best.*

      a. People seem to remember the outline of an image more than its details.

      b. Use line drawings, symbolic representations rather than realistic drawings, simple clip art, photocopies of simple images, and children's art.

     2. *Make sure the drawing clarifies the verbal message.*

     3. *Use audience centered humor.*

  e. **Photographs** *help you show your audience what something really looks like or what really happened* (pg. 253).

   i. Photographs can add color and drama to your speech.

   ii. Photographs are most often shown on slides or computer-projected images.

          iii.   They can also be photocopied onto a transparency or a handout.

          iv.   There are several guidelines you can follow when using photographs.

              1.   *Describe the photograph.*

              2.   *Don't pass out photographs.*

              3.   *Do not display photos in a book.*

   f.   **Maps** *are visual representations showing the physical layout of geographical features, cities, road systems, the night sky, and the like* (pg. 254).

       i.   They can help you show your audience the physical layout and characteristics of a place, its location in relation to other places, and the route between places.

       ii.   Use a map to show your audience the physical details that are best understood when presented both verbally and visually.

       iii.   There are several guidelines you can follow when using maps.

              1.   *Draw your map to scale.*

              2.   *Include the most important details.*

              3.   *If you hand out a map, show a larger visual aid of that same map.*

              4.   *Speak to the audience, not to the map.*

IV.   **Formats for visual aids** (pg. 256).

   a.   **Font style and size** (pg. 256).

       i.   **Font** *is a type or style of print.*

              1.   Choose a simple font over a fancy one.

              2.   Select *serif fonts* because they create a baseline for the reader's eyes, leading them easily from letter to letter.

              3.   To emphasize words, use a boldface version of your font to make the letters heavier and darker.

       ii.   **Font size** *is the size of the letters and measured points.*

              1.   Headings should be in 30 to 36 point font.

              2.   Main points should be in 24 point font.

              3.   Subpoints should be in 18 point font.

              4.   Varying font size can clearly indicate to audiences which are your main and subordinate points.

   b.   **Color** helps you to tap into three main design principles (pg. 257).

       i.   Color helps an audience make associations.

       ii.   Soft tones tend to set a calm, soothing mood.

       iii.   Bright colors tend to set an exciting mood.

       iv.   Meanings of colors vary across cultures.

              1.   Red in Western cultures can bring to mind anger or sinful activity.

              2.   In China, red often symbolizes good fortune.

              3.   In Mexico red symbolizes the sun and its awesome power.

       v.   Different colors help your audience differentiate objects or items on a list.

       vi.   Color creates hierarchies.

              1.   Darker to lighter progressions indicate the level of importance.

              2.   The darkest being the most important.

   c.   **Balance** *is the visual relationship of the items on your visual aide to one another* (pg. 259).

       i.   You establish balance by the way you use space to arrange your ideas.

       ii.   A balanced visual aide helps your audience find information easily and not feel like their eyes are tipping in a certain direction.

V.   **Guidelines for effective and ethical use of visual aids** (pg. 259).

   a.   **Prepare in advance.**

   b.   **Practice in advance.**

Students are often challenged by distinguishing between the different organizational patterns. This InfoTrac activity can be very helpful, giving them practice outside class and lecture. Have students do this activity as a homework assignment, or you can have students work on this with partners, reporting their answers to the full class.

3. **InfoTrac College Edition Activity 13.3: Discussing Human Cloning**

   Purpose: To evaluate how objectively the information about a concept can be presented.
   Directions: Use InfoTrac College Edition to locate two articles about human cloning. Search on the term cloning, and then follow the Moral and Ethical Aspects subdivision. Assess the degree to which each article follows the three tips for effective, informative speaking. Consider how each article informs its audience about the complex issue of human cloning. Which article do you think was presented in the more ethical way? Why?

   Students are often challenged to understand an informative speech about a concept. They often slip into persuading their audience about the value of the concept rather than informing. Assign this activity to help clarify how they can more effectively give an informative speech about a concept.

Interactive Student and Professional Speech Videos

1. **Video Clip 1: Student Speech, NASA and the Mars Exploration Rovers, Process Speech**
   Watch this video clip where NASA scientists discuss the process that they use for checking the cameras on the Mars Exploration Rovers. Do they discuss each step of the process in a clear concise manner? How is their explanation useful to you as you consider using the chronological pattern of organization to give an informative speech about a process?.

   Show this video clip in class, and begin the clip using the questions listed here. Emphasize for students the importance of making each step of a process clear during their speech. Also, remind them that using visual aids during a process speech can also help informative speakers to remain audience centered.

2. **Video Clip 2: Student Speech, Rachel Rota, Informative Speech**
   Watch Rachel's speech, and identify the organizational pattern she used for her informative speech. Are her main points clearly structured? Is this the strongest organizational pattern she could have used? Would you recommend a different pattern? Was her demonstration effective?

   Show this clip in class, and have students address the questions listed here. Direct them to also consider if Rachel's main points reflect a clear organizational pattern, and have them consider also options for patterns of organization as well.

3. **Video Clip 3: Student Speech, Cindy Gardner, Informative Speech**
   As you watch Cindy's speech about folding a flag, consider how she organized her speech. What type of informative speech does she present? Which organizational pattern does she use? Was her choice of patterns effective? What other organizational patterns might she have used?

   Show Cindy Gardner's speech in class, especially if you are requiring students to give a process speech. Have students respond to the questions listed here. As students discuss the speech, make sure to clearly indicate your grading criteria for their speeches. A useful tip is to have students follow along with the critique sheet you will be using to grade them. Also see the "Additional Exercises and Resources" section at the end of this chapter for ideas on how to show video clips in your class.

Additional Exercises and Resources

1. **Animal Art**
   Go to http://www.fotoclipart.com/frame/animals.htm. Bring your informative speech about an animal to life by using one of Fotoclipart's images. Why do you think images like these might keep an audience's attention? Besides keeping an audience's attention, what are some other advantages of using images to illustrate your informative speech? What are some limitations to using images in a speech?

   As was mentioned in chapter Twelve, students are challenged to find appropriate visual images to use in a speech. Encourage students to access this website if they are looking for visual images to enhance their speech. Before they select an image, have them consider the reasons they think the image enhances the speech and helps them make their point.

2. **Evaluating a Process Speech**
   Purpose: To consider how processes can be clearly explained.
   Directions: When you give a process speech, your audience must be able to follow your points easily. To learn how to create a PowerPoint presentation for a kiosk, visit
   http://office.microsoft.com/assistance/2002/articles/ppCreateAPresentationForAKiosk.aspx.
   As you read the page, think about how clearly it communicates the process of creating the presentation. If you have access to PowerPoint, try to complete the process described. Can you? If you don't have access to PowerPoint, do you think you could complete the task? What additional information could the site provide? Does it provide too much information?

   This can be a great activity to have students do if you are requiring a process speech and if you are requiring that students use PowerPoint. Have students access the website here and respond to the questions listed.

3. **Describing the Race of a Lifetime**
   Purpose: To learn how examples can bring informative speeches about events to life.
   Directions: Go to http://ww5.komen.org/ Susan G. Komen for the Cure. As you read through the site, think about how you would describe this race series to your class audience. Where possible, read the stories of participants. How does it communicate the significance of the race to its participants? Is the story vivid?

   If you are having students do service learning as an option, this can be a great activity for them to do. Many of the nonprofit organizations for which students will volunteer, sponsor or put on certain events. This website can help students determine if this type of information will be useful in their speech.

4. **Critiquing Videos**

Students have a much easier time grasping how the different components of a speech come together when they can actually see a video clip. When you show the sample video clips that come with the *Invitation to Public Speaking* textbook, have students follow along with a copy of the critique sheet you will use to grade them. After the clip is over, have students "grade" the speech based on that critique sheet. Not only do students get a clearer sense of how you will grade them on their own speeches, but they learn to identify specific components of a speech and to look for them in their own speeches. Many students will also ask you what kind of grade you would give the sample speech. Be sure to have a response ready, depending on your own criteria.

5. **Handout: Selecting a Topic and Identifying the General Purpose, Specific Purpose, and Thesis Statement for Informative Speeches**

It can be hard for students to select and then narrow their speech topics, and then identify their general and specific purposes as well as their thesis statements for informative speeches. Use the handout at the end of this chapter to help them in this process. Have students fill this out and turn in this information when beginning to prepare their speeches. This handout can be adapted for other speech types, as well. This handout can also help the instructor keep track of topics so that you do not get the same topic more than twice.

6. **Informative Speech Assignments**

There are a number of different ways you can assign an informative speech. Use the following three ideas as models adapting them to your own classes as necessary. Each option is followed by a sample speech.

A) *A Basic Informative Speech*

Define the different types of informative speeches and have students choose the type they will use for their informative speech. With this assignment you will get a full range of informative speeches. Students like this type of assignment because it gives them a lot of flexibility. Instructors like this type of assignment because they get to hear a variety of different speeches. However, some students will struggle with this type of assignment because it is "too" open and they have difficulty settling on a topic.

Speech Assignment: An informative speech on the topic of your choice (review the different types discussed in Chapter 13 of your *Invitation to Public Speaking* textbook).

Time: 4 to 6 minutes in length.

Source requirement: Cite at least 4 different sources in your speech.

Visual Aid requirement: At least one visual aid.

Outline: Turn in a preparation outline, with a works cited page, on the day you speak.

Delivery: Extemporaneous.

Informative Speech
U.S. Flag Etiquette
by Cindy Gardner

Topic: The U.S. Flag
General Purpose: To inform
Specific purpose: To inform my audience about the rules and regulations for handling the U.S. flag.
Central Idea: The flag, a symbol of much that is great about this nation, should be hung, handled, and folded in a specific manner.

Introduction

I. "The flag is the symbol of our national endeavor, our aspiration, our unity. The flag tells of the struggle for independence, of our union preserved, and of the sacrifices of brave men and women to whom the ideals and honor have been dearer than life." This is a quote from Charles Hughes, a teacher of flag etiquette. *(capture attention and reveal topic with a quote)*

    A.   The U.S. flag is more than a piece of material; it symbolizes all that is great in this nation.

    B.   In the wake of the recent tragedies in New York and Washington, D.C., many feel the flag represents humanity, liberty, and justice.

II.   Today I would like to educate you on how to display the flag, some important rules to remember when using the flag, and how to fold it. *(internal preview)*

Body

I. When hanging a flag, it is important to remember its symbolism and significance and hang it in a specific manner.

    A.   Each part of the flag has a specific meaning that symbolizes patriotic ideas.

        1.   The red stripes stand for blood and the fearless courage of those who gave their lives for our country.

        2.   The white stripes represent purity and faith.

        3.   The blue field represents heaven and our courage.

        4.   Each star represents one state of the union.

    B.   There are many rules and regulations regarding how to hang the flag.

        1.   When displaying the flag when it is not on a staff, place the union (blue field and stars) at the uppermost left corner.

        2.   When hanging the flag at an angle from the side of a building, place the union to the top of the staff unless the flag is flown at half-staff.

        3.   When flown with other flags, the U.S. flag is always the uppermost flag.

        4.   The biggest mistake people make when displaying the flag is positioning it to the wrong side of a speaker.

            a.   It should always be to the speaker's right.

            b.   If you are viewing it from the audience, it should be to your left.

Transition: I have given you tips on how to hang the flag, and now I would like to explain some rules regarding its use.

II.   Flag etiquette is more than just stories told from generation to generation.

    A.   The United States has developed a special code regarding its use: Title 36, Chapter 10.

    B.   The U.S. Code states that when a flag is no longer fit for display, it should be destroyed in a dignified way, preferably by burning.

    C.   According to the *Rocky Mountain News*, September 2001, "The flag should only be displayed from sunrise to sunset unless you have a spotlight on it."

    D.   It should never be used as clothing or a costume.

    E.   In honor of the flag, we place our right hand over our heart and face the flag during the national anthem.

Transition: Now that I have explained some rules regarding the flag, you might be wondering what to do when you are done using it.

III.   When putting the flag away, you fold it in such a way that each fold represents something. *(signposts used throughout this main point)*

    A.   First, fold the flag in half from bottom to top to represent life.

    B.   Second, fold it in half again to symbolize eternal life.

    C.   Third, begin folding the flag in a triangle in remembrance of our veterans.

    D.   The fourth fold represents out trust in God.

    E.   The fifth fold is a tribute to our country.

    F.   The sixth fold represents where our heart lies when we say the Pledge of Allegiance.

    G.   The seventh is a tribute to our armed forces.

    H.   The eighth fold is to the one who entered the valley of the shadow of death.

    I.   The ninth is a tribute to our womanhood, who has given us sons and daughters.

    J.   The tenth is a tribute to our fathers.

    K.   The eleventh is to the eyes of our Hebrew citizens.

    L.   The last one is a tribute to all the Christians and their eyes to the Father, the Son, and the Holy Ghost.

    M.   Lastly, the flag is tucked in to show four stars remaining of the front, symbolizing the motto "In God we trust."

Conclusion

I. I hope you have found some valuable information in my speech. *(internal summary)*

    A.   When we look at the flag, it is important to remember the rules regarding it and why they are there.

    B.   The flag stands for something different to every person and so is to be respected.

II.   Today I talked about how to display the flag, the rules regarding its use, and how to fold it.

    A.   When hanging the flag, the union and its position are most important.

    B.   The U.S. Code is helpful in deciding how to use the flag respectfully.

    C.   When finished using it, it is proper to fold the flag, with each fold representing something different.

III.   I would like to end with a quote from the poem *My Name Is Old Glory*: "But my finest hour comes when I am torn into strips to be used [as] bandages for my wounded comrades on the field of battle, and when I lie in the trembling arms of a grieving mother at the grave site of her fallen son [or daughter]."

Works Cited

Butchko, Angela. *The Foundation of the United States Air Force.* New York: U.S. Government Printing

Office, 1999.

"Flag Etiquette." Accessed 21 September 2001. http://www.annin.com/etiquette.htm.

Franklin, Peter. "Red, White and Blue: Give Your Flag Its Due." *Rocky Mountain News*. 19 September 2001: 8–9.

Rous, Ruth. "I Am the Flag." Accessed 21 September 2001. http://www.usflag.org/I am.the.flag.html.

Schnauber, Howard. "My Name Is Old Glory." Fort Collins Public Library Local History Archive, oral history interview of Howard Schnauber, 17 November 1994. City of Fort Collins, Colorado. Accessed 13, February 2002.

http://library.ci.fort-collins.co.us/local_history/topics/WWII/hist3b15.htm

If you are incorporating service learning into your course, consider the following simple option for an informative speech about a place. You can also assign this speech even if you are not having students participate in service learning, but do want them to give speeches about local, national, or international nonprofit agencies.

Speech Assignment: An informative speech about a health and human service agency in your community, a national service agency, or an international agency.
Time: 5 to 7 minutes.
Source Requirement: Cite at least 4 different sources in your speech.
Visual Aid Requirement: At least 2 visual aids.
Outline: Turn in a preparation outline, including a works cited page, on the day you speak.
Delivery: Extemporaneous

Informative Speech
Planned Parenthood

Topic: Planned Parenthood
General Purpose: To inform
Specific Purpose: To inform my audience about services provided at Planned Parenthood.
Central Idea: In order to have an understanding of the services provided at Planned Parenthood my audience needs to first understand the myths associated with this agency, then have an understanding of the family planning and birth control services, and the testing and treatment done for sexually transmitted diseases.

Introduction

I.   Two years ago, I found out that my ex-husband had been cheating on me over the year that we had been married.
    A.   I lived with the fear that he had given me AIDS.
        1.   Living with this fear, I realized I needed to be tested.
        2.   I went to a place where I received the help and compassion I needed during that time.
II.   I want to tell you about Planned Parenthood Federation of America because they can help you, too.
    A.   This is a place, here in Fort Collins that can help men and women through some challenging times in their lives.
    B.   No matter your background, they can offer everyone some help.
III.   I have been a patient there for three years, and have experienced their services first hand.
IV.   They offer many different services at reasonable prices, of which I will focus on three.
    A.   First, I will give some background information about Planned Parenthood that will help dispel some misconceptions.
    B.   Second, I will tell you about their family planning and birth control services.
    C.   Lastly, I will tell you about sexually transmitted disease testing and treatment.

Body

I.   In a recent interview with John Legman, a pro-life advocate, I learned that the misconception of Planned Parenthood is that it is only an abortion clinic.

    A.   It is possible to be pro-life and still take advantage of other services without compromising your beliefs.

        1.   Planned Parenthood offers many different services, depending on their patients' needs.

        2.   Going to Planned Parenthood does not mean that you subscribe to a specific set of values, it is there for *your needs*.

    B.   Planned Parenthood's mission, accessed from their website (www.plannedparenthood.org) reflects their openness to all.

        1.   They believe that it is each individual's right to manage his or her fertility.

            a.   Within this right is the right to privacy and respect.

            b.   All people will be helped without regard to income, marital status, race, ethnicity, sexual orientation, age, national origin, or residence.

            c.   Planned Parenthood also believes that their respect for diversity is essential to carry out their goals.

        2.   They believe that their goals will contribute to quality of life, strong family relationships, and population stability.

        3.   Planned Parenthood provides high quality affordable reproductive health care to men and women in 875 local health centers across the country.

[I have experienced their dedication to their mission statement. Let me now tell you about the services they offer.]

II.   Family planning and birth control often go hand-in-hand.

    A.   Family planning is a way for women and men to plan out how and when they want to have their family develop.

        1.   One method is by using birth control devices, such as oral contraceptives, barrier methods and internal methods.

            a.   These different ways help the person to control his or her fertility, keeping them from getting pregnant.

            b.   Some of these methods also help from sexually transmitted diseases.

            c.   Birth control is a personal choice.

                (1)   Planned Parenthood will talk with you about your lifestyle, habits, needs and issues to determine what contraceptive method is best for you.

                (2)   Many of the methods are offered through Planned Parenthood at a reasonable price.

        2.   Another method of birth control they inform their patients about is Natural Family planning.

            a.   This method is based on a woman's menstrual cycle, her body temperature and various other means according to the book, *The Art of Natural Family Planning*.

            b.   There are no drugs or "unnatural" means used, making it a good choice for people who want to plan out their family based on religious principles.

        3.   Planned Parenthood is also equipped to assist you with yearly gynecological screenings to ensure that your method is right for you.

[This now leads me into the last service I want to inform you about.]

III.   The last service is sexually transmitted disease testing and treatment.
    A.   There are 15 million new cases of STD's diagnosed each year in the United States.
        1.   You could be at risk and not even know it because two-thirds of these cases occur in the 15 to 24-age bracket.
        2.   A dear friend of mine (who wants to remain anonymous) was diagnosed with Human Papillomavirus about seven years ago.
            a.   In an interview with her last Monday, she told me she switched her primary care to Planned Parenthood after her diagnosis.
            b.   She was treated with more respect and compassion by Planned Parenthood than by her regular doctor.
    B.   Any test for any STD is available from Planned Parenthood, at no risk to you.
        1.   Confidentiality and respect is foremost on their mind.
        2.   Counseling sessions are conducted before any test so that you know what will happen.
        3.   All tests and results are confidential and are offered at a reasonable price.
        4.   If you do test positive for anything, do notify your primary care physician, but Planned Parenthood can treat you just as easily.

Conclusion

I.   I have told you only a piece in a large pie of what is Planned Parenthood.
    A.   You know the standard this agency holds itself to.
    B.   You know the different options of family planning and or birth control they offer.
    C.   You know where to go for STD testing and treatment.
II.   If you have further questions or concerns, please contact our local Planned Parenthood.
    A.   They treated me with the compassion I needed.
    B.   Thankfully, my HIV test was negative.
III.   I leave you with a quote: "In many communities around the world, Planned Parenthood is the only source of affordable, quality reproductive health care services and information . . ."

Works Cited

Kippley, John F., and Sheila K. Kippley. *The Art of Natural Family Planning.* 4th ed. Ohio: Couple to

    Couple League, 1996.

Kippley, John F. *The Legacy of Margaret Sanger.* Ohio, 1998.

Longeman, John. Personal interview. 16 October, 2000.

Personal interview. 14 October, 2000.

Planned Parenthood Federation of America website. 16 October 2000.

http://www.plannedparenthood.org/about/thispp/mission.html

Serotta, Betty. *Colorado Religious Collation for Abortion Rights.* Denver: 1998.

Informative Topic Choices

Name _____

Refer to Chapter 3 of your text to help you.

Topic Choice #1

Topic:

General Purpose:

Specific Purpose:

Thesis Statement:

Main Points:

Topic Choice #2

Topic:

General Purpose:

Specific Purpose:

Thesis statement:

Main Points:

Supplemental Bibliography

Anholt, Robert R. H. <u>Dazzle 'em With Style: The Art of Oral Scientific Presentation</u>. New York: W.H. Freeman and Company, 1994.

A practical guide to informative speaking that covers preparation and structure of the presentation. A good resource for material for lectures.

Davis, Martha. <u>Scientific Papers and Presentations</u>. New York: Academic Press, 1997.

Davis covers many aspects of informative writing and speaking including organization, documentation, style, and ethical issues. A nice supplement for lectures and for information on technical presentations.

Forbes, Mark. <u>Writing Technical Articles, Speeches, and Manuals</u>. New York: Wiley, 1988.

This is a helpful manual for technical or informative speaking for nonspeakers. It includes topics such as when people might be asked to speak and things to consider when writing your speech.

Morrisey, George L., and Sechrest, Thomas L, and Warman, Wendy B., <u>Loud and Clear: How to Prepare and Deliver Effective Business and Technical Presentations</u>. 4th ed. Reading, Mass.: Addison-Wesley Publishing, 1997.

This text addresses considerations for informative presentations including identifying your message objective, establishing message structure, and analyzing the audience. A nice resource for lectures as well as for students as they begin to prepare their group presentations.

Rowan, Katherine E. "A New Pedagogy for Explanatory Speaking: Why Arrangement Should Not Substitute for Invention." *Communication Education*, 44 (1995), 236-250.

Rowan highlights the importance of invention during the creation of the informative speech. An excellent resource for additional material during lecture and discussions with students about the organization of speeches.

http://writing.colostate.edu/guides/speaking/infomod/

Colorado State University web page guide to Informative Speaking.

Chapter Fourteen: Invitational Speaking

Chapter Goals

Chapter Fourteen introduces a new type of speech, the invitational speech. It includes a discussion of an invitational environment, and the different types of invitational speeches. As students reach the end of this chapter, they should understand the following goals:

- To identify the three conditions for an invitational speaking environment.
- To describe the two types of invitational speeches.
- To apply the four most common patterns of organization for invitational speeches.
- To identify three tips for giving effective invitational speeches.
- To identify two principles for giving ethical invitational speeches.

Chapter Outline

I. **Invitational speaking** is a type of public speaking in which *a speaker enters into a dialogue with an audience to clarify positions, explore issues and ideas, or articulate beliefs and values* (pg. 286).
   a. To speak invitationally is to do something other than inform or persuade.
   b. To speak invitationally is to decide to continue the public dialogue and seek mutual recognition, despite firm differences in opinions, values, and beliefs.
   c. To speak invitationally is to try and understand why your audience sees things as they do by exploring a topic civilly and with openness.

II. **The invitational speaking environment** *is one in which your highest priority is to understand, respect, and appreciate the range of possible positions on an issue, even if those positions are quite different from your own* (pg. 286).
   a. In invitational speaking, you want to begin a dialogue with your audience.
   b. You offer your position as one viable stance and encourage your audience to express their positions so that everyone might come to a fuller understanding of the different positions.
   c. It is best suited for situations in which speakers have some time with an audience to allow for the fullest expression of the various positions possible.
   d. A key to creating a successful invitational speaking environment is to alter the traditional roles of the speaker and audience.
       i. Rather than taking on the role of the "expert" and assigning the role of the "listener" to the audience, you consider both yourself and the audience as the experts and the listeners.
       ii. The traditional distance between the speaker and the audience is replaced with a feeling that everyone is free to express his or her views without risk of attack or ridicule.
   e. In order to create a *invitational environment*, three conditions must exist (pg 288.).
       i. **The condition of equality** is created when *you acknowledge that all audience members hold equally valid perspective worthy of exploration* (pg. 288).
          1. You use language, delivery, and presentation of ideas to let your audience know that you recognize them as people whose knowledge, experiences, and perspectives are as valid for them as yours are for you.

2. Your audience is able to offer their perspectives, share their experiences, and even question you, in the same way you do with the audience.

  ii. **The condition of value** is created by *recognizing inherent value of your audience's views, although those views might be different from the speaker's views* (pg. 288).

   1. You let your audience know that they will be encouraged to express their views and opinions, even if they are vastly different from yours.

   2. You communicate that you will try to step outside your own standpoint in order to understand another perspective and see the world as your audience sees it.

  iii. **The condition of self-determination** is created by *recognizing that the members of your audience are experts in their own lives--that they know what is best for them and have the right to make choices about their lives based on this knowledge* (pg 288).

   1. Although you may not make the same choices as your audience, they are free to decide how to think, feel, and act.

   2. You will not close off conversation or try to persuade your audience to do something they may not feel inclined to do.

III. **Two types of invitational speaking** (pg. 290).

 a. **Speeches to explore an issue** occur when *you attempt to engage your audience in a discussion about an idea, concern, topic, or plan of action* (pg. 290).

  i. Your goal is to gather information from your audience so you might understand the subject more fully and from the audience's perspectives.

  ii. You begin these speeches by stating your intent to explore the issue.

   1. Then, lay out the positions of an issue, trying to go beyond presenting it as having only two sides.

   2. You may also share your opinions, even if they are tentative ones.

 b. **Speeches to articulate a position** occur when *you invite an audience to understand an issue from your perspective* (pg. 292).

  i. This is similar to informative speaking in that you share information with an audience.

  ii. Articulating a position is different from informative speaking in that you are open to conversation with the audience about their views on the topic.

  iii. Both the audience and the speaker leave the exchange with a richer understanding of a complex issue.

  iv. You invite the audience to enter your world for a moment, and you return the gesture by entering their world during the discussion.

  v. Your goal is that you and members of the audience gain a better understanding of different views and frame the issue in more complete and inclusive ways in the future.

   1. Change may occur, but that is not your goal.

   2. The simple exchange of information might occur, although that is not your primary goal.

IV. **Organizational patterns for invitational speeches** (pg. 293).

 a. **Chronological organizational pattern.**

  i. The chronological pattern allows you to trace a sequence of events or ideas.

  ii. It can be used for both types of invitational speeches.

   iii. By tracing the evolution of your perspective or an issue over time, you establish common ground as well as openness to seeing how the perspective or issue might continue to evolve.

  b. **Spatial organizational pattern.**
   i. The spatial pattern can help you organize your ideas according to location or geography.
   ii. This pattern can be used with both types of invitational speeches.
   iii. It can be useful when you want to discuss what various locations (communities, for example) have in common with your topic, or how the issue differs across countries, nations, states, or cities.
   iv. You can also use this pattern in speeches in business settings to compare how other businesses have dealt with a problem.

  c. **Topical organizational pattern.**
   i. The topical pattern allows you to discuss the aspects of your topic point by point.
   ii. A topical pattern can work very well in an invitational speech to articulate a position.

  d. **Multiple perspectives organizational pattern.**
   i. **The multiple perspectives pattern** *allows you to systematically address the many sides and positions of an issue before opening up the speech for dialogue with the audience* (pg. 297).
    1. This works well when you want to explore an issue with the audience.
    2. You can go beyond dividing an issue into only two opposing sides and illustrate the multiple perspectives possible on the issue.
    3. There are three guidelines to using the multiple perspectives organizational pattern.
     a. Do your research so you can explain the various sides to your audience.
     b. Present each perspective fairly so the audience members can make their own assessment of the different perspectives.
     c. Make room for even more perspectives to be offered from the audience.

V. **Tips for giving effective invitational speaking** (pg. 300).
  a. **Use invitational language.**
   i. Use appropriate language to create an environment of equality.
    1. "I came to this view because . . ."
    2. "For me, this position makes sense because . . ."
    3. "Because of that experience, I began to see this issue as . . ."
    4. Use phrases that display respect and openness to other positions throughout your speech.
   ii. During discussion with the audience, encourage dialogue about differences and disagreements.
    1. Offer positive reinforcement to the ideas of others so the dialogue can develop openly and freely.
    2. Use phrases like "can you elaborate on that idea?" "How might that work?" and, "Can you explain why you prefer that solution?"
   iii. Draw audiences out and get them to elaborate on their views.
    1. Use a flip chart or write ideas on a white board.
    2. Return the focus to ideas when the discussion gets heated.
   iv. A speaker's language can help diffuse a hostile audience member.

b. **Allow time for discussion.**
    i. Be patient, do not rush through your part of the presentation and/or hurry your audience through the discussion.
    ii. In a classroom, however, you do have time constraints.
        1. If you have only a small amount of time, consider reducing the scope of your presentation.
        2. Decide what you can address in a shorter period of time.

c. **Know your own position.**
    i. Take time to figure out how you really feel about an issue and why you feel as you do.
    ii. You need to do thorough research in order to help you explore how you feel about the issue, and present the information with clarity and detail to your audience.

VI. **Ethical invitational speaking** (pg. 302).
a. When you choose to speak invitationally, stay true to your purpose.
    i. Although value, equality, and self-determination can be created in other speeches, in invitational speaking your fundamental goal is the exchange and appreciation of perspectives, not persuasion.
b. If you really want to change your audience, do not pretend to offer an invitational approach. If you choose to share your own perspectives and listen fully to the perspectives of others.
    i. Your topic needs to be one to which you are truly open.
    ii. Ethical speakers do not say they are open about a given topic when they are really not.
    iii. This means you have to be willing to listen with respect to other views, but not necessarily change your own view.
    iv. If you cannot grant value and self-determination to someone who disagrees with you, then it would be more ethical for you to give an informative or persuasive speech.

End of the Chapter Activities and Discussion Questions

The following questions can be found at the end of Chapter Fourteen.

Review Questions and Activities

1. Can you identify situations in which you might have preferred giving an invitational speech but gave another type instead? What might have been different if you had given an invitational speech rather that the type of speech you did give?

After defining invitational speaking, or after assigning the reading, use this question as a discussion prompt. Ask students to explain why they would have preferred the invitational approach and what the specific outcomes might have been.

2. Imagine you are giving an invitational speech on the subject of gays and lesbians serving in the military. How might you create conditions of equality, value, and self-determination in this speech?

   Have students address this question in small groups. After you have given students time in class, have them report their ideas to the whole class. Compare the different options students choose and, as a class, identify what made each of the options invitational using the conditions of equality, value, and self-determination as your guidelines. Ask students to identify whether they are giving speeches to articulate a position or explore an issue.

3. Identify a person or group with whom you strongly disagree. Consider whether you might speak invitationally with that person or group and what benefits or disadvantages might result from such an interaction.

   Many topics are not suited for invitational speeches because a speaker cannot be invitational—they hold values or positions that are more suited for persuasive speeches than invitational ones. This question encourages students to think carefully about appropriate invitational speech topics before they get too far in their preparation process. Use this question as a discussion prompt or a homework assignment to encourage students to be realistic about the topics that are suitable for them. Remind them that it is ok not to select a certain topic; invitational speaking is not appropriate for all situations and this is a good time to make that distinction for students.

4. Develop an invitational speech to give to the person or group you identified in question 3. Would you prefer to articulate a position or explore an issue with them? What is it about your position that you would like them to understand, and what aspect of their position would you like to explore? Did you allow time for these types of interactions in your speech?

   Pose this question as a discussion prompt to your class. You can also assign this question to students as homework, and have them come to class prepared to discuss their responses. Encourage students to look at these topics as potential invitational speech topics for their in-class speeches.

5. Suppose that while you are giving the speech you developed in question 4, a member of your audience strongly disagrees with the position you articulate. What kind of language could you use to acknowledge his anger and frustration, but also continue to have a productive dialogue with him and other members of the audience? (You might role-play this scenario with members of your class.)

   Because there are many excellent options for handling this situation, place students into groups of three or four, and have them role-play this scenario. After they have had time to identify the language they would use, bring the class back together. Have students share as many varied examples as they can. You can even assign one or two groups to deal with the situation in a not so appropriate way so that students can compare what works well and what does not.

6. Check out Speech Studio to see other students deliver their invitational speeches. Or record a speech you're working on, upload it to Speech Studio, and ask your peers for their feedback. What feedback could you use to fine tune your invitational speech before you give it in class?

Web Activities

1. **Hecklers, Hardliners, and Heavy Questions**
Go to http://www.expressionsofexcellence.com/ARTICLES/DifficultQ.html. Read Craig Harrison's article, "Hecklers, Hardliners, and Heavy Questions: Handling Difficult Questions and Questioners with Eloquence and Ease." Which of his advice agrees with what your book has said about invitational speaking? Which of his advice disagrees with the advice in the book? How have you handled hostile audiences? Were you successful? Why or why not?

In general, students will be quite nervous engaging their audience in a dialogue (although they often report this is their favorite part of the speech after they are done). They seem especially concerned about hostile questions or emotional disagreements. Have them access this website for ideas on how to deal with potential hostile audience members. Once they identify the strategies ask them to share what they learned in class discussions so that they can feel like they have several strategies at their disposal when they go into the discussion.

InfoTrac College Edition Activities

1. **InfoTrac College Edition Activity 14.1: Identifying Invitational Speeches**
Purpose: To learn how to identify invitational speeches.
Directions: Find a speech in *Vital Speeches* that is invitational. What makes this speech different from one that is informative or persuasive? What is the central idea? What do you think were the attitudes of the audience? Did the speaker use the invitational style effectively?

This can be a very effective activity to help students distinguish between the different types of speeches. Students can work on this individually or with partners. Direct students to use the questions listed above to help them locate an invitational speech. Keep copies of their speeches in your files for future use or, identify several on your own and give copies of them to students and ask them to answer the questions above.

2. **InfoTrac College Edition Activity 14.2: Articulating a Position**
Purpose: To understand one of the types of invitational speeches.
Directions: Use your InfoTrac College Edition account to locate Benjamin Olaakande's article, "My Perspective on the "F" Word," *Vital Speeches* (March 1, 2001), p. 311. The speaker addresses failure and offers his perspective for dealing with it. How does the speaker encourage discussion with the audience? What examples does the speaker offer to help articulate his position? Was the speech effective as an invitational speech?

This activity can help students with effective strategies on how to articulate a position and how to set the stage for an open dialogue. Have students read the speech and respond to the questions listed here. Give time in class to hear the other students' responses and compare them to their own. Note, some students may not see Olaakande's speech as entirely invitational—this is a good time to review audience centered strategies and how speakers can try to create invitational environments. If they do not think his speech is the best example of an invitational speech, ask them to offer specific suggestions for how they would change the speech to make it invitational.

3. **InfoTrac College Edition Activity 14.3: Using Invitational Language**

   Purpose: To appreciate the importance of using invitational language.

   Directions: Use your InfoTrac College Edition account to look up Judy Olian's speech, "The Past and Prologue," *Vital Speeches* (April 15, 2001), p. 398. How does the speaker use invitational language? Does the speaker articulate effectively that he or she is offering only one potential viewpoint on the topic discussed? What advice might you give this speaker concerning invitational language?

   Students can be uncertain about the specific use of invitational language in their speeches. This activity can illustrate for them specific and effective invitational language.

Interactive Student and Professional Speech Videos

1. **Video Clip 1: Student Speech: Creating a Condition of Equality**

   How does Shelly create a condition of equality as she's giving her speech? Do you think she does so effectively? As an audience member listening to her speech, would you be willing to offer your perspective or experience on the subject? Why or why not?

   Show this clip in class, and have students respond to the questions listed here. Students may have different responses and will catch different strategies that Shelley used, so make a list of the specific ways they see her speech as being invitational (language, organization, delivery, etc). Make sure to clarify your own criteria of what you consider to be effective, so that students understand how to best meet your requirements.

2. **Video Clip 2: Student Speech: Condition of Self-determination**

   How does Melissa create a condition of self-determination as she's giving her speech? Do you think she does so effectively? As an audience member listening to her speech, would you think Melissa recognized that you knew what was best for you and had the right to make choices about your life? Why or why not?

   Some students struggle with the condition of self-determination. Show this video clip, and discuss with students the specific ways they can create an environment of self-determination when giving their invitational speeches.

3. **Video Clip 3: Student Speech, Amanda Bucknam**

   Watch Amanda's speech and consider the way that she establishes the conditions of equality, value, and self-determination. Also, pay close attention to her use of language. Can you identify specific phrases that she uses in her speech to assist her in creating an invitational speaking environment?

   Show this clip in class, and have students address the questions listed here. Emphasize to students the very important role that language plays in creating an invitational speaking environment.

4. **Video Clip 4: Student Speech: Invitational Speech**

   How fairly does Cara present the three theories of evolution and creationism, given that she favors only one of them? How do you think her discussion with her audience helps her clarify her own position and understand the positions of people in her audience? Do you think her invitational speech was effective? Why or why not?

For students to better understand how all of the different components of effective invitational speaking work together, show Cara's speech in class. Have students follow along with their own critique sheets that you will use to grade them. After the speech, have students respond to the questions listed here. Ask them to consider organization, language, delivery, and the like as they respond to the questions and fill out the critique sheet.

5. **Video Clip 5: Student Speech, David Barworth**
   Watch David's speech and consider the way that he establishes the conditions of equality, value, and self-determination. Also, pay close attention to his use of language. Can you identify specific phrases that he uses, or should have used, in his speech to assist him in creating an invitational speaking environment? Is his invitational approach effective?

   Show this clip in class, and have students address the questions listed here. Emphasize to students the very important role that language plays in creating an invitational speaking environment.

Additional Exercises and Resources

1. **Report versus Rapport**
   Go to http://www.time.com/time/time100/artists/profile/winfrey.html. Read linguist Deborah Tannen's article, "The TV Host: Oprah Winfrey." What is the difference between "report-talk" and "rapport-talk?" How does the style of Oprah's show reflect the ideas we have discussed about speeches to explore an issue? Is this style beneficial to Oprah's viewers?

   Have students access this website and respond to the questions listed here. Have them bring their lists to class and then put all the examples on the board. As many examples as you can provide for students, the better. If you have access to the internet in your classroom, you can pull up this site and answer the questions as a full class or in small groups.

2. **Cultural Rhythms**
   Go to http://www.trinity.edu/~mkearl/time-c.html. To learn more about how cultures think differently about time, visit The Cultural Rhythms of Life web page. The page describes polychronic and monochronic cultures. Which best describes your general orientation toward time? Which view of time is reflected in how you think about public speaking and time constraints?

   This is a good website for students to access, even before the invitational speeches. Ideally, it would be nice to not have such rigid time constraints on the invitational speech; however, in classroom settings we need to. This is a great site to help with the discussion of staying invitational under even the tightest time constraints. Also refer to the "Additional Exercises and Resource" section at the end of this chapter for options on how to time the invitational speech.

3. **Keeping an Open Mind**
   Go to http://www.mendosa.com/openmind.htm. The Reasons to Keep an Open Mind web page contains several statements made by people who had a very narrow sense of the future. What do these statements say about truth and certainty? What lessons can we learn from them?
   This website can be valuable for students to read as they prepare their invitational speeches. Students in class will nod and say they understand the concept of "keeping an open mind"; however, putting it into practice is another story. Have students look through this website to help with the practice component of this concept. Also, refer to the end of the chapter section "Additional Exercises and

203

Resources" for an activity you can do in class that will help students practice the dialogue component of the invitational speech and keep an "open mind" as they engage their audience in a dialogue.

4. **Thinking about Attitudes**
   Purpose: To think critically about attitude formation.
   Directions: Read the attitude formation page of the Hypertext Development Project at Wayne State University. As you read the page, consider how you have formed attitudes toward racism, affirmative action, or feminism. How were these attitudes formed? Are there any specific experiences you've had that formed these attitudes? How might these attitudes play a role in your interaction with an invitational speaker? http://sun.science.wayne.edu/~wpoff/cor/grp/formatio.html

   This is a great website to help students think about how they feel on certain issues and how they came to believe what they do. This will assist students in formulating stronger invitational speeches and in identifying topics on which they will have a difficult time staying invitational. Assign this activity as homework and then use their answers to assist you in a discussion of invitational topic selection.

5. **Detecting Hidden Agendas**
   Purpose: To understand the effects of hidden agendas.
   Directions: Access the "Decision Process Guidebook" by the U.S. Department of Reclamation at http://www.usbr.gov/pmts/economics/guide/index.html. The page listed here describes hidden agendas. What is a hidden agenda? How can you protect yourself from others who might have a hidden agenda? How do hidden agendas impede the dialogue that can occur between a speaker and an audience?

   Some students might slip into persuasion when giving invitational speeches. Have them access this website as a way to uncover any hidden agendas they may have before they give their speeches. As students prepare the invitational speeches, you might also want to have them review the differences between the different kinds of speeches to help them avoid any hidden agendas.

6. **The differences between informative, persuasive, and invitational speeches** (Prepared by Jennifer Emerling Bone, University of Colorado, Boulder). Divide students into groups of three. Write a topic on the board. Have the students write a specific purpose, thesis statement for an informative, persuasive, and invitational speech (using same topic). This assignment allows students to understand the difference between the different speech rounds. Example:

   On Board Write: Music

   Informative Speech

   Specific Purpose: I will inform my audience about the people who shaped jazz music.
   Thesis Statement: Duke Ellington and Miles Davis are two of the most important musicians that helped shape jazz as we know it.

   Persuasive Speech

   Specific Purpose: I will persuade my audience that warning labels should be strictly enforced on record labels.

Thesis Statement: More warning labels are needed on records and parents should monitor what type of music their children listen to.

Invitational Speech: Exploring an Issue

Specific Purpose: I will invite my audience to discuss whether warning labels are beneficial in keeping obscene and violent lyrics from reaching the hands of children.
Thesis Statement: Warning labels were introduced to keep parents informed of the content of albums and CD's but I'd like to discuss with my audience the research related to the sales of music with these labels in order to explore the effectiveness of these labels.

Invitational Speech: Articulating a position

Specific Purpose: I will invite the audience to understand why I feel warning labels can be beneficial to keeping under aged children from hearing the explicit language contained in some lyrics.

Thesis Statement: I think warning labels do help parents identify records that contain language that is inappropriate for their children and I'd like to share and then discuss this position with my audience.

7. **Making a Distinction Between the Types of Invitational Speeches**
   At the end of this chapter you will find a handout that can help students distinguish between the two different types of invitational speeches. These topics are included in the textbook, but are in condensed form so that students can easily see the differences.

8. **Open Dialogue**
   Practicing the Open Dialogue (full class period)
   In the invitational speech, the open dialogue tends to make students the most anxious. At the end of this chapter is an activity that students can do in small groups in class to feel more confident about this aspect of invitational speaking. You will want to allow a full class period for this activity. Make sure that each group is keeping track of time to ensure that all students have a turn. As the students work, listen in on each group to make sure that each group understands the importance of the invitational speaking environment (creating conditions of equality, value, and self-determination). With this activity, instructors can sometimes pose as the more "hostile" audience members to give students practice on how to handle these situations should they arise in class. Students should provide each other with constructive feedback in order to be successful the day they give their speech.

   Facilitating a Dialogue (20 minutes)
   (Prepared by Jennifer Emerling Bone, University of Colorado, Boulder)

   Using one of the sample speeches in this chapter (or one that you have from previous classes) have students read a sample invitational outline or view an invitational speech. Ask the class to write down five possible questions they would ask if they were a member of the audience for that speech. Choose a student to facilitate the discussion. Have that student come forward and lead a discussion around the sample speech. Help students identify open-ended versus fixed-alternative questions. Be sure students stay invitational, use inviting language, and continue to express civility towards their classmates. Be sure the speaker contributes to the conversation, rather than just agree with all the information given. Make sure the speaker manages the dialogue well, allowing all students to participate. After 5-7 minutes, ask the speaker to sum up the dialogue in a conclusion format. Allow more students the opportunity to become the facilitator if time allows.

9. **Impromptu conclusions: (20 minutes, 5 min./person)**
(Prepared by Jennifer Emerling Bone, University of Colorado, Boulder). Divide students into groups of four. Have each person in the group select a question from a bag. Spend a minute answering the question silently and providing reasons for the answer (may record on paper). The instructor starts timing (5 minutes). The first person acts as the speaker, reads the question to the group, explains their answer to the question, and then asks the question of the group members. Each person in the group will respond to the question. Once everyone has participated (5 minutes), and the instructor calls time, the speaker will conclude by summarizing the discussion. Have three participants critique the speaker's conclusion. Remind students to think about managing discussion!

Possible Questions:
A. How do you feel about the death penalty and why?
B. How do you feel about making a year round school system mandatory (no summers off)?
C. How do you feel about euthanasia and why?
D. Should fast food be allowed in schools? Why/why not?
E. How do you feel about gay adoption?
F. How do you feel about public schools versus private schools?
G. How do you feel about school uniforms?
H. What is your opinion on the electoral college system?
I. What is your opinion on censorship in the music industry?
J. What is your opinion on taking the SAT/ACT/GRE to get into school?

10. **Being a "Good" Audience Member and Speaker**
While it is very important to review speaker strategies to effectively manage an open dialogue, it can also be quite useful to go over how to be an effective audience. At the end of this chapter, you will find guidelines you can share with students on how to be "good" audience members and speakers. You can place these guidelines on an overhead or PowerPoint slide.

11. **Generate a list of possible speech topics for an invitational speech (20 minutes)**
(Prepared by Jennifer Emerling Bone, University of Colorado, Boulder, CO)
Place the following list on the board. You can start the list by using the topics listed below, then have the class add to it. Discuss what topics may be better for a different speech or not used at all.
Possible topics:
A. Articulate a position on mandatory STD testing.

B. Exploring an issue on the current debate of "under God" in the Pledge of Allegiance.

C. Articulate a proposal on new admission standards for colleges, discuss removing requirement of SAT and ACT scores.

D. Articulate a proposal on incorporating mandatory parenting classes and child development classes for new parents.

E. Explore the issue of gay and lesbian adoption.

F.   Articulate my perspective on bi-racial adoption.

G.   Discuss a proposal on urban redevelopment to help reduce urban sprawl.

H.   Explore an issue of lowering age for children to begin their education (lower age from 5 to 4).

I.   Articulate a position on limiting fighting forest fires.

J.   Explore an issue of cloning animals.

K.   Explore whether juveniles should be tried as adults.

L.   Explore the issue of prayer in schools.

Then discuss whether students could respect and validate others' opinions on the following topics (add to this list additional topics many people can't remain open about):

A.   Abortion

B.   Death penalty

C.   Teaching evolution in classrooms

D.   Spanking and other forms of discipline used with children

E.   Topics based on certain religious beliefs

12. An Invitational Speech Assignment

Following is an example of an invitational speech assignment. Included is a description of the assignment, a breakdown of the requirements, ideas on how to grade the speech, and a sample preparation outline. (Note: At the end of the chapter you will find another sample invitational outline, and a sample critique form).

Speech Assignment: Invitational Speech.

In the invitational speech you are not attempting to change your audiences' perspectives or positions or to simply offer them new information. You are attempting to come to a fuller understanding of an issue through openness and respect. This speech is designed so that you enter into a dialogue with the audience about a position you wish to articulate or explore or an issue/proposal you wish to offer regarding your topic. In this speech you are not acknowledging only one side, or two-sides of the issue, but all sides of an issue. Although you use many of the same principles learned in informative and persuasive speeches (introductions, conclusions, organization, reasoning, delivery) unlike the other speeches, this speech allows you to engage the audience in a dialogue.

This will be a three part speech: 1) Speech; 2) Dialogue with the audience; 3) Summary/conclusion. In your introduction, you should clearly identify whether you are articulating a position or exploring an issue, (but still accomplishing the four objectives needed in an introduction). You also will explain that you are assuming an invitational stance and wish to hear other possibilities. In the introduction (and the remainder of the speech) you will need to use invitational language. The body of your speech develops according to the principles you learned in this text (organization, supporting materials, reasoning, delivery, etc). This is followed by the discussion component of the speech. Finally, you will deliver a conclusion that also follows the principles for effective conclusion, incorporating a summary of the key ideas raised in the speech. If your speech is only 5 minutes long, you can transfer the extra minute to the open dialogue of the speech. Formal requirements:

Time: **10-12 minutes total.**
- **Opening speech: 5-6 minutes**
- **Dialogue with audience: 4-5 minutes**
- **Summary/Conclusion: 1 minute**

Source requirement: You need to cite at least **five** different sources in your speech.
Visual Aid requirement: You need to use PowerPoint (at least 4 slides).
Outline: You will turn in a preparation outline, including a works cited page.
Delivery: Extemporaneous.

Topic: Physician Assisted Suicide
General Purpose: To invite
Specific Purpose: To invite my audience to join me in a dialogue about their perspectives on physician assisted suicide.
Thesis Statement: My personal experiences with death and my point of view on the religious, ethical, and legal issues that surround P.A.S. have shaped my views on this topic and I'd like to invite my audience to understand these views and to discuss why I believe society should have the legal choice of physician assisted suicide available to them.

Introduction

I.   *"The tears rolled down her face as she struggled to communicate. Frustrated, she grabbed a pen and a note pad and tried to write what she so wished me to know 'I don't want this anymore.' My father-in-law's life ended much as Grandmother's had. Body riddled with cancer, joy of life extinguished by the constant bouts of pain and sickness brought about by the disease itself and the endless rounds of medical treatments that continued until his death. Both of them suffered immeasurably the last six months of their lives."*

II.   Physician assisted suicide or P.A.S. is an issue I have thought a lot about in the last several years after facing the deaths of my Grandmother and father-in-law.

    A.   It is from these two experiences that I set about deciphering my own attitude about P.A.S.

    B.   After much mental wrestling I have come to the conclusion that I personally would like to see physician assisted suicide laws passed for the terminally ill.

III.   One thing that played a major role in my decision-making is my strong belief in freedom of choice.

    A.   In this class we learned about self-determination, where we must recognize that audience members have a right to choose what is best for them, even if those choices are not ones we would make for ourselves.

    B.   As a society, we understand that it is necessary to respect the choices of others even if we disagree with those choices.

IV.   I would like to invite you to express your perspectives on P.A.S. after I share with you in greater detail how and why I arrived at my decision.

    A.   I will share with you some of my thought process and research about the legal, religious, and ethical issues surrounding P.A.S. that went into making my decision.

    B.   I would then like to hear your perspectives on the issue.

Body

I.   For both my Grandmother and father-in-law, when the end was near and the suffering became unbearable it seems to me that they should have had the legal option to end their suffering in a humane and dignified way.

    A.   I don't believe that my Grandmother or Ken's life would have been less rich had they spared themselves the very painful end.

        1.   Currently, the only state that allows for this option legally is Oregon.

        2.   Oregon voters passed the Death with Dignity Act in 1994 according to information I accessed on March 29, 2002 on http://www.finalexit.org.

    B.   I believe that laws that make suicide illegal actually deny us the right to live and make choices about our own lives.

1. From my perspective, it denied Grandmother and Ken the right to end their suffering if they would have chosen to do so.
2. I believe as Thomas Bowden does, an attorney who authored *Assisted Suicide: A Moral Right,* "if you have a duty to live, despite your better judgment, than your life does not belong to you" (March 29, 2002 on the Ayn Rand Institute's website at http://aynrand.org).
3. The Declaration of Independence proclaimed that each person exists as an end in himself, my perception of this is that I have the guaranteed right to choose what is best for me.

{The next issue I needed to consider for myself related to my religious beliefs.}

II. From a religious standpoint, I personally believe that life is a gift from God but I do not believe that God punishes those who commit suicide under these circumstances.
   A. We know that not all people believe in the same religious doctrines, some people believe in none at all, and that is, after all, each person's choice.
   B. But I wonder, is it fair to assume that every human considers suicide as something that goes against their faith or that every faith subscribes to the same point of view or that every person subscribes to some type of faith?
      1. Part of my religious belief is supported by a quote from the Ninth Circuit Court of Appeals in 1995: "those who believe strongly that death must come without physician assistance are free to follow that creed, be they doctors or patients" (March 2, 2001, Compassion in Dying Federations website http://compassionindying.org).
      2. The Court of Appeals goes onto to discuss that people, however, do not have the right to force their religious beliefs onto others.
         a. As members of a democratic society, we should have the right to make choices that are right for us.
         b. Having the right to choose P.A.S. I believe, is a more democratic approach, rather than not having the choice to begin with.

{The last issue I have considered is that of ethics}

III. I do not believe suicide is wrong under these circumstances, nor do I believe that to allow physician assisted suicide is to have doctors murdering patients.
   A. In my view, the protocol that doctors would follow would be one that does not reflect murder, but, rather, guidance.
      1. The definition of P.A.S. states that the doctor provides an individual with the information, guidance, and the means to take his or her own life (March 29, 2002 http://www.euthanasia.com).
      2. Doctors such as Richard MacDonald, oncologist, also agree with this perspective.
         a. In an article to the editor of the *Journal of the American Medical Association,* Dr. MacDonald stated "Sometimes physicians not only must help patients face dying but also assist them in finding a death that is more peaceful and dignified" (http://jama.org).
         b. All lives cannot be saved and I believe that when that life involves someone who is terminally ill, it is ethical to allow a doctor to help end the suffering, if that is the patient's wish.

B.   If my Grandmother and Ken had the choice, then it may have saved them from experiencing the most excruciating pain.
        1.   Ultimately, the question I ended up asking myself was, who has the final right to make decisions about my life and body: is it God, society, the government, or me?
        2.   If you were to ask yourself that question what would your answer be?

[ENGAGE THE AUDIENCE IN AN OPEN DIALOGUE]

Conclusion

I.   I have shared with you my perspectives on P.A.S. and I have invited you to share yours with me.
    A.   I began by telling you about my experience with two deaths related to a terminal disease.
    B.   I also talked to you about how I arrived at my decision by considering the religious issues, the legal issues, and the ethical issues.
II.   We entered into a dialogue that provided me with the basis to see this issue from your perspective.
    A.   [SUMMARIZE KEY IDEAS FROM THE DIALOGUE]
III.   Is P.A.S. the best option? For me it is an option I would like to have available.

Recommendations for the length of the Invitational Speech Round

There are various methods for scheduling the invitational speech. For the sample speech on physician-assisted suicide, the round was organized as follows: Class of 20-22 students; class meets twice a week for 75 minutes; 4-5 days of speeches; 5 speeches per class. This leaves time for instructor and peer critiques.

Recommendations for grading the Invitational Speech

The invitational speech can be the speech that is worth the most points in the semester, or it can easily be weighted between the persuasive and informative speeches on the total point scale. If this speech is the longest, you might consider giving it the highest point value. However, if it runs the same length as one of the other speeches, or slightly shorter, then weight the speech accordingly. Whatever your preference, you will use some of the same criteria with this speech as you would for the other speeches, which might include, but is not limited to the following:

- ✓ A clear introduction
- ✓ A clear organizational pattern
- ✓ Clear connectives
- ✓ Appropriate use of reasoning
- ✓ The required number credible sources
- ✓ The effective use of visual aids
- ✓ Staying audience centered
- ✓ Clear delivery
- ✓ Clear conclusion
- ✓ A thorough preparation outline
- ✓ Adhering to time limits

The additional elements you will need to consider when grading the invitational speech include the following:

- ✓ Did the speaker clearly indicate the TYPE of invitational speech?
- ✓ Is there a consistent organizational pattern? (NOTE: students often get so focused on the open dialogue that they lose sight of the need for clear organization in an invitational speech).
- ✓ Did the speaker create conditions of equality, value, and self-determination at all points of the speech (the introduction, body, open dialogue, and conclusion)?
- ✓ Did the speaker use invitational language throughout the speech (the introduction, body, open dialogue, and conclusion)?
- ✓ Did they speaker successfully incorporate audience perspectives into their conclusion?

Given these criteria, some basic guidelines for an A, B, C, D, or F speech are as follows (A sample invitational critique sheet can be found at the end of this chapter):

The "F" speech

The "F" speech will be a speech that students actually do not give, a speech that is of the wrong type (informative or persuasive rather than invitational), or a speech in which the student disregards your criteria for an invitational speech (no beginning speech, for example, or a persuasive or hostile dialogue, a one-page hand-written preparation outline).

The "D" speech

In this speech, the student may have prepared ahead of time (they do have sources, they do engage their audience in an open dialogue), however, the student is, in fact, obviously not open to other perspectives and their language and reasoning reflects a much stronger persuasive speech than an invitational one. In the D speech, the student often uses biased or unsound evidence and their preparation outline often is not in complete sentence format (which likely prevented them from recognizing they were wanting to persuade rather than invite) or very well-structured.

The "C" speech

This is perhaps the hardest to describe, but the most common speech we hear. In a C speech, students usually have a clear statement of purpose, an introduction that satisfies the basics of our criteria, and during the speech the student does one or two of the following (doing most or all of the following usually results in a D grade): has a sloppy or weak organizational pattern; does not use the required number of sources; goes significantly over or under the time requirements; relies on a manuscript delivery (when extemporaneous was required); switches their speaking goal or only meets the basics for establishing conditions of equality, value, and self-determination; uses only a few connectives; shows evidence of not having done just the basics in terms of research; and/or shows evidence of not having thought carefully about perspectives other than their own. Although they do engage their audience in a dialogue, and attempt to use invitational language, they primarily ask the audience "yes" and "no" questions (versus drawing more in-depth answers out of their audience) and may simply agree with most everything the audience offers rather than engaging in actual dialogue and discussion. Their preparation outline often has organizational flaws, which reflects the lack of organization of their speech. Again, one or two of these "errors" makes a C speech; that is, they meet the basics of most of these expectations and fall short on only a few.

The "B" speech

Students have an engaging introduction and clear statement of purpose, a clear organizational pattern, an effective use of invitational language, shows evidence of careful research and sound reasoning, and a clear understanding of the different perspectives possible on their topic. They clearly attempt to establish conditions of equality, value, and self-determination, although there may be times when this could have been more evident. Delivery during the open dialogue (or even the speech itself) perhaps could have been stronger, and there may have been places where they easily could have drawn out more in-depth responses from their audience. Their conclusion met the basics, but perhaps could have been stronger by more clearly incorporating the audience's perspectives. The preparation outline is clean and carefully organized.

The "A" speech

While it is easy to say that the "A" speech is perfect . . . we would be kidding ourselves and we would not be good public speaking instructors! The "A" speech satisfies all basic requirements, and does so with creativity and an "above average" effort. The student clearly indicates their purpose, they have a clear and effective organizational pattern, and they do their best to establish conditions of equality, value, and self-determination. The student uses reasoning and evidence. There is clearly no hidden agenda. They do their best to draw more in-depth responses from their audience during the open dialogue. They do incorporate some of the audience perspectives into their conclusion. Delivery may not be "perfect" but they do establish direct eye contact, they are as extemporaneous as they are going to get, and they can be heard in the classroom. They have a clean and well-organized preparation outline.

13. **Frequently Asked Questions** (Prepared by Jennifer Emerling Bone, University of Colorado, Boulder). Because invitational speaking is new to many instructors, what follows is a summary of the most frequently asked questions by both instructors and by students. The answers to these questions are included so that you can use them to answer your own questions as well as those of your students.

Questions asked by Instructors

What exactly is an invitational speech?

An invitational speech is a speech in which a speaker shares their perspective on an issue and then engages in a conversation with their audience about that issue. This might be an issue they would like to explore, an idea they would like to share, or a proposal they would like to discuss. Although the speaker does give an actual speech, the speaker is not the only "expert" on the subject. The invitational speech allows the audience to express their ideas and opinions and to be seen as just as valid as the speaker's ideas and opinions. This speech allows both the speaker and the audience to better understand the perspectives held by one another.

Is the invitational speech harder to teach than the other traditional speeches?

No, the invitational speech is just *different* from traditional speeches. It has a structure and format in the same way informative or persuasive speeches do. In fact, once an instructor fully understands the mechanics of an invitational speech, it becomes easy to teach. Students can relate the invitational speech to situations they have previously encountered when they were seeking information to help them make decisions or formulate opinions. Instructors can build on this and create interesting and fun lectures to explain the structure and format of invitational speaking.

*The invitational speech seems like **one more** speech I have to teach now, how do I decide which speeches to include in my curriculum?*

As an instructor, it is important to provide students with a variety of possibilities to choose from as they encounter future public speaking situations. An instructor needs to decide which speech types may be of use to the students in their future and offer them the skills to turn theory into practice. Students often comment that they will use the invitational speech quite often in their future, so it is an important one to consider teaching to them. With some minor adjustments, you probably can teach an informative, invitational, and persuasive speech in a single semester and may be able to also teach a short commemorative speech, as well.

214

How can I explain the difference between an informative, persuasive, and invitational speech?

Explain to the students the goal of each speech type. Tell students that informative speeches, while staying neutral, give the audience information about a certain topic that they don't already have, persuasive speeches are designed to make audience members change their attitudes and/or behaviors to match the speaker's attitudes and behaviors, and the invitational speech is designed to explore an issue and engage in a discussion. This is the only speech type that does not force the speaker to be the sole expert on the topic; instead, it seeks input from audience members. In an invitational speech, the speaker shares their perspective on the topic being discussed, but also often explains the many sides people take on the topic, and the speaker allows each student in the class the right to his/her own opinion. Refer to Activity #1 to help students understand better the differences between each speech type.

How do I manage the time requirement for an invitational speech in my curriculum?

Invitational speeches do take up more time than the other types of speaking (10-15 minutes, on average). One option is to limit both the speech content and dialogue to a specific time frame. Have students prepare a 5-7 minute speech and then manage a discussion for another 5-7 minutes. This leaves students time for a conclusion that lasts no more than one minute. This allows each student up to 15 minutes for his or her invitational speech. You also will need to make adjustments to the length of other speeches and many instructors shorten other speech rounds by a few minutes to make room for the invitational speech. The sample syllabi at the beginning of this IRM should help you manage your time.

Why should I teach the invitational speech round?

Teaching the invitational speech round offers students another option for speech making. Many students have reported the invitational round is a realistic speech for day-to-day interactions. Several students have found themselves incorporating invitational speaking in their work place and have been successful in making decisions without conflict. The invitational speech provides students with a new perspective on how to communicate with others when they see the world very differently and when they are seeking input or wanting to share their own perspectives with others.

Is there a list of possible invitational speech topics to share with the students?

Yes, see Activity #4.

Are there any topics students should not use as invitational speech topics?

YES, there are many topics that students may feel VERY strongly about (i.e., reproductive rights, religion, death penalty) these topics can make it very difficult for students to understand and appreciate opposing viewpoints. If a speaker feels strongly for or against an issue, they should use that topic for an informative or a persuasive speech rather than an invitational speech. A student needs to choose a topic that they (and their audience) are likely to understand and appreciate those holding a differing opinion. Students should have someone play "devil's advocate" to help them discover whether they can remain appreciative of opposing viewpoints or not. Students have also suggested that instructors should mention topics that may work well as invitational speeches (see Activity #4). This usually turns into a wonderful class discussion.

Questions asked by Students

When is this type of speech used?

An invitational speech is frequently used in day-to-day interactions or "mini-speeches." People use it to make decisions about what college to attend, what job to accept, even what items to purchase. Invitational speeches are often given in the work place, during round table discussions or when employees need to work together to make decisions, solve problems, or set goals for the future. When people can understand why their co-workers hold the opinions they hold, less conflict tends to occur and more productive decision-making is often the result. Invitational speeches also are given as environmentalists speak to representatives from the timber industry, member of pro-life and pro-choice groups attempt to work together, and as individuals respond to crises in their communities. In fact, an invitational speech was given when the architects of the proposed plans for the new World Trade Center rolled out the options to the New York community.

When do you include the dialogue with the audience?

A speaker can decide when the dialogue would be the most productive. Typically, students like to enter into the dialogue after they have given the complete body of their speech. This way, the audience is well informed on the proposal, or the idea being explored, and then can engage in a detailed discussion.

Can you use visual aids?

Of course, but invitational visual aids should be chosen carefully. If visual aids are used, they should provide clarity to the information presented. Often, visual aids can be very persuasive, so be sure to use them to clarify your position or to help the audience keep track of information. In an invitational speech, the speaker must be certain that the visual aid does not persuade, but rather adds clarity or insight to the content.

What do I do when I disagree with what someone is saying?

As members of a community, it is important to understand others' viewpoints while staying true to your own. An invitational speech teaches us to respectfully state our opinion without forcing it upon others. One way of doing this is by saying "I understand you see the benefits to . . . however, based on my experience I have to say I don't agree. Let me explain why I see it another way . . . ." Remember, the goal is to discuss the implications of opinions and options, not persuade others of the correctness of them.

Isn't this speech just being nice?

No, it is respecting others and appreciating all the possible viewpoints to a single topic. By respecting others, audience members will likely continue to engage in conversation. Oftentimes when people become insulted or offended, they will shut down and not listen to what others have to say. By respecting opposing viewpoints, while holding onto your own, you have a better understanding of the topic and a more productive conversation. Many invitational speeches are quite passionate and full of energy and even differences of opinion, but they also incorporate respect for those strong views and differences rather than attempting to argue with them.

What if nobody responds during the dialogue?

Although this rarely happens, speakers can bring questions with them to the speech in case their audience does not ask them questions. Speakers should bring several open-ended and a few closed-ended questions for the class to consider. This helps begin the discussion, and focus the audience's thoughts. After this, the discussion seems to take on a life of its own. Remember, though, the speaker manages the discussion and is in charge of facilitating an open and respectful dialogue. Speakers should also feel comfortable calling on their fellow classmates to participate.

Why do I need sources in my speech if we are exploring ideas with the audience?

Invitational speeches are researched, just like other speeches. Although we do have views and ideas of our own as speakers, additional sources can help us learn more about the issue. They also help the audience fully understand the possible viewpoints to the topic and add credibility to the speech. It is important for the audience to understand more about the topic than just the speaker's point of view. Sources can clarify an issue and lend to a better discussion.

Can we include sources during the dialogue?

Definitely. Including sources in the dialogue can help the audience understand where the information is coming from and can provide a more rounded viewpoint.

When it comes to the dialogue, does the class just voice their opinion or do I ask them questions?

Both. You can expect the audience to state their opinions, answer direct questions, and ask questions of you and/or the topic being discussed.

What happens if everyone agrees with me?

If everyone is in agreement, be prepared to ask a few students to expand on why they hold their opinion, and possibly explore other viewpoints. Bringing well-written questions to class should help the discussion continue for the time required. Remember the goal of an invitational speech; it is to explore and/or articulate a perspective. If a speaker chooses a topic that everyone is in agreement with, perhaps another topic would be more beneficial.

What is the easiest way to start this speech?

The speaker should first decide the goal of the invitational speech (to explore an issue or to articulate a position). Once the speaker has decided the goal, the easiest way to start this speech is to remember and follow the objectives to an effective speech introduction.

What are good topics for the invitational speech?

Good topics are those topics in which a speaker can be open to the perspectives of others if they differ from their own, has not formed a strong opinion on, or has an idea for a proposal, but is willing to listen to ways to improve it. Be sure to select a topic in which you can appreciate others' point of view. See Activity #4.

Is this speech normally the hardest type of speech to give?

No, it is just different from the other more familiar speeches. Students have reported in the past that once they understood the idea behind the invitational speech, it was the easiest and most enjoyable speech to give. Many students like the fact that they do not have to have ALL the answers, but can rely on their audience to help out.

Why does the invitational speech need to be so long?

Because the speaker does not claim to have all the answers, there needs to be time to listen to others' opinions to help clarify the issue. Although 15 minutes sounds like a long time, you will soon see that many people want more time to explore the issue in greater detail. Many discussions take time to develop.

217

What are good topics to stay away from?

Topics that speakers feel very strongly about should not be used. This makes it difficult to keep the conditions necessary for an invitational setting. See Activity #4.

Can we have questions during the body section of the speech? For example, can I talk about my first main point and discuss it with my audience, then talk about my second main point and enter into a second discussion with the audience?

Yes, the speaker must decide the best way to engage in a dialogue. Remember, you are the facilitator, but you also must be able to manage the time so that you can give your full speech.

Is it a good idea to pick a topic that I already know a lot about?

It depends. Having a great deal of information can help you explain great detail to the audience. On the other hand, if you have all the answers, why discuss it with the class?

How do we keep track of the dialogue so we can work it into the conclusion?

It is okay for the speaker to take *brief* notes during the discussion. Feel free to bring a pen and piece of paper to the podium. This can help you retain the information being discussed and summarize it in your conclusion.

Is there a specific format we need to use?

The format may seem more flexible than the other traditional speeches; however, this speech does require organization. There should be a distinct introduction, body, and conclusion. The body should follow one of the organizational patterns discussed in Chapter 16, and the speaker should use connectives and speak from a speaking outline. Also, the speaker should be prepared to manage the dialogue by bringing in questions, calling on a range of audience members, and by keeping the dialogue respectful and open.

How do we create a preparation outline for an invitational speech? What about the conclusion?

The preparation outline should follow the same format as the other speeches, with exception to the conclusion. The speaker needs to allow room to add information from the dialogue into the conclusion (this cannot be pre-determined because a speaker will not know exactly what will be said during the dialogue). Students can write the introduction, body, and the questions intended for the discussion. Then, students can decide if they want to include a brief conclusion, or leave it open. Don't forget the works cited.

14. **The Types of Invitational Speeches.** Students often ask for more examples of the differences between invitational speeches to articulate a position compared to invitational speeches to explore an issue. Use the following examples (either handout, overhead, or PowerPoint slide) to help you explain those differences.

To Articulate a Position

Topic: The Equal Rights Amendment

General Purpose: To invite

Specific Purpose: To invite my audience to understand the powerful impact that ratifying the Equal Rights Amendment could have on all our lives.

Thesis Statement: I have learned from my family the importance of the amendment and the significant impact it could have on our lives.

Main Points:

I.   The Equal Rights Amendment has a long, intriguing history.

II.   For over seventy years, the women in my family have played a role in the effort to see the amendment pass.

III.   I have learned many important lessons from watching and hearing about their efforts, including how important the Equal Rights Amendment is.

IV.   I personally believe the amendment could significantly advance the status of both women and men in our society.

V.   I'd like to discuss my position with my audience and learn about their views of the amendment.

To Explore an Issue

Topic: The Equal Rights Amendment

General Purpose: To invite

Specific Purpose: To invite my audience to explore, and to explore myself, possible reasons to ratify or not ratify the Equal Rights amendment.

Thesis Statement: I know there are some good reasons to support the Equal Rights amendment, but many people feel it should not be supported and I'd like to discuss these reasons with them.

Main points:

I.   Many people argue that the Equal Rights Amendment should be ratified because men and women should be viewed and treated as equal.

II.   Other individuals suggest that ratifying the Equal Right Amendment would have a harmful effect on society.

III.   I respect women, but we are different and I value those differences.

IV.   I'd like to discuss these views with my audience and learn more about this issue.

219

To Explore an Issue

Topic: Evolution and Creation

General Purpose: To invite

Specific Purpose: To invite my audience to explore, and to explore myself, three theories of evolution and creation and their role in public education.

Thesis Statement: I'd like to describe for my audience the controversy over three theories of how the universe was created—creationism, the big bang theory, and intelligent design—then explore which theory should be taught in our schools.

Main Points:
I.   The debate between evolution and creationism has existed since the theory of evolution was proposed by Darwin and brought to the public's attention in the Scopes "Monkey Trial" in 1925.
II.   The creationist theory holds that God created the universe and all living things, including humans, whom God made in his image.
III. The theory of evolution, also known as the big bang theory, argues that the universe was created through a compression of matter and intense heat.
IV.   A new theory, known as the intelligent design theory, accounts for the origins of RNA and DNA and recently has become part of this debate.
V.   Discussion about the appropriateness of each theory in public schools would help us make decisions about what to teach our children in our classrooms.

To Articulate a Position

Topic: Evolution and Creation

General Purpose: To invite

Specific Purpose: To invite my audience to consider my views on the need to teach creationism in the public schools.

Thesis Statement: My belief in creationism comes from many years of studying the bible, anthropology, and religion and I believe that it is a viable position to teach our children as they attend school.

Main Points:
I.   I have studied the bible for over twenty-five years in order to understand this rich and valuable text.
II.   I also have studied anthropology and religion so that I can have a broader understanding of our existence as humans.
III. Although not everyone agrees, I believe that the lessons of creationism are lessons children from any background would benefit from learning.
IV.   Because this view is so controversial, I welcome questions, insights and suggestions from the members of my audience.

220

Sample Invitational Speech: To Explore an Issue
Evolution/Creationism/Intelligent design
By
Cara Buckley-Ott

Introduction

I.   By the end of a toothbrush's life (usually 1-3 months) there is more microscopic bacteria collected within its bristles than in the average public toilet.

    A. Considering investing in more new toothbrushes?

        i.   Well, maybe you should reconsider.

        ii. After all, it is commonly believed that those microscopic mouth invaders are nothing more than distant relatives of everyone in this room today.

    B. This belief stems from the theory of evolution that believes that humans have evolved over time from tiny microscopic organisms formed in the big bang that created the universe.

    C. However, this theory is not alone in its explanation of the creation of the universe, and in fact it has been enveloped in controversy and debate since, well, basically the beginning of time.

II.   Recently, however, a new argument has been added to this debate, making it a newly charged issue, but also making it more difficult than ever to reconcile.

    A. This new argument, surrounding the theory of intelligent design, is giving new life to the evolution/creationism debate, and, for this reason, it is my feeling that this issue deserves to be considered and discussed in order to determine how it should be handled.

III.   Today, in order to give us all a grounding for discussing this issue together, I'd like to invite you to consider the history of this debate, as well as a detailed explanation of the opinions that inform each side of this argument.

    A. Also, I'd like to bring you up-to-date on the most recent version of this debate, intelligent design.

    B. Following this, I'd like to discuss this issue as a class and gather the thoughts and opinions of all of you so that we may all better understand the various sides of this issue.

    C. However, please feel free at any time during the speech to ask me questions or voice your own opinions as points of clarification, because, as you will see, the origins of the universe are nowhere near being undisputed fact.

    D. It is important that we understand and discuss this issue so we are better informed in our opinions, as it is an issue that has the potential to affect us all, whether directly or indirectly.

IV.   I am not sure where I stand on this issue. I'd like to discuss this debate with you so that I may form a better opinion myself.

Body

I.   According to *The Plain Dealer* of March 12, 2002, although the debate between evolution and creationism has existed since the theory of evolution was first proposed by Darwin, the controversy that continues to surround this debate actually began in 1925 with the "Scopes Monkey Trial."

    A. John Scopes was a science teacher in Tennessee who taught Darwin's theory of evolution in a public school system.

   i. Many people don't realize that he agreed to teach evolution in order to be arrested and tried, in an effort to bring the issue to the public's attention.

   ii. The trial became a larger public spectacle than anyone ever expected, partially due to the high profile lawyers representing each side: Clarence Darrow and William Jennings Bryant.

 B. Although Scopes was convicted of teaching evolution, the decision was overturned a year later in an appeal.

   i. However, it took 43 years after the Scopes Monkey Trial for the Supreme Court to deem the restriction on teaching evolution unconstitutional.

 C. With evolution a legal and viable option, and creationism considered unteachable in public schools due to the separation of church and state, evolution became the accepted norm in public science education.

Transition: I'd like to continue on now by discussing the competing theories.

II. According to Robert Pennock's 1999 book, *Tower of Babel,* creationism is the belief that God created the universe and all living things, including humans, whom God made in his image.

 A. There are many versions of creationism that range from "New-Earth" creationists who believe that the world was literally formed by God in six-24 hour days, as Genesis describes it, to the "Old-Earth" creationists who still believe in the six days of Genesis but believe that the days were much longer, allowing the earth to be millions of years old.

   i. There are even some creationists who believe that God set evolution in motion, set some rules for it, and then let the process proceed on its own.

 B. However, no matter what the specific sect of creationism believes, all creationists stand by the notion of the universe, and humans specifically, having been created by God to serve him.

 C. And many believe that the Godless approach to universe creation found in evolution contributes to many of the societal ills we face today, such as school violence.

   i. As Jordan Reed-Thomas, a freshman at a high school with a creationism focus pointed out in the Newsday of March 11, 2002, "Evolution teaches us that we're animals, so who cares if we do something that's wrong or right."

Transition: On the other side of this argument are the supporters of evolution—which supports the Big Bang theory of creation, as opposed to divine creation.

III. The Big Bang theory says that the universe was formed through a compression of matter and intense heat causing a massive explosion, or bang.

 A. According to the Big Bang Chronology website, this intense bang set in motion the creation of the life forming elements on our planet.

 B. With the creation of these elements, life, at a microscopic level, was allowed to begin millions of years after the big bang.

   i. Over time, the life evolved from microscopic, single-celled organisms into complex multi-celled creatures, and eventually into humans.

 C. Evolution contends that there is overwhelming evidence that all living things share a common ancestor in the fossil record, the genetic code, distribution of life on earth, and results of comparative anatomy and biology, according to the *Plain Dealer* of February 24, 2002.

 D. Evolutionists further contend that theories of creation based on faith should not be taught in public schools. As Vic Walczack, the Executive Director of the Pittsburgh Chapter of the ACLU points out in the Pittsburgh Post Gazette of March 17, 2002, "We live in too pluralistic a society for the public schools to be indoctrinating children with a particular faith."

Transition: However, recently, a new argument has been added to this age-old debate, bringing new heat to the never-quite-extinguished fire of the evolution/creation debate.

IV. The newest argument in the creation debate revolves around what has come to be known as "Intelligent Design."
   A. This theory looks to what some say is the biggest gap in scientific knowledge—the origins of RNA and DNA, the building blocks of life.
   B. Believers in intelligent design theory claim that the "irreducible complexity" of both human and animal DNA and RNA leads to the conclusion that these items couldn't just be acts of spontaneous occurrences where all of the items needed just happened to line up right at the right time.
   C. Instead, according to *The Columbus Dispatch,* of March 17, 2002, Intelligent Design believers say that "the complexity of biological structures require an intelligent creator, God or otherwise."
   D. The key to these arguments seems to be avoiding the "faith based" issues surrounding evolution/creationism—instead Intelligent Design proponents are arguing for the acceptance of this new theory into the US American classroom on the basis of science—it serves as an answer to the missing origins of DNA and RNA and other previous unexplainables.
      i. And the creators leave the identity of the "intelligent designer" open to interpretation.

Discussion

I. At this point, I'd like to open the floor to discussion.
   A. In my mind, this is an important issue for all of us.
      i. More and more school boards are being asked to consider the inclusion of intelligent design in their schools.
      ii. It is important that the people who influence these school boards have informed opinions and have considered all sides of this issue.
   B. We are all products of the United States education system, and furthermore, we are affected by changes in this system.
      i. Before any drastic changes are made to this system that could affect our children, nieces and nephews, or brothers and sisters, we should form intelligent, informed opinions and be aware and respectful of the opinions of others.
   C. By discussing this issue in a classroom environment we are able to hear others' opinions and voice our own.
      i. Hopefully in doing so, we can all walk away feeling more comfortable with this topic and ready to address it in whatever capacity we may have to.

Dialogue
Conclusion

I.   As you can see, the issue of creationism versus evolution has always been an interesting and messy one.

     A. And with the introduction of Intelligent Design theory, this issue only becomes more complex.

     B. Hopefully, through hearing the history of this issue, the two main arguments historically involved, the newest argument, as well as the comments and insights of your classmates, you have been able to better understand all sides of this issue.

     C. Perhaps what makes this issue so intriguing and has kept it controversial for so long is the interesting and compelling nature of all sides involved. And maybe you've been left not knowing whether to throw away that old toothbrush or throw a family reunion.

Critique Sheet: *Invitational Speech*

Name _____ _____ **Time:** _____ **Grade:** _____ **Points:** _____

Key: + Excellent; √ Satisfactory; - Needs improvement; 0 Failed to complete

INTRODUCTION   **Time:**

    Captured attention/interest _____
    Introduced the topic   _____
    Established credibility   _____
    Previewed main points   _____

BODY

    Main points clear _____
    Main points explained clearly _____
    Connectives _____
    Source citation_____
    Audience centered _____
    Use of invitational language _____
    Clarity of PowerPoint   _____
    Management of PowerPoint _____

DIALOGUE WITH AUDIENCE   **Time:**

    Condition of equality   _____
    Condition of value   _____
    Condition of self-determination _____
    Listening and response _____

SUMMARY/CONCLUSION   **Time:**

    Signaled the speech is ending _____
    Summarized main points _____
    Final conclusions _____
    Closed decisively _____

DELIVERY

    Volume _____
    Eye contact _____
    Avoided distracting mannerisms _____
    Articulation _____
    Rate _____
    Extemporaneous/conversational style _____
    Enthusiasm _____

OUTLINE

    Complete sentence form   _____
    Logical subordination   _____
    Grammar   _____
    Works Cited   _____

Practicing the Open Dialogue

To prepare you for the open dialogue of the invitational speech, respond to the first two questions with your group members. After you have discussed the questions, move on to the practical component of this activity. Make sure that you time yourselves so that each group member has a turn. Provide each other with effective feedback, keeping in mind the tips your textbook provides for effective and ethical invitational speaking.

1) Consider the times you, as an audience member, have been from a background very different from the other audience members, a very similar background to other audience members, or held different or similar beliefs. How did this affect your experience? Did the speaker address these differences or similarities? What was the effect of the speaker's actions?

2) What are your biggest fears regarding discussions and questions and answer sessions? Based on what you have read in this chapter and what we have discussed in class so far, identify three ways you might ease some of your fears? Which strategies do think will be the most helpful?

3) In your small groups, each of you will practice a timed discussion/questions/answer period using the strategies you discussed above. Take only 2-3 minutes to express your position on a subject, or to explore an issue, and then engage your audience in dialogue for 3-4 minutes.

How to Be a "Good" Audience Member

1) **Raise your hands to speak**

   Do not blurt out questions or answers!
   Wait your turn—do not interrupt.

2) **Ask questions respectfully**

3) **Be concise**

   Avoid long anecdotes because of time constraints.

Advice for both Speakers and Audience Members

4) **Know your own position.**

5) **Why do you feel the way that you do?**

   Does your upbringing, your career choice, your sex, your religion, etc., play a role in your perspective? (consider your master statuses)

6) **Use Invitational Language**

   No name calling
   Maintain composure and respect
   Have a positive attitude
   Use phrases such as:
   "I feel this way because . . ."
   "I learned this through . . ."
   "From my perspective . . ."
   "This may not work for everyone, but it works for me . . ."

7) **Offer Positive Reinforcement**

   Use phrases such as:
   "Interesting, can you elaborate on that?"
   "How might that work?"
   "Why do you think so?"
   "What benefits do you see with that position?"

Supplemental Bibliography

Anderson, Rob, and Cissna, Kenneth N., and Ronald, Arnett C., (Eds.). <u>The Reach of Dialogue: Confirmation, Voice, and Community</u>. New Jersey: Hampton Press, 1994.

> This twelve-chapter volume is an excellent resource for background on the call for dialogue, a critique of dialogue, and the practice of dialogue. See part one for a discussion of an invitation to dialogue and part three for interesting examples of dialogue as well as the ethical implications of dialogue.

Barrett, Harold. <u>Rhetoric and Civility</u>. Albany: State University of New York Press, 1991.

> Although the book as a whole is useful, in chapter nine, Barrett offers an excellent overview of the various definitions of civility, giving this complex term both context and a historical perspective.

Carter, Stephen L. *Civility:* <u>Manners, Morals, and the Etiquette of Democracy</u>. New York: Basic Books, 1998.

> Carter provides an excellent overview of the practice of civility, relating it to both manners and community and marking civility as different from simply being nice or going along with decisions and actions with which you don't agree. A great resource for discussions of civility in general, and difference and disagreement in particular.

Ellinor, Linda, and Gerard, Glenna. <u>Dialogue: Rediscovering the Transforming Powers of Conversation</u>. New York: John Wiley & Sons, 1998.

> Ellinor and Gerard take the practice of dialogue into organizational communication. Great examples and discussion that are applicable to the public speaking classroom as well as the group speaking assignment.

Foss, Sonja K., and Karen A. Foss. <u>Inviting Transformation</u>, 2nd ed. Prospect Heights, IL: Wavelend, 2003.

> Foss and Foss offer a presentational speaking text framed in the context of transformation. The chapter on invitational speaking is a nice resource for background and lecture material.

Foss, Sonja K., and Griffin, Cindy L.. "Beyond Persuasion: A Proposal for an Invitational Rhetoric." *Communication Monographs,* 62, (1995): 2-18.

> The challenge to the strict idea of rhetoric as always and only persuasive is first presented in this article. The framework for this chapter is an adaptation of this original essay.

Gearhart, Sally Miller. "The Womanization of Rhetoric." *Women's Studies International Quarterly,* 2 (1979): 195-201.

Gearhart's article, although quite controversial, opened the door for invitational rhetoric. In this essay Gearhart suggests that all persuasion is harmful, and that rhetoric can be reconceptualized to include a more feminine and feminist perspective.

Issacs, William. Dialogue and the Art of Thinking Together. New York: Doubleday, 1999.

Issacs offers excellent chapters on listening, allowing multiple perspectives, as well as pragmatic suggestion for how to dialogue in everyday life as well as the work place.

Makau, Josina M., and Marty, Debian L., Cooperative Argumentation: A Model for Deliberative Community. Prospect Heights, IL: Waveland, 2001.

Makau and Marty provide a fresh approach to the practice of argumentation suggesting that "cooperative argumentation," which is similar to invitational rhetoric, provides a useful framework for discussing complex and controversial resources. A great resource for lectures.

Shepherd, Gregory J. "Communication as Influence: Definitional Exclusion." *Communication Studies,* 43 (1992): 203-209.

Shepard offers a compelling argument for expanding the strict definition of rhetoric and communication suggesting that both terms have been defined from gendered perspectives. A great resource for those with debaters in their classes or an interest in alternative definitions of rhetoric and communication.

Spano, Shawn. Public Dialogue and Participatory Dialogue. New Jersey: Hampton Press, 2001.

Written from the perspective of a communication scholar, Spano offers wonderful information on the theory and practice of public dialogue as it was lived-out in a community project in Cupertino, California. An excellent resource for lectures and discussion.

Tannen, Deborah. The Argument Culture: Stopping America's War of Words. New York: Ballantine, 1999.

Tannen's book offers a clear discussion of the current emphasis on argument in our culture and encourages an alternative, dialogue to that emphasis. The book is an excellent resource for background, examples, and lecture ideas.

Walton, Douglas N., and Krabbe, Eric C.W.. Commitment in Dialogue: Basic Concepts of Interpersonal Reasoning. Albany: State University of New York Press, 1995.

Although written from an interpersonal perspective, chapters three, four, and five, offer useful information on dialogue, addressing types, goals, rules and the evaluation of arguments.

Chapter Fifteen: Persuasive Speaking

Chapter Goals

Chapter Fifteen introduces students to persuasive speaking, and the different types of persuasive speeches. Students should have an understanding of the following goals after the end of this chapter:

- To describe the three types of persuasive speeches
- To apply the most common patterns of organization for persuasive speeches
- To understand the importance of the elaboration likelihood model (ELM)
- To identify three tips for giving effective persuasive speeches
- To identify the principles for giving ethical persuasive speeches

Chapter Outline

I. **A persuasive speech** *is one whose message attempts to change or reinforce an audience's thoughts, feelings, or actions* (pg. 361).
   a. **Types of persuasive speeches** (pg. 308).
      i. **Persuasive speeches addressing questions of fact** (pg. 309).
         1. A **question of fact** *addresses whether something is verifiably true or not.*
      ii. **Persuasive speeches addressing questions of value** (pg. 309).
         1. A **question of value** *addresses the merit or morality of an object, action, or belief.*
            a. The speaker moves from asserting that something is true or false to advocating that one thing is better or worse than another.
               i. Values cannot be answered simply be analyzing facts.
               ii. Values are grounded in what people believe is right, good, appropriate, worthy and ethically sound.
            b. When speakers speak on questions of value, their claims must be justified.
      iii. **Persuasive speeches focusing on questions of policy** (pg. 310).
         1. A **question of policy** *addresses the best course of action or the best solution to a problem.*
            a. They go beyond just fact and value to offer solutions and plans of action.
            b. They present an audience with a specific solution or plan to a problem and try to persuade them that the solution or plan will eliminate the problem satisfactorily.
II. **Organization of speeches on questions of fact** (pg. 310).
   a. Questions of fact can be organized chronologically, spatially, and topically.
III. **Organization of speeches on questions of value** (pg. 312).
   a. Questions of value can be organized chronologically, spatially, or topically.

IV. **Organization of speeches on questions of policy** (pg. 314).
    a. The organizational pattern used will depend on the kind of change expected from the audience.
        i. When you attempt to **gain immediate action,** *your goal is to encourage an audience to engage in a specific behavior or take a specific action* (pg. 314).
            1. Speakers move beyond asking an audience to alter a belief.
            2. Speakers should be as specific as possible in stating what they want to the audience to do.
            3. Speakers should have a clear **call to action** or *an explicit request that an audience engage in some clearly stated behavior* (pg. 314).
        ii. When you attempt to **gain passive agreement** *your goal is to ask an audience to adopt a new position without also asking them to act in support of that position* (pg. 314).
            1. Speakers still advocate a solution to a problem, but do not call the audience to action.
            2. The speaker simply encourages the audience to adopt a new position, perspective, or view.
    b. There are different patterns of organization used for speeches focusing on questions of policy.
        i. The **problem-solution pattern of organization** *focuses on persuading an audience that a specific problem exists and can be solved or minimized by a specific solution* (pg. 314).
            1. These types of speeches are organized generally with two main points.
              a. The first point specifies the problem.
                i. Define the problem clearly.
                ii. The problem must be relevant to the audience.
              b. The second point is the solution.
                i. Offer a solution that really does help solve the problem.
                ii. The audience should be able to reasonably support and implement the solution.
              c. These speeches are an excellent vehicle for persuading an audience to support a cause or take action.
        ii. The **problem-cause-solution organization** *focuses on identifying a specific problem, the causes of that problem, and a solution for the problem* (pg. 316).
            1. This type of speech can be effective if a speaker feels they will be more persuasive by explaining how a problem came about.
            2. Explaining the causes of a problem can help an audience see the merits of a proposed solution.
            3. This speech has three main points.
              a. The first identifies a clear and relevant problem.
              b. The second identifies the relevant causes of that problem.
              c. The third details a clear and appropriate solution to the problem.
        iii. **Causal Organization** will work well to persuade an audience when a problem is based on a cause-and-effect relationship (pg. 317).
            1. There are two possible ways to arrange a speech using a causal pattern:"
              a. moving from cause to effect, and
              b. moving from effect to cause.
        iv. **Narrative Organization** is when a speech to persuade is organized using one or more stories (pg. 318).

       1. Depending on the topic, a speaker may share an extended narrative to help personalize an argument that may seem difficult for some audience members to fully comprehend.

  v. The **comparative advantages organization** *illustrates the advantages of one solution over others* (pg. 320).
       1. Each main point explains why the speaker's solution is preferable to other possible solutions.
       2. Explain why the alternatives will not work, without degrading or belittling them.

  vi. **Monroe's motivated sequence** *is a step-by-step process used to persuade audiences by gaining attention, demonstrating a need, satisfying that need, visualizing beneficial results, and calling for action* (pg. 321 - 322).
       1. In the **attention** step, the goal is to motivate the audience to listen and see the personal connection they have to the topic.
       2. In the **need** step, the goal is to encourage the audience to become invested in the problem, feel affected by it, and want to find a solution.
       3. In the **satisfaction** step, the goal is to define the specific solution and why it solves the problem.
       4. In the **visualization** step, the speaker describes the benefits that will result from the audience's need being satisfied.
       5. In the **action** step, the goal is to outline exactly what the audience should do.

v. **Connecting with Your Audience** (pg. 323).
       1. Petty and Cacioppo's **Elaboration Likelihood Model (ELM)** explains that receivers process persuasive messages in either a *central processing* or a *peripheral processing* route depending on how motivated the audience is to think critically about a message.
          a. The more a speaker encourages listeners to become consciously engaged to think about a persuasive message, the more likely listeners are processing information in the **central route**.
            i. listeners are evaluating the overall quality of the argument, evidence and supporting material included, and any call for action presented in the speech.
            ii. Listeners may research additional information on the topic after they listen to the speech because they want more details. Before deciding if they will support the speaker's argument.
          b. When listeners lack motivation to think critically about a topic, they move toward using the **Peripheral Route**.
            i. In this situation listeners consume messages in a passive manner.
            ii. They may focus on parts of the speech without thinking critically about the message in its entirety.
            iii. In addition, listeners may be influenced by the speaker's style of dress or delivery, not the

quality of speech structure and content.

    c.   To encourage listeners to process information in the central route, speakers should connect their topic to their audience, explain the reasons that the audience should be concerned about the speech topic, and continuously work toward keeping the audience actively and critically thinking about the speech information.

    d.   Listeners using the central processing route tend to be more heavily influenced by a speaker than those using the peripheral route.

VII. **Tips for effective persuasive speaking** (pg. 323).

    a.   Although it is natural to want others to share in our commitments and beliefs, persuasion is a complex process. There are specific tips that can assist a speaker.

        i.   **Be realistic about changing your audience's views** (pg. 323).

            1.   Think carefully about the position your audience holds and choose realistic arguments before attempting to change their views.

            2.   Advocate a position or some aspect of a position the audience can be open about.

            3.   Try to not elicit radical changes.

        ii.   **Use evidence fairly and strategically** (pg. 324).

            1.   Use **two-sided messages** *to address two sides of an issue, refuting one side to prove the other is better.*

            2.   Use **counterarguments** *or arguments against the speaker's own position.*

            3.   When using a **fear appeal,** which *is the threat of something undesirable happening if change does not occur* (pg. 326), use caution.

                a.   If a fear appeal is so extreme that the audience feels immobilized, they may avoid or deny the problem.

                b.   Use fear appeals so that the audience sees the problem, but also feels there is a solution to the problem and that the solution will actually work.

        iii.   **Use language that encourages an audience to change** (pg. 326).

            1.   Use language that indicates what an audience "should do," what the "best" solution would be, and how something is "better than" something else.

            2.   Persuasive language often appeals to emotions.

            3.   Avoid telling an audience you "will persuade" them, because when they hear this phrase they are more likely to hold firmly to their positions.

VIII. **Ethical persuasive speaking** (pg. 327).

    a.   To persuade ethically is to persuade others without threatening or challenging their sense of self-determination and freedom to choose what is best for them.

        i.   When you persuade ethically, you act as an advocate and not a bully who tries to force or threaten an audience to see things your way.

        ii.   When you persuade ethically, you recognize the complexity of the issues you speak about and the possible impact of your proposed solutions on your audience.

    b.   There are four questions a speaker can keep in mind when persuading ethically.

        i.   What is my position on this topic and why do I hold this position?

doubled in the last decade.
- a.   This increase in obesity has led to Type 2 Diabetes in significant numbers of children and adolescents.
- b.   Type 2 Diabetes usually comes on after the age of 45.

2.   Dr. Gerald Bernstein predicts that left unchecked, the onset of more diabetes could have a huge impact.
- a.   More than 500 million people worldwide could develop diabetes in twenty-five years.
- b.   We're looking at a tidal wave of suffering and an avalanche of healthcare bills if people don't change their ways.

Transition: Now we've seen that Americans are consuming too much sugar, and it's destroying their health, one bite or sip at a time.

III.   To improve our health, we need to decrease our sugar intake, both at a national and a personal level.

    A.   On a national level, we need to increase awareness about the hazards of sugar and decrease soda pop consumption.

      1.   Kelly Brownwell, director of Yale University's Eating and Weight Disorders, suggests we increase awareness and provide incentives to eat more healthily by regulating food advertisements and amending the cost of food.
- a.   Regulate food advertisements directed at children so they provide equal time for pro-nutrition and physical activity messages.
- b.   Change the price of food to make healthier foods less expensive.

      2.   We can decrease soda pop consumption by making it more difficult to purchase soft drinks, especially in schools.
- a.   Nationwide, schools should turn off school vending machines during class time, strip them of sweets, or impose new taxes on soda pop machines.
- b.   We can also impose new taxes on soft drinks in general.

    B.   To get rid of our addiction to sugar, we must make a personal commitment to health.

      1.   Start off slow and eat sugar in moderation.
- a.   Dr. Ralph Golan, author of *Optimal Wellness*, suggests that dessert a few times a week or a can of pop once or twice a week isn't going to hurt anyone's health.
- b.   The World Health Organization suggests that between 0 to 10 percent of your daily calories can come from sugar and you'll still be safe.
- c.   Try to stick to good foods like fruits, vegetables, and fruit juices that don't have any added sugar.

      2.   Become a label reader and be aware of what you're eating.

Conclusion

I. Today we've explored the hazards of sugar and how we can avoid these hazards.
- A.   We've looked at common misconceptions about sugar.
- B.   We've looked at the health problems that can result from these misconceptions.
- C.   We've explored some solutions to our sugar addiction.

II. Americans have become unhealthy because they're eating too much sugar.
- A.   Americans need to decrease their sugar intake.
- B.   If they don't, more of them will end up like fifteen-year-old Arnell Scott, having to take daily insulin injections just to stay alive.

Works Cited

Brody, Jane E. "Don't Lose Sight of Real, Everyday Risks." *New York Times*. 9 October 2001.

Condon, Garret. "Diabetes Epidemic Menaces the U.S.: Costs, Suffering Expected to Soar." *Hartford Courant*. 9 September 2001.

Diet, Nutrition, and the Prevention of Chronic Diseases. Posted 26 April 2002. World Health Organization. Accessed 29 June 2002. http://www.who.int/hpr/nutrition/26Aprildraftrev1.pdf

Geiger, Debbe. "Diabetes' Changing Face: Number of Type 2 Cases among Children Is Increasing." *Newsday*. 20 July 1999.

Golan, Ralph. *Optimal Wellness*. New York: Ballantine Books, 1995.

National Desk. *New York Times*. "Extra Soft Drink Is Cited as a Major Factor in Obesity." 16 February 2001.

"Not Diabetic? Glucose Still Counts." *Consumer Reports on Health*. August 2001.

Overweight and Obesity: Health Consequences. U.S. Department of Health. Accessed 30 June 2002. http://www.cdc.gov/nccdphp/dnpa/obesity/consequences.htm.

Sevrens, Julie. "The *Mercury News* Food Group Volunteers Put Their Diets to the Test." *San Jose Mercury News*. 17 January 1999.

Winter, Greg. "States Try to Limit Sales of Junk Food in School Buildings." *New York Times*. 9 September 2001.

Critique Sheet: *Persuasive Speech*

Name _____ Time _____ Grade _____ Points _____

Key: 5 Excellent; 4 Good; 3 Satisfactory; 2-1 Needs improvement; 0 Failed to complete

INTRODUCTION

Captured attention and interest/related to the audience _____
Introduced the topic _____
Established credibility _____
Previewed main points _____

BODY

Main points clear _____
Established a need for change _____
Clear solution _____
Attempted to gain immediate action _____
Main points supported _____
Sources cited _____
Connectives _____
Audience centered _____
Avoided fallacies _____
Clarity of PowerPoint _____
Managed PowerPoint _____

CONCLUSION

Signaled the finish _____
Summarized main points _____

DELIVERY

Volume _____
Eye contact _____
Avoided distracting mannerisms _____
Articulation _____
Rate _____
Extemporaneous/conversational style _____
Enthusiasm _____

OUTLINE

Complete-sentence form _____
Logical subordination _____

249

Grammar _____
Works Cited _____

Peer Evaluation

Name _____ Points_____

1.   Did the speaker clearly indicate the type of persuasive speech? Where could they have improved?

2.   Did the speaker use a clear pattern of organization? Where could they have improved?

3.   Was the problem clearly indicated? Where could they have improved?

4.   Did the speaker cite sources throughout the speech? Where could they have improved?

5.   Did the speaker use *logos, ethos, pathos, and mythos* effectively?

6.   What suggestions do you have for delivery?

Additional comments:

Supplemental Bibliography

Baker, Sherry. "Five Baselines for Justification in Persuasion" *Journal of Mass Media Ethics* 14 (1999): 69-81.

> Baker offers a discussion of five baselines of ethical justification in persuasive communication. She also provides a means to analyze underlying motives in persuasive communication. This is a great article for an extra credit assignment (students can review the article or report on it as an impromptu or extra speech) as well as for your lectures.

French, Tom. "Ethics and Persuasion: Right Makes Might in the Courtroom" *Trial* 31 (Apr 1995): 86-90.

> How to be an ethical persuader in the courtroom is discussed here. Three rules for ethical behavior are suggested.

Johannesen, Richard L. Ethics and Persuasion; Selected Readings. New York: Random House, 1967.

> This is a useful volume of readings about the problem of ethics in persuasion. While the text may seem a little dated, the ideas and concerns discussed here are still relevant.

Rybacki, Karyn Charles, and Rybacki, Donald Jay. Advocacy and Opposition: An Introduction to Argumentation. 3rd ed. Boston: Allyn and Bacon, 1996.

> This volume covers questions of fact, value, and policy as well as the need to consider the audience of your persuasion. This book offers a very nice overview of persuasion.

O'Keefe, Daniel J., Persuasion: Theory and Research. 2nd ed. Thousand Oaks, CA: Sage Publications, 2002.

> The fundamentals of how persuasion works are covered here. This is not a book about persuasive speaking, but is a book about how and why people are persuaded. This is excellent background information for any discussion on persuasion and why it works the way it does.

Sproule, J. Michael. Argument: Language and Its Influence. New York: McGraw Hill, 1980.

> For solid information of basics of argumentation form including the questions of fact, value, and policy see this text. Also included is a discussion of ethics in persuasion.

Storey, Richard. *The Art of Persuasive Communication*. Brookfield, VT: Gower, 1997.

> This book asks the reader to evaluate her or his own goals, needs, and experience in persuasive speaking. Includes many tests and exercises that could be useful in the classroom. This book is a little less academic in tone and style, but is a fun way to approach the subject.

Walton, Douglas N. Plausible Argument in Everyday Conversation. Albany: State University of New York Press, 1992.

Often, a discussion of how students use, and are used by, persuasion in their everyday lives is helpful as they think about their persuasive speeches. This book discusses argumentation theory in conversation and can help students understand that they use persuasion on a regular basis.

Chapter Sixteen: Persuasion and Reasoning

Chapter Goals

Chapter Sixteen continues the discussion of the importance of sound reasoning begun in chapter seven, specifically discussing the importance of sound reasoning as it relates to persuasive speaking. Students should have an understanding of the following goals after the end of this chapter:

- To use evidence effectively in a persuasive speech
- To enhance credibility before, during, and at the end of a speech
- To use emotional appeals effectively and ethically to persuade an audience
- To appeal to mythos effectively and ethically to persuade an audience
- To avoid five of the most common fallacies in persuasive arguments

Chapter Outline

I. Arguments used in persuasive speeches are based on reasoning (pg. 334).
   a. Speakers can accomplish sound reasoning when using Aristotle's modes of proof.
      i. **Logos** or logical arrangement of evidence in a speech.
      ii. **Ethos** or the speaker's credibility.
      iii. **Pathos** or emotional appeals made by the speaker.
   b. Students are introduced to a fourth component of reasoning.
      i. **Mythos**, to which speakers appeal when they want to tap into common cultural beliefs and attitudes to persuade an audience.
II. **Evidence and Persuasion** (pg. 335).
   a. There are three aspects of the effective use of evidence that are especially important.
      i. **Use specific evidence** when you want to convince your audience that something is true, good, or appropriate (pg. 335).
         1. Your evidence must address and support your claims as explicitly as possible.
         2. Your evidence must address and support your claims as unambiguously as possible.
      ii. **Present novel information** to be more persuasive to an audience (pg. 335).
         1. In this age of information overload, audiences already have been exposed to enormous amounts of information.
         2. When you go beyond what an audience knows, you capture their attention in new ways and cause them to listen more carefully to your ideas.
      iii. **Use credible sources** to persuade an audience (pg. 336).
         1. When wanting to persuade an audience, evidence must come from truthful and dependable sources.
         2. There are two guidelines for using credible sources persuasively.
            a. Provide the audience with enough information about the source so they can assess its credibility.
            b. Select sources the audience will see as trustworthy and fair.

III. **Credibility and Persuasion** (pg. 336).
    a. A speakers **credibility** comes from *the audience's perception of a speaker's competence and character*.
        i. The most important aspect of credibility is that it is attributed to a speaker by an audience.
        ii. Without it, a speaker will have a hard time persuading an audience.
        iii. There are two important components to credibility.
            1. **Competence** is *the audience's view of a speaker's intelligence, expertise, and knowledge of a subject* (pg. 336).
                a. Competence is expressed through research.
                b. Competence is expressed through organization.
                c. Competence is expressed through delivery.
            2. **Character** is *the audience's view of a speaker's sincerity, trustworthiness, and concern for the well being of the audience* (pg. 336).
            3. Character is communicated through language and logic to express integrity and values.
    b. **There are three types of credibility** (pg. 337).
        i. **Initial credibility** is *the credibility a speaker has before giving the speech.*
        ii. **Derived credibility** is *the credibility a speaker develops during a speech.*
        iii. **Terminal credibility** is *the credibility given to the speaker at the end of a speech.*
    c. There are three ways **to enhance your credibility** (pg. 338).
        i. **Establish your competence** by revealing any credentials, training, experiences, or research that make you competent to speak on the topic. Or, you can explain what research you have done.
        ii. **Establish common ground** by identifying similarities, shared interests, and mutual perspectives with the audience.
        iii. **Deliver your speech effectively.** Enhance your credibility through delivery.
            1. Be prepared, energetic, speak moderately fast, and appear comfortable.
            2. Practicing and working on delivery should contribute to an increase in credibility.

IV. **Emotion and persuasion** (pg. 339).
    a. Appeals to emotion can be powerfully persuasive because these appeals encourage an audience to relate to an issue on an internal and personal level.
    b. Likewise, research suggests that an inappropriate appeal to emotion can cause an audience to shut down in an instant.
    c. **Emotions** are *'internal mental states' that focus primarily on feelings* (pg. 340).
        i. Research distinguishes emotions from three other states: bodily, cognitive, and behavioral.
            1. **Emotions** include *internal states such as fear, anger, and sadness* (pg. 340).
            2. **Bodily states** include *tiredness and hunger* (pg. 340).
            3. **Cognitive states** include *confusions and uncertainty* (pg. 340).
            4. **Behavioral states** include *timidity and aggressiveness* (pg. 340).
        ii. There are six primary emotions that tend to be expressed similarly across cultures.
            1. **Fear** is an unpleasant feeling of apprehension or distress and the anticipation of danger or threat.

2. **Anger** is a feeling of annoyance, irritation, or rage.
3. **Surprise** is a feeling of sudden wonder or amazement, especially because of something unexpected.
4. **Sadness** is a feeling of unhappiness, grief, or sorrow.
5. **Disgust** is a feeling of horrified or sickened distaste for something.
6. **Happiness** is a feeling of pleasure, contentment, or joy.

   iii. There are three secondary emotions, which are not expressed similarly across cultures.
1. **Pride** is exhibiting an appropriate level of respect for a person, character trait, accomplishment, experience, or value; feeling pleased or delighted.
2. **Guilt** is an awareness of having done wrong, accompanied by feelings of shame and regret.
3. **Shame** is a feeling of dishonor, unworthiness, and embarrassment.

   iv. A final emotion common in persuasive speeches is **reverence** which is defined as the expression of feelings of deep respect, awe, or devotion.

d. In persuasive speaking, speakers make appeals to emotion to accomplish four things.
   i. *Gain attention and motivate listening* through stories, testimony or examples.
   ii. *Reinforce points* with examples after a statistic is used.
   iii. *Express personal commitment* through delivery and a more passionate or intense tone, or by personalizing claims and arguments.
   iv. *Call to action or conclude memorably* by sharing a story that also causes an audience to envision the action.

e. Speakers want to consider several aspects of emotional appeals to use them more effectively (pg. 340).
   i. **Stay Audience Centered** (pg. 341).
1. Almost every element of our master status affects how we respond to the emotional side of an issue.
2. One of three errors can be made if a speaker misjudges the appropriateness of an emotional appeal and the master statuses in the audience.
   a. *Overly graphic and violent appeals* are appeals, either visual or verbal, that describe wounds and injuries, deaths, attacks, or harm to another being in extensive detail.
   b. *Overly frightening or threatening appeals* cause an audience to feel so threatened or fearful that they can no longer listen to the speech or they feel immobilized.
   c. *Overly manipulative appeals* are appeals to an emotion, either positive or negative, that rely on theatrics, melodrama, and sensation rather than fact and research.

   ii. **Use Vivid Language** (pg. 342).
1. The language a speaker uses should help the audience connect with profound experiences.
2. Speakers can use vivid language to help listeners connect with feelings and create images that are rich with feeling.

   iii. **Balance Emotion and Reason** (pg. 342).
1. Overly emotional speeches may get an audience stimulated, but without sound reasoning, audiences are less likely to be persuaded.
2. Use emotional appeals to elaborate on reasons for a particular argument or to show the more personal side of your evidence.

V. **Mythos and persuasion** (pg. 343).

    a. **Mythos** is *the interrelated set of beliefs, attitudes, values, and feelings held by members of a particular society or culture.*

        i. We learn mythos through the "whisperings of Mother culture" as children, adolescents, young adults, and adults. (Marian Friestad and Peter Wright)

        ii. These "whisperings" come to us through anecdotes, customs, events, and accepted norms for behavior.

        iii. The cultural narratives in the United States stress the importance of specific values.

            1. The mythos of the United States stresses the importance of freedom and democracy.

            2. It describes the United States as the land of opportunity and tells of journeys from rags to riches.

            3. This mythos emphasizes the value of progress and the exploration of new frontiers.

            4. Not all cultures share this same mythos.

        iv. Mythos and persuasion are tightly connected.

            1. When we use mythos, we call to mind history, tradition, faith, feelings, common sense, and membership in a community or culture.

            2. We tap into certain emotions, attitudes, and values.

            3. We encourage our audience to accept our claims based on stories told over lifetimes and generations.

    b. Because mythos is so integral to persuasion, it is important to consider several guidelines for using this form of persuasion.

        i. **A part of a story can tell the whole story** (pg. 343).

            1. When tapping into the mythos of a culture, you rarely need to tell the full story to the audience.

            2. Speakers can call forth a complete myth with only a few words from the familiar story.

            3. In using a few words from a story, a speaker tells a full, familiar story that has been repeated over and over again.

        ii. **Mythos has logic** (pg. 345).

            1. Fairy tales, folklore, or science fiction are myths that describe heroes and villains, elaborate adventures, death-defying feats, supernatural powers, and romance and relationships.

            2. They tell of events that seem unreal, but contain the logic of their culture or the everyday common sense of people.

            3. When speakers use mythos, they should think carefully about what logic they are appealing to and how it makes sense to their audience.

        iii. **Different Cultures Have Different Myths** (pg. 345).

            1. When appealing to mythos, speakers should try to understand the differences between cultures.

            2. Speakers should stay audience centered and consider the different experiences and perspectives audience members have as a result of cultural differences.

VI. **Fallacies** (pg. 346).

    a. **A fallacy** is *an argument that seems valid, but is flawed because of unsound evidence or reasoning* (pg. 346).

    i.   Fallacies are a problem in persuasive speeches because they are incorrect arguments but they still can be quite persuasive.

    ii.   They can seem reasonable and acceptable on the surface, but when analyzed further the flaw in logic is evident.

b. There are **five common fallacies**.

    i.   An **ad hominem fallacy** is *an argument in which a speaker attacks a person rather than that person's arguments* (pg. 346).

        1. They are persuasive because they turn the audience's attention away from the content of an argument and toward the character and credibility of the person offering the argument.

        2. Ad hominem fallacies cloud an issue, making it hard for an audience to evaluate the ideas the speaker challenges.

    ii. The **bandwagon fallacy** occurs when a speaker *suggests that something is correct or good because everyone else agrees with it or is doing it* (pg. 346).

        1. Even though a solution or plan works for one community, it may not work for all.

            a. A speaker needs to spend time explaining exactly why a plan might work for a particular community.

            b. A speaker also needs to use sufficient evidence illustrating why it will work well.

        2. Just because "lots of others agree" does not make a particular thing "good."

    iii. An **either-or fallacy** presents a false dilemma which *is an argument in which a speaker claims our options are either "A or B" when actually more than two options exist* (pg. 348).

        1. To identify a false dilemma, listen for the words "either-or."

        2. Either-or arguments are fallacious because they oversimplify complex issues.

    iv. A **false cause fallacy** is an argument mistaking a chronological relationship for a causal relationship. There are two types of false cause fallacies (pg. 348).

        1. The first type occurs when a speaker assumes that one event *caused* the second to occur.

        2. The second type of false cause fallacy is known as a *single cause fallacy*. It occurs when speakers oversimplify and assume a particular effect has only one cause. This is misleading because many problems are complex, resulting from multiple causes.

    v. A **hasty generalization fallacy** is an argument based on too few cases, or examples, to support a conclusion (pg. 350).

        1. For example, when speakers rely only on personal experiences to draw conclusions, they may fall into the trap of a hasty generalization because personal experiences often are not enough to prove a claim is true.

        2. In addition to relying solely on personal experience, hasty generalization fallacies also consist of too few external cases, or examples, to support a claim.

        3. Speakers using examples to support a claim must provide enough specific instances to convince their audience that the claim is true (See Chapter 7).

iv. With a **red herring fallacy** the speaker raises an irrelevant issue *by introducing irrelevant information into an argument in order to distract an audience from the real issue* (pg. 350).

    1. This is fallacious because the fallacy turns the audience's attention from one important issue to another.

    2. Red herrings are hard to spot because both issues usually are quite important and the audience feels pulled to attend to the most recently raised issue.

    3. If you are being introduced to a new and important topic in a persuasive speech, you may be listening to a red herring.

v. The **slippery slope fallacy** is an argument in which a speaker claims that taking a first step in one direction will lead to inevitable and undesirable further steps (pg. 351).

    1. Slippery slopes can be persuasive because the first claim gets wrapped up in bigger issues, when the two may not be linked.

    2. If you think you are hearing a slippery slope fallacy, stop and consider the chain of effects before you accept a full claim.

End of the Chapter Activities and Discussion Questions

The following questions can be found at the end of Chapter Sixteen.

Review Questions and Activities

1. You have been asked to give a speech on the topic of living wills to your classmates. Your position is that living wills are good and you want to persuade audience members to arrange for their own living wills, regardless of their age. How will you establish ethos, or credibility, on this topic? How will you make appeals to emotion, or pathos? What ethical considerations do you think you'll have to grapple with in this speech?

You can have students address this question as a discussion, or actually create a mini-speech where they address these questions. If you do have students create a mini-speech, place them into small groups and assign them this task. Give them time in class to prepare, or have them come ready for the next class to present their "speeches." Remind them that each member of the group should contribute to the idea, although only one will speak, or assign this as a group speaking assignment (appendix B) and have them prepare so that each person gives a part of the presentation. Have them practice the mini-speech, and then have each group perform their mini-speech to the class. After each speech, have the class discuss if the speech established ethos and pathos effectively. You might also have the audience listen for fallacies in their arguments.

2. Using the topic you have selected for your in-class persuasive speech, review Chapter 7 to identify three of the five possible types of arguments you might make in a persuasive speech (inductive, deductive, cause, analogy, and sign). Then use the suggestions from this chapter's section on evidence and persuasion to find ways you might make these patterns of reasoning more effective.

You can have students address this question during a speech workshop day. Have students bring in rough drafts of their outlines. Place them into small groups and have the students consider the above questions. Visit with each group to check their understanding of the different types of reasoning and offer specific help. Remind students that they should also be watching for potential fallacies.

3. Using the topic you have selected for your in-class persuasive speech, list the appeals to mythos you might make in the speech. After you've identified these appeals, consider your audience carefully. Determine which appeals likely will resonate strongly with your audience and which may not be appropriate given their cultural backgrounds.

   This question can also be incorporated into a workshop day, along with question #3. Be sure to discuss cultural differences and the ways students can adapt to those differences in their appeals to mythos.

4. Bring a copy of the morning newspaper or your favorite magazine to class. In groups, identify as many different types of fallacies of the five most common fallacies as you can find (ad hominem, bandwagon, either-or, red herring, and slippery slope). Now that you recognize these fallacies, evaluate the strength of the argument being advanced.

   This activity can also work well as a homework assignment. If you do this activity in class, place students into small groups and have each group look through the paper or magazines and generate good examples of each fallacy. Ask students to report their findings back to the class.

5. As a class, select a topic that is given considerable attention nationally or locally. Identify several positions or perspectives on this issue and divide the class into groups, with each group taking a different position or perspective. In your groups, develop five fallacious arguments in support of your position (ad hominem, bandwagon, either-or, red herring, and slippery slope). Present these to the class and see if they can find the fallacies and identify or name the type you are using.

   This can be a very engaging and interactive class activity and students learn a great deal about fallacies by trying to "sneak" them by their classmates. Encourage students to think of complex topics for this activity so that their fallacies are not easily spotted. You may want to allow the whole class period for this activity.

6. Check out Speech Studio to see how other students use reasoning in their persuasive speeches. Can you spot instances where they rely on logical fallacies? Or record a speech you're working on, upload it to Speech Studio, and ask your peers for their feedback. What feedback could you use to fine tune the reasoning in your persuasive speech before you give it in class?

Web Activities

1. **Freedom House**
   To understand further how you can support democracy and democratic processes, access http://www.freedomhouse.org. Freedom House was founded by Eleanor Roosevelt in an effort to promote democracy and freedom around the world. Like E-Democracy, this organization is nonprofit and nonpartisan.

This web resource can be quite helpful to students, particularly if they are involved in service learning. By participating in service learning, students can gain knowledge about the democratic process, given the extent to which many nonprofit organizations rely on this process.

InfoTrac College Edition Activities

1. **InfoTrac College Edition Activity 16.1: Using Specific Evidence**
   Purpose: To appreciate the impact of using specific evidence.
   Directions: Use InfoTrac College Edition's PowerTrac to locate an interesting speech in the journal *Vital Speeches*. Pay particular attention to the evidence used by the speaker. How novel is the evidence? Is it detailed? How effectively does the speaker use it? Based on what you have learned in this chapter, what advice would you give the speaker about using his or her evidence even more effectively?

   Encourage students to find a speech about a topic they know little about or get very "heated" about. For instance, some students may not really know about United States' foreign policy in the Middle East. You can have students access a speech about an issue, and respond to the above questions as a homework assignment. On the due date of the assignment, have students share what they learned with the class. This may also be a good assignment for students to work with partners. If you do place them with partners, you may consider giving them in-class time to work in the library.

2. **InfoTrac College Edition Activity 16.2: Establishing Credibility**
   Purpose: To understand how a speaker establishes credibility.
   Directions: Use InfoTrac College Edition to locate Farah M. Walters's speech, "Prize and Embrace What Is America," *Vital Speeches* (December 15, 2000). How does Walters establish her competence? How does she establish common ground with her audience?

   You can begin this activity by having students access this speech a few days before you plan on having a discussion about it in class. If you can, you may consider getting an audio or video tape of the speech to show in class so that you can discuss delivery and credibility. Ask students to identify specific examples of her attempts to establish credibility and discuss whether any of those can be adapted and used in their own speeches.

3. **InfoTrac College Edition Activity 16.3: Drawing on Mythos**
   Purpose: To understand how speakers use mythos to appeal to a culture's logic.
   Directions: Use InfoTrac College Edition to locate President George W. Bush's speech, "The Spirit of Respect and Cooperation," *Vital Speeches* (March 15, 2001). Which cultural beliefs does Bush appeal to? What is the logic of those beliefs? Would this speech be effective if given to audiences who belonged to other cultures? Are there members of the U.S. culture who may not be persuaded by this speech? Why or why not?

   Have students read this speech a few days before you plan on having a discussion about it in class. During an in-class discussion, have students respond to the above questions. Also emphasize to students that not all members of a culture agree with the mythos of their culture. You may have students consider why that is during this discussion, and how that might affect their response to a speaker's argument. For instance there are several groups in the United States who may feel that the United States does not represent freedom and democracy for all.

Interactive Student and Professional Speech Videos Website

1. **Video Clip 1: Mary Fisher's Speech to the Republican National Convention**
   As you watch Mary Fisher's speech to the 1992 Republican National Convention, consider how she uses emotional appeals. How does she use emotion to gain her audience's attention? How does she use emotion to reinforce her main points? How does she move the audience to action? How does she demonstrate her commitment to her topic?

   You can also show this video in class and have students respond to the above listed questions. You can also incorporate a discussion about Mary Fisher's credibility into this activity. Remind students that ethos, pathos, and logos are all used together in effective persuasive speeches.

2. **Video Clip 2: Student Speech, Jessica Fuller, Reasoning**
   Watch Jessica's speech, and focus on her reasoning. What different forms of reasoning does she use? Does she have fallacies in her speech? How does she avoid fallacies? How does her delivery help to enhance her reasoning strategies?

   Show this video clip in class, and have students consider the questions listed here. You may also want to consider having students address any improvements they might want to see in this speech, as well as how they will adapt their persuasive speech after having watched this one.

3. **Video Clip 3: Student Speech, Carol Godart, Reasoning**
   Watch Carol's speech, and focus on her reasoning. What different forms of reasoning does she use? Does she have fallacies in her speech? How does she avoid fallacies in certain areas? How does her delivery help to enhance her reasoning strategies, or detract from them?

   Show this video clip in class, and have students consider the questions listed here. You may also want to consider having students address any improvements they might want to see in this speech, as well as how they will adapt their persuasive speech after having watched this one.

4. **Video Clip 4: Student Speech, Amanda Konechy, Reasoning**
   Watch Amanda's speech, and focus on her reasoning. What different forms of reasoning does she use? Does she have fallacies in her speech? How does she avoid fallacies in certain areas? How does her delivery help to enhance her reasoning strategies, or detract from them?

   Show this video clip in class, and have students consider the questions listed here. You may also want to consider having students address any improvements they might want to see in this speech, as well as how they will adapt their persuasive speech after having watched this one.

Additional Exercises and Resources

1. Statements Used to Provoke Pathos
To check out a list of statements that can be used to appeal to an audience's emotions, go to http://humanities.byu.edu/rhetoric/ (created by Gideon Burton of Brigham Young University). Select the *Pathos* page from the list of choices in the left column. Now select *Figures used to provoke emotional response (pathos)* Which of these statements have you used in the past? Which have you heard recently? Which statement was most effective in eliciting an emotional response?

Encourage students to access this website for ideas on how to phrase emotional appeals in their speeches. Remind them of the potential errors that can be committed by speakers when appealing to an audience's emotions but also the power of appealing to emotions ethically and appropriately.

2. **Graphic Appeal to Emotion**
The Truth is an anti-smoking organization that, by its own admission, airs aggressive television and radio commercials. Go to The Truth's website at http://thetruth.com to view some of this organization's television ads, or listen to some of its radio ads. To what extent does the sensational nature of these ads help Truth's cause? To whom might the ads appeal? Who might be turned off by their advertising?

If you have access to the internet in your classroom, you may consider accessing this website and showing some of the ads to students during class. You can also place some of the ads on PowerPoint slides and ask students to respond to the above questions. This web link activity can generate good discussion about emotional appeals and the importance of using these appeals effectively and ethically, as well as the specifics of what makes an appeal too graphic or harsh.

3. **Identifying Fallacies**
Purpose: To learn the basic fallacies of reasoning and how to identify them in a speaker's argument.
Directions: Stephen Downes's Guide to the Logical Fallacies at:
  http://www.intrepidsoftware.com/fallacy/toc.php explains some of the more common fallacies of reasoning. Choose three of the fallacies, click on their links, and read more about them. Where have you heard speakers use these fallacies? Why do audiences sometimes fall victim to a speaker's use of fallacies?

To encourage students to access this website to help them identify fallacies, and to help their homework assignments about fallacies, you can assign this as an extra-credit assignment. Direct students to log on, to make notes about one or more of the fallacies discussed, and then to come to class with those notes. In class, ask students to give impromptu reports (or speeches) about the material they found on this site. To keep the activity interesting, and to encourage students to take detailed and careful notes, tell them that if someone has already shared a particular piece of information about a particular fallacy, they must present new information or speak about a different fallacy. Remind students that this website can also be helpful for other classes they may be taking, such as Logic and Critical Thinking, where fallacies are also discussed.

4. **Did they use Ethos/Pathos/Logos/Mythos Effectively?**
Show a short speech given by a politician or celebrity (state of the state or union addresses are good examples, as are award ceremonies) or even someone playing the role of politician or celebrity in a film. Write on the board "Ethos," "Pathos," "Logos," and "Mythos." Facilitate a class discussion about how the speaker used ethos, pathos, logos, and mythos effectively, or how he or she could have used any of those components effectively. Write their ideas on the board under each category. This can be a very helpful review for students, and can also help them have a clearer understanding of how all of these concepts function together to create an effective persuasive speech. Bill Clinton's apology speech works well for this activity; however, students may complain that his speech is dated (remind them of the public dialogue and the fact that issues get raised again and again, over time, and the issue of appropriate behaviors for presidents has been raised in the past). **NOTE:** a chart has been included at the end of this chapter to help students follow along in lecture and during this activity. This chart has been adapted from a chart originally created by Courtney Pederson at Colorado State University, 1997.

5. **Rating the Different Types of Credibility**

   In order to have students discuss the different types of credibility, have them think of a speaker they have seen. Have students then go through and discuss their impression of the speaker's initial credibility. For example, had they heard about the speaker before, what were the speaker's credentials and did those credentials contribute to their initial credibility? Would they rate the speaker's initial credibility as low, medium, or high? Have students provide specific examples for their "rating." Do the same for derived and terminal credibility. This is a good review for students, and it helps them to identify the different types of credibility while providing specific examples for their own claims about a speaker's credibility.

6. **Rating Your Own Credibility**

   Do the same as with question #2 above, but have students discuss their own credibility. This will be initially challenging for students so you will need to prompt them a bit. Ask them to think about their own master statuses, for example, and the master statuses of their audience. They can then consider age, sex, ethnicity, etc., as it may affect their initial credibility. Then move the discussion to introductions as they establish credibility, the appropriateness and realistic nature of their persuasive goals, etc. This activity helps students to evaluate themselves and be more aware of how they can enhance their credibility in future speeches. Tell students that they can use their first speeches as an example.

7. **Identifying Fallacies**

   As a homework assignment, have students list and define each of the fallacies defined in this chapter (ad hominem, bandwagon, either-or, red herring, and slippery slope). Students should then provide an example of each, other than what appears here in the textbook. You can either simply collect the assignment (some of these examples are great resources for future lectures) or have students present one or two of their fallacies in class and then collect the assignment. At the end of this chapter you will find a checklist for avoiding the fallacies discussed in this chapter. For a similar activity, including more fallacies, refer to Chapter 7.

Avoiding Fallacies

As you work on in-class assignments, and your own speeches, be sure to avoid fallacies. This handout has the definitions for each type of fallacy discussed in this chapter. Use the checklists as a guide to check your own reasoning.

1. **Ad hominem:** *an argument in which a speaker attacks a person rather than that person's arguments.*

    _____ What ideas, claims, and arguments are you arguing against?

    _____ Are you actually attacking the person rather than the ideas and claims?

    Write an example of an ad hominem fallacy:

2. **Bandwagon:** *suggesting that something is correct or good because everyone else agrees with it or is doing it.*

    _____ Are you asking yourself "if it is good for them, is it good for me?"

    _____ Are you asking yourself: "even though so many others are doing something, is it something I support?"

    Write an example of a bandwagon fallacy:

3. **Either-or:** *an argument in which a speaker claims our options are either 'A' or 'B' when actually more than two options exist.*

    _____ Do you hear or see the words "either-or" in the argument (or the words, "if we don't do X, then Y will surely happen")?

    _____ What other options might exist?

    Write an example of an either-or fallacy:

5. **False Cause**: *an argument mistaking a chronological relationship for a causal one.*

    _____ Did you assume that one event caused the second to occur?

_____ Did you oversimplify and assume that a particular effect has only one cause?

6. **Hasty Generalization**: *an argument based on too few cases, or examples, to support a conclusion.*

    _____ Are there enough specific instances to convince your audience that your claim is true?

7. **Red herring:** *when we introduce irrelevant information into an argument in order to distract an audience from the real issue.*

    _____ Are you being introduced to a new important issue?

    _____ Do you feel your attention being pulled between two important issues, but also forced to consider the new issue?

    Write an example of a red herring fallacy:

8. **Slippery Slope:** *an argument in which a speaker claims that taking a first step in one direction will lead to inevitable and undesirable further steps.*

    _____ What is the inevitable next step?

    _____ Is it really inevitable?

    _____ Are the claims linked together logically?

    Write an example of a slippery slope fallacy:

265

Sample Speech Outline: Persuasive Speaking
Fat Discrimination
by
Carol Godart

Topic: Fat Discrimination
General Purpose: To persuade
Specific purpose: To persuade my audience to help eliminate the prejudice against overweight people.
Thesis statement: Fat discrimination exists because of stereotyping, misconceptions, and fear, but through education and awareness, we can each help break down the prejudice against overweight people afflicted with the disease of compulsive overeating.

Introduction

I. Let me tell you a true story.
    A.   After I was in weight-loss recovery and lost much of my excess weight, I attended a convention, where I noticed a man who weighed about 400 pounds.
        1.   In my mind, I condemned him for not working harder to lose weight.
        2.   He was the keynote speaker, which I thought must be a mistake, because he was so obese.
        3.   In his speech, he gave his name, said that he had been abstinent for over a year and lost 250 pounds.
        4.   I sat humbled because I knew I was still fat-prejudiced—I judged him because he didn't look the way that I thought he should.
    B.   I have been on both sides of fat prejudice.
        1.   I have been discriminated against for being fat.
        2.   I've been a perpetrator of the same discrimination.
    C.   Fat discrimination is one of the last acceptable prejudices in this society.
        1.   You might think this is an exaggeration.
        2.   However, research indicates that today, three or four women and three men in this room, or 35 percent of this audience, are on a diet right now.

II.   I am here to persuade you to open your minds to the issue of fat discrimination so we can start to heal the disease of compulsive overeating that leads to obesity.
    A.   Fat discrimination exists because of stereotyping, misconceptions, and fear.
    B.   Compulsive overeating is a disease, but through education and awareness we can break down barriers of prejudice to allow people afflicted to find help.

Body

I. Fat discrimination exists.
    A.   The media stereotype of an ideally thin female body is prevalent in our society.
        1.   According to the 2001 text *Mass Media/Mass Culture* by James and Roy Wilson, in 1995 American television was introduced to the island of Fiji, "where eating was thought of as a cultural norm and big was considered beautiful for women."
        2.   A little more than three years later, after being exposed to television shows like *Melrose Place, The Bold and the Beautiful,* and *Seinfeld,* "studies showed that teens at risk from eating disorders had more than doubled and the

266

number of high school girls who vomited for weight control went up five times."

        3.   Stereotyping people with such a narrow focus creates barriers of exclusion for a majority of the population.

B.   Stereotyping can be very harmful and can stem from miscommunication.

        1.   One of the greatest misconceptions about overweight people is that they should be able to control their weight.

            a.   I could not control my own eating or weight.

            b.   I tried most diets, starting with my first one, unsupervised, at the age of nine.

        2.   Thirty-five percent of the people in this class could be on a diet right now, according to the statistics I obtained on October 20, 2001, at *www.ephedrafacts.com* from a recently released study by the U.S. Center for Disease Control and Prevention.

            a.   The study shows that 25 to 30 percent of adult American women and 20 to 24 percent of American men are trying to lose weight at any given time.

            b.   That does not count the people who just got off a diet, want to diet, plan on dieting, or will diet.

        3.   If people could control compulsive overeating, don't you think they would?

        4.   Jerome Hass, our classmate and a diabetic, said in a personal interview on November 5, 2001, that he cannot control his disease, but with education and daily treatment he can maintain a fairly normal life.

C.   Misconceptions and stereotyping are generated from the emotional response of fear.

        1.   According to the 1999 textbook *Interpersonal Communication: Everyday Encounters* by Julia T. Wood, one of our most basic human needs is self-esteem as depicted in Maslow's hierarchy of needs.

            a.   Our self-esteem "needs to be satisfied before we can focus on those [needs] that are more abstract."

            b.   "We gain our first sense of self from others who communicate how they see us."

        2.   When we are educated about differences, we see that obesity doesn't threaten our basic needs, and we can then show compassion and not react with prejudice.

        3.   Jerome Hass stated that the reaction of people who find out he has diabetes is sympathy because most people have been educated about the disease.

        4.   Edmund Burke, a famous seventeenth-century philosopher, was quoted at ***www.bluepete.com***, accessed November 30, 2001, as saying, "No passion so effectively robs the mind of all its powers of acting and reasoning as fear."

Transition: Now that I have identified the problem, I will focus on the solution.

II.   To minimize fat prejudice, we must use understanding, education, and awareness as the keys for change.

        A.   We must understand that compulsive overeating is a disease.

            1.   According to the 1939 book Alcoholics Anonymous, "We believe . . . that the action of alcohol on these chronic alcoholics is manifestation of an allergy; that the phenomenon of craving is limited to this class and never occurs in the average temperate drinker."

2.   Compulsive overeating also results from the allergy of addiction, whether the substance is food, drugs, alcohol, or gambling.

B.   People who suffer from this disease and the general population must speak out so fat discrimination can be minimized through education.

1.   According to the article "The Ryan White Story: A Shift From Confusion, Fear, and Ignorance to Acceptance and New-Found Knowledge of AIDS" by Deepa Channiah, obtained on November 10, 2001, at www.engl.virginia.edu, in just a short time, Ryan White "played a major role in changing people's views concerning the disease and AIDS patients."

2.   "Education and behavior change [were] our only weapons."

C.   By being aware of how each of us contribute to the problem, we can instead help create the solution.

1.   Awareness takes practice.

a.   For the next two weeks, please be aware of the thoughts, feelings, and behaviors we have when encountering obese or overweight people.

b.   When we walk into the grocery store and see an overweight person, stop and focus on automatic thoughts and reactions, then shift them into positive actions.

c.   You can do this by smiling, holding the door open, sitting at the same table to eat, giving a nod of your head, saying hello, or initiating a conversation.

d.   No gesture is too small or too large if it is different than it will have been prior to the next two weeks.

2.   Doing something differently is what makes change.

a.   The Ephedra statistics show that 58 million of our adult population is overweight.

i.   Each of us in this class could touch one person a day differently for fourteen days.

ii.   This would total 300 people affected in a short time.

b.   With awareness, change will happen.

Conclusion

I. Fat prejudice and discrimination must be addressed in order for those afflicted to reach help.

II.   I discussed two main points in my speech.

A.   Fat discrimination exists through stereotyping, misconceptions, and fear.

B.   Each of us can have an impact on solving the problem.

1.   We can help through education and the awareness that compulsive overeating is a disease.

2.   We can help by being aware that one person can make a difference.

3.   We can help by turning our prejudicial behavior around.

III.   I remind you of my story about the obese man I encountered at the convention.

A.   If you had seen this person in this classroom today, my hope is that you would have treated him as you would anyone else.

B.   My experience tells me that usually this sort of treatment is not the norm.

1.   More often there is silent condemnation of overweight people, self-righteous judgment, and hurtful discrimination.

2.   I can say this because prior to recovery, I was one of those overweight people.

268

Works Cited

Alcoholics Anonymous. New York: Alcoholics Anonymous World Service, 1939.

Channiah, Deepa. "The Ryan White Story: A Shift From Confusion, Fear, and Ignorance to Acceptance and New-Found Knowledge of AIDS." University of Virginia. Accessed 10 Nov. 2001. http://www.engl.virginia.edu/.

Ephedra Education Council. "Consumer Information: View Some Obesity Statistics." Accessed 20 October 2001. http//:www.ephedrafacts.com/obesitystats.htm.

Hass, Jerome. Personal interview. 5 November 2001.

Landry, Peter. "Edmund Burke: Quotes." *Biographies*. Revised September 2000. Dartmouth, Nova Scotia. Accessed 30 November 2001. http://www.blupete.com/Literature/Biographies/Philosophy/Burke.htm.

Wilson, James R. and S. Roy Wilson. *Mass Media/Mass Culture*. 5th ed. New York: McGraw-Hill, 2001.

Wood, Julia T. *Interpersonal Communication: Everyday Encounters*. 2nd ed. Belmont, CA: Wadsworth Publishing, 1999.

Supplemental Bibliography

Booth-Butterfield, Steve and Gutowski, Christine. "Message Modality and Source Credibility Can Interact to Affect Argument Processing." *Communication Quarterly,* 41 (Winter 1993): 77-89.

> This article discusses the results of an experiment designed to see how source credibility contributes to argument processing and understanding by the audience. Helps to show the importance of credibility.

Cohen, Jodi R. Communication Criticism: Developing Your Critical Powers. Thousand Oaks, CA: Sage Publications, 1998.

> Units four, five, and six investigate the three modes of proof. This book stresses the importance of critical reasoning and good argumentation. A great resource for lectures.

Corbett, Edward P. J., and Connors, Robert J. Classical Rhetoric for the Modern Student. New York: Oxford University Press, 1999.

> This easy-to-use book covers argumentation and the three modes of proof and places them in the larger picture of classical rhetorical theory. A nice resource for your lectures.

Garrett, Mary M. "Pathos Reconsidered from the Perspective of Classical Chinese Rhetorics." *The Quarterly Journal of Speech*, 79 (February 1993): 19-39.

> Garrett argues that traditional Aristotelian persuasion theory privileges logos while deemphasizing pathos. She suggests that to reconceptualize and understand better the use of pathos we should look to non western rhetorical theories. An interesting resource to help with a discussion of cultural differences and the ways they affect strategies of persuasion.

Garver, Eugene. Aristotle's Rhetoric: An Art of Character. Chicago: University of Chicago Press, 1994.

> This book offers a thorough background of Aristotle and the three modes of proof presented as rationality, emotion, and ethical discourse. A great resource for lectures.

Kahane, Howard, and Cavender, Nancy. Logic and Contemporary Rhetoric: The Use of Reason in Everyday Life, 8th ed. Belmont, CA: Wadsworth Publishers, 1998.

> A helpful look at fallacies. By presenting them in "everyday life" situations, it can make them easier to understand and easier to see why fallacies should be avoided. A nice resource for examples and for activities.

Little, Joseph. "Confusion in the Classroom: Does Logos Mean Logic?" *Journal of Technical Writing & Communication,* 29 (1999): 349-353.

> According to Little, the redefinition of logos as an appeal to logic is mistaken. Little describes how logic contributes to all three methods of persuasion and that Aristotle used "logos" to refer to the argument itself.

Pauley, John L., II. "Reshaping Public Persona and the Prophetic Ethos: Louis Farrakhan at the Million Man March." *Western Journal of Communication,* 62 (Fall 1998): 512-536.

This is an examination of how, in this particular speech, Farrakhan addressed problems with his ethos and helps to show that ethos is a central part of persuasive speaking. A great resource for lecture material or for a homework or an extra credit assignment.

Walton, Douglas N. Ad Hominem Arguments. Tuscaloosa: University of Alabama Press, 1998.

An in-depth look at what ad hominem arguments are and what makes up a person's character. Walton also includes an evaluation of ad hominem arguments, which is a useful resource for lecture material.

Walton, Douglas N. The Place of Emotion in Argument. University Park, Pa: Pennsylvania State University Press, 1992.

Walton presents a thorough investigation of the use of emotion in reasoning and the role emotions play in fallacies.

Witte, Kim "Putting the Fear Back into Fear Appeals: The Extended Parallel Process Model." *Communication Monographs,* 59 (December 1992): 329-349.

Witte offers a nice discussion of the potential of fear appeals, why so many fear appeals fail, and how to make them better so that they are more persuasive.

Chapter Seventeen: Speaking on Special Occasions

Chapter Goals

Chapter Seventeen introduces students to the different types of special occasion speeches. Students should have an understanding of the following goals as they finish reading the chapter:

- To describe the four types of special occasion speeches
- To identify at least four tips for giving effective special occasion speeches

Chapter Outline

I. **Special occasion speeches** are given when people come together to celebrate, reflect, remember, or establish a common purpose or goal (pg. 359).
   a. These speeches are given when we want to acknowledge someone's accomplishments.
   b. They are also given when we want to celebrate events or transitions.
   c. Speakers also give them when we come together after difficult events.
      i. There are several different types of special occasions.
      ii. Special occasions include weddings, awards ceremonies, banquets, and memorials.
         1. Special occasions often bring an audience together, reminding people of what they have in common.
         2. These events mark an occasion as special and as unique from the familiar events of our lives.

II. **Speeches of Introduction:** When speakers give an introductory speech *they provide an audience with a unique perspective on the person being introduced* (pg. 360).
   a. Speeches of introduction are organized around three goals.
      i. Acquaint the audience with a person,
      ii. Establish the credibility of the person being introduced.
      iii. Generate enthusiasm for the person.
   b. To accomplish these goals, speeches of introduction should do the following:
      i. *Introducing yourself.*
         1. State your name and any of your credentials or titles.
         2. Identify any qualification, experiences, or expertise.
         3. State your pleasure at being invited to speak.
      ii. *Introducing another person.*
         1. State your own name and credentials.
         2. Indicate that you will introduce the other person.
         3. Provide accurate relevant details about the person.
         4. Identify the topic of the person's speech.
         5. Provide closure to your remarks and welcome the person to the podium.
   c. There are several tips you can follow to give an effective speech of introduction (pg. 361).
      i. *Be brief and concise.*
      ii. *Be accurate.*
      iii. *Be appropriate.*

272

III. **Speeches of commemoration** are *speeches that praise, honor, recognize, or pay tribute to a person, an event, an idea, or institution* (pg. 362).

    a. **A speech of tribute** is *a speech given to honor someone* (pg.362).

    b. **A speech of award** is *a speech given to present a specific award to someone and describe why that person is receiving the award* (pg. 362).

    c. Speeches of commemoration are organized around two goals.

        i. To help an audience appreciate the importance of a person, an event, an idea, or an institution.

        ii. To illustrate for an audience a person's unique achievements or the special impact of an event, idea, or institution.

    d. To accomplish these goals, a commemorative speech should do the following:

        i. Identify who or what you are commemorating.

        ii. Identify and describe the qualities or activities that make this person, event, idea, or institution special.

        iii. Identify and describe the contributions made by the person, event, idea, or institution.

        iv. Identify and describe any obstacles the person, event, idea, or institution had to overcome to be successful.

        v. Identify and describe your relationship to the person, event, idea, or institution.

    e. There are several guidelines to follow when giving a speech of commemoration.

        i. *Share what is unique and special* (pg. 364).

        ii. *Express sincere appreciation* (pg. 364).

        iii. *Tell the truth* (pg. 364).

IV. **Speeches of acceptance** are *speeches in which you express your gratitude, appreciation, and pleasure at receiving an honor or a gift* (pg. 364).

    a. Speeches of acceptance are organized around three goals.

        i. First, thank an audience for the award.

        ii. Second, show your awareness of the significance of the award.

        iii. Third, acknowledge the people who helped you accomplish what you're being honored for.

    b. There are several guidelines to follow when giving speeches of acceptance.

        i. *Understand the purpose of the award* (pg. 365).

        ii. *Recognize others* (pg.365).

        iii. *Respect the time limitations* (pg.365).

V. **Speeches to entertain** are *lighthearted speeches that address issues or ideas in a humorous way* (pg. 366).

    a. A speech to entertain may be informative, invitational, or persuasive and is organized around two goals.

    b. There are two goals in a speech to entertain:

        i. Entertain the audience.

        ii. Make the audience think.

    c. Humor is one of the most complicated communication phenomena.

        i. What is funny to one person may not be funny to another.

        ii. Different audiences may not react in the same way to the same joke.

        iii. To make something funny is the result of a successful combination of three elements.

            1. *Timing* is the way you use pauses and delivery for maximum effect.

            2. The *objective of the joke.*

a. Jokes are told to make light of something, to remind us of our humanity, to highlight the silly or bizarre, to tease others playfully, and even to relieve tension in difficult times.

b. Humor is also used to belittle others, make fun of them, and put them down; which is the type of humor you want to avoid in speeches to entertain.

c. Women and men respond differently to different types of jokes.

3. *The audience* also contributes to successful humor.

a. Stay audience centered as you consider humor.

b. Use jokes that respect the different master statuses in your audience.

d. There are several guidelines you can follow when writing a speech to entertain.

    i. ***Use humor carefully*** (pg. 370).

    ii. ***Speak about meaningful issues*** (pg. 370).

    iii. ***Pay careful attention to your delivery*** (pg. 370).

End of the Chapter Activities and Discussion Questions

These questions can also be found at the end of chapter Seventeen.

Review Questions

1. Pair up with someone in class whom you do not know well. Talk with each other for ten minutes to discover answers to these questions: Who is this person? What are his or her accomplishments? What makes those accomplishments significant? Now write a one-minute speech to introduce your partner. Share your speeches with each other and discuss whether your introductions are accurate and appropriate.

   Use this as a homework assignment or an in-class activity to get students thinking about speeches that introduce others. Although the speeches may take a light hearted tone, be sure to identify the components of speeches of introduction you want them to use in their actual speeches.

2. Identify an award you would like to receive during your lifetime. What is the purpose of this award? If you were to receive this award, who would you identify as playing a significant role in assisting you in getting the award?

   This question can be used for a homework assignment, or an in-class discussion. You could even have students take notes and present these awards to one another at the end of the semester.

3. Identify your favorite public figure and write an outline for a speech commemorating this person. Check that your outline identifies the traits that make this person unique and special. Identify the places in your speech where you express your sincere appreciation for this person. Finally, check to be sure your representation of this person is true and that your facts and stories are correct.

   During class discussion or in small groups, ask students to offer up ideas for who they might commemorate. Discuss some of the characteristics they might want to highlight, the language they

Fill in the Blank

13. Communication among members of a team or a collective about topics such as goals, strategies, and conflict is _____.

ANS: group communication
REF: pg. 7

14. A/an _____ speaker considers the moral impact their ideas and arguments have on their listeners.

ANS: ethical
REF: pg. 4

15. When speakers consider the audience's positions, beliefs, values, and needs they are being _____.

ANS: audience centered
REF: pg. 8

16. When we translate ideas and feelings into words to say, we are _____.

ANS: encoding
REF: pg. 10

17. If an individual in the audience is worrying about the coffee pot left on at home, it is _____ that is impeding them from receiving the message.

ANS: internal noise
REF: pg. 10

List/Define

18. Define public dialogue.

ANS: Public dialogue is the civil exchange of ideas and opinions among communities about topics that affect the public.
REF: pg. 3

19. List and define two types of communication other than public communication.

ANS: Intrapersonal communication is communication with ourselves via the dialogue that goes on in our heads. Interpersonal communicationis communication with other people that ranges from the highly personal to the highly impersonal. Group communication: Communication among members of a team or a collective about topics such as goals, strategies, and conflict. Mass communication is generated by media organization that is designed to reach large audiences.
REF: pg. 7

20. What does the word context mean in public speaking? List and define two components that contribute to creating the speaking context.

ANS: Context is the environment or situation in which the speech occurs. Components include: Time of day; place given; audience expectations and/or the traditions associated with the kind of speech. The student may also mention that these are interconnected.
REF: pg. 11

21. List and define the different components of the public speaking process.

ANS: Speaker: the person who stimulates public dialogue; Message: The information conveyed by the speaker to the audience. This can be verbal or nonverbal. ; Feedback: verbal and nonverbal signals an audience gives a speaker. Encoding: translating ideas and feeling into words, sounds, and gestures. Decoding: translating words, ideas, sounds and gestures into ideas and feelings to attempt to understand the message. Audience: the complex and varied group of people the speaker addresses. Channel: means by which the message is conveyed. Noise: anything that interferes with understanding the message being communicated. Context: environment or situation in which a speech occurs.
REF: pgs. 10-11

22. What are five ways to reduce your anxiety as a speaker?

ANS: Do your research. Practice your speech. Have realistic expectations. Do affirmations and visualizations. Connect with your audience.
REF: pg. 14-17

Essay

23. The book discusses the influence that culture has on our speaking style. What is one aspect of your culture that impacts your speaking style? What feedback have you received about your speaking style from people you consider to share your culture? From people you consider outside your culture?

ANS: Students should use what has been outlined in the textbook as a guideline for identifying their style. The aspects of culture they should choose from include those listed in the book: nationality, race, ethnicity, religion, work environment, peer group, sex or gender. They should list at least one of these aspects, but may list more than one (i.e. Asian, Catholic, female). Examples do not have to be long and involved, but should reflect their understanding of how culture impacts their communication.
REF: pg. 5-6

24. Explain the three elements that make public speaking different from other forms of communication.

ANS: Students should know the differences, and should provide an explanation that illustrates their understanding of each. The first difference is that public speaking creates a community. The second difference is that public speaking is audience centered. The third difference is that public speaking encourages ethical dialogue.
REF: pg. 7-9

25. Think about your insecurities as a public speaker. Write three of your most common negative thoughts about speaking, and then transform each of your negative thoughts into a positive affirmation.

ANS: Students should write three distinct negative thoughts, then turn them into positive thoughts. REF: pg. 16-17

Chapter Two

<u>**Multiple Choice**</u>

1. The active process of attending to and understanding a spoken message is
a. confirming.
b. hearing.
c. listening.
d. interference.

ANS: c
REF: pg. 22

2. Anything that hinders or stops a listener from attending to and receiving a message
a. confirming.
b. hearing.
c. listening.
d. interference.

ANS: d
REF: pg. 22

3. Which of the following is a poor listening habit?
a. Trying to identify the speaker's main points.
b. Tuning out difficult or disagreeable information.
c. Taking notes over new and unfamiliar information.
d. Engaging the speaker with nonverbal feedback.

ANS: b
REF: pg. 23

4. Li was caught in a surprise rainstorm just before class. As a result, she had to present her speech in wet clothes. Her speech opener humorously addressed this misfortune. What type of audience reaction did she adapt to?
a. the disruptive audience
b. the audience who responds rather than listens
c. the confused audience
d. the audience distracted by the speaker

ANS: d
REF: pg. 38

5. This language choice causes listener interference because the words are very informal, nonstandard and very subject to change in meaning.
a. slang
b. jargon
c. colloquialisms
d. euphemism

ANS: a
REF: pg. 26

True/False

6. A listenable speech is a speech that has a sufficient amount of volume so that all audience members can hear it.

ANS: False
REF: pg. 23

7. In class and the workplace, an individual will spend more time listening than speaking.

ANS: True
REF: pg. 22

8. When a classroom speaker (who is also an Emergency Medical Technician) talks about her experience "bagging" someone then moving to "BLS" without explaining those words, she is using jargon

ANS: True
REF: pg. 26

9. When a speaker taking about learning how to change a tire says, "I was helped by a Mexican mechanic" they are using culturally inclusive language by spotlighting.

ANS: False
REF: pg. 27

10. A speaker's values can cause speaker interference.

ANS: True
REF: pg. 31

Fill in the Blank

11. A speaker concerned with making his/her speech listenable and easy to process has developed a/an_____ speech.

ANS: considerate
REF: pg. 23

12. _____ is language that recognizes that both women and men are active participants in the world.

ANS: Gender-inclusive language
REF: pg. 27

13. The physical phenomenon of sound vibrations being delivered to the brain is _____.

ANS: hearing
REF: pg. 22

14. Extra words that pad sentences and claims but don't add meaning, such as "like" "you know" and "OK" are examples of _____.

ANS: verbal clutter
REF: pg. 30

15. A/an _____ listener overcomes listener interference in order to better understand a speaker's message.

ANS: careful
REF: pg. 32

16. A/an _____ listener focuses on the accuracy of a speech's content and the implications of a speaker's message.

ANS: critical
REF: pg. 33

List/Define

17. Define interference.

ANS: Interference is anything that stops or hinders a listener from receiving a message.
REF: pg. 22

18. List three "problem audiences" and a suggestion for dealing with each.

ANS: The uninterested audience; Distracted/disruptive audience; Audience distracted by the speaker; The confused audience; The audience who plans a response before listening.
REF: pgs. 36-40

19. List four tips for becoming a careful listener.

ANS: Listen for the speaker's purpose, main ideas and support; Listen for consistency; Write down new information; Offer nonverbal feedback; Listen for conclusion.
REF: pgs. 32-33

20. List and define the three types of casual language.

ANS: Slang, colloquialism, euphemism
REF: pg. 26

21. Define gender-inclusive language and provide two examples.

ANS: Gender inclusive language recognizes that both women and men are active participants in the world. For example, if I am not sure of the sex of a person—like a doctor—I would not assume they are male. I would say something like "when a doctor chooses his or her specialty." The student might also choose something like saying "fire fighter" instead of "fireman."
REF: pg. 27

22. List reasons why speaker interference can be caused because of differences between the speaker and the audience.

ANS: Style of speaking; background; appearance; values.
REF: pg. 31

Essay

1. Think about a time when you were listening to a speech and experienced interference because of the way the speaker handled information or used language. What specific words or statements caused the interference? What could the speaker have done to make their speech considerate? (Note: This example could be of a classmate's speech or a different presentation.)

ANS: Students responses will vary, but should be informed by information from pages 23-30.
REF: pgs. 22-23

2. Identify and define three strategies for listening effectively you will you use this semester. Choose one general listening tip, one critical listening tip and one ethical listening tip.

ANS: Students should be able to clearly identify strategies outlined in the textbook. They should be able to distinguish between the different types of strategies.
REF: pgs. 32-36

3. As a speaker, you know that you will also be a listener. Which three of the six steps of careful listening will be most helpful for you? Why?

ANS: Students responses will be personal but should specifically mention the steps outlined on pgs 32-33: listen for the speaker's purpose; listen for the main ideas; listen for supporting evidence and sources; write down new words, ideas and questions; listen for the conclusion; offer nonverbal feedback.
REF: pgs. 32-33

Multiple Choice

1. The speaker concerned about knowing the positions, perspectives and prior knowledge of their listeners is being audience
a. agreeable.
b. centered.
c. compromised.
d. manipulated.

ANS: b
REF: pg. 65

2. These reflect a person's likes or dislikes of events, people or ideas.
a. standpoint
b. beliefs
c. attitudes
d. values

ANS: c
REF: pg. 68

3. Understanding that an audience is a/an _____ helps speakers stay audience centered.
a. captive audience
b. temporary community
c. technology driven audience
d. group of experts

ANS: b
REF: pg. 70

4. A speaker is informing an audience about different services the community provides for individuals with out health care. An audience member who appears to be Mexican-American asks the speaker "Is there an age requirement to receive services?" The speaker responds: "Your kids will easily qualify, and so will you. I get a lot of Latina single moms like you asking me about services." The young woman in the audience replies: "I have health insurance through the University I am attending. I do not have any children. I am actually asking this question for my grandparents who have no health coverage." This situation best illustrates which of the following concepts?
a. belief
b. ethnocentrism
c. attitude
d. stereotyping

ANS: d
REF: pg. 70

5. Which term best describes what a survey asks or does when they ask an individual about their age, nationality, ethnicity, sex, or religious orientation?
a. standpoint
b. demographic audience analysis
c. close-ended questions
d. master status analysis

ANS: b
REF: pg. 69

6. When a speaker gives a speech about what is good, worthy or important they are relying mainly on
a. attitudes.
b. values.
c. beliefs.
d. norms.

ANS: b
REF: pg. 68

True/False

7. All master statuses are considered equally valuable in US society.

ANS: False
REF: pg. 68

8. An effective speaker stays audience centered by being open to compromising their message.

ANS: False
REF: pg. 65

9. Ethnocentrism is the belief our own cultural perspectives, norms, and ways of organizing society are superior to others.

ANS: True
REF: pg. 68

10. If you are speaking to members of an involuntary audience, then there is no way to capture anyone listener's attention.

ANS: False
REF: pg. 71

11. Chronemics is a form of nonverbal communication that considers issues of time.

ANS: True
REF: pg. 75

Fill in the Blank

12. A/n _____ is a complex and varied group of people the speaker addresses.

ANS: audience
REF: pg. 66

13. _____ are significant positions occupied by a person within society that affect that person's identity in almost all social situations.

ANS: Master statuses
REF: pg. 66

14. A _____ is a perspective from which a person views and evaluates society.

ANS: standpoint
REF: pg. 68

15. A person's perception of an idea being real or not real, true or false is a/an _____.

ANS: belief
REF: pg. 68

16. A _____ question is limited in the number of responses that can be made.

ANS: closed-ended question
REF: pg. 69

17. _____ is working to see and understand the world as another sees it, and can motivate an involuntary audience to welcome you as a speaker.

ANS: Empathy
REF: pg. 72

List and Define

18. List and define the three audience expectations to which speakers adapt.

ANS: Expectations about the speaker, the form of the speech and discussions
REF: pgs. 77, 79, 80

19. Define stereotype and identify one stereotype that people who share one of your master statuses might face.

ANS: A stereotype is a broad generalization about an entire group based on little knowledge or exposure to only certain members of that group. For example, people might think that all women want to have children.
REF: pg. 70

20. List and briefly explain the three temporal factors you need to consider when thinking about your speaking environment.

ANS: Time of day; Speaking order; Length of speech
REF: pgs. 75-77

21. Explain what it means to engage in a dialogue.

ANS: To engage in a dialogue is to interact, connect and exchange ideas and opinions with others.
REF: pg. 66

22. Define speaking environment, then list and briefly explain three factors that can affect your speaking environment.

ANS: Size and physical arrangement; Technology; Temporal factors. See text for explanations of each.
REF: pgs. 72, 73-4, 75

Essay

23. Identify one master status that will impact you as a speaker. What is one stereotype that an audience might make about you? What is one standpoint you have related to that stereotype? How might you address your master status and stereotype in your introduction?

ANS: Students are likely to identify race, ethnicity or gender as a master status. Depending on what came up during the class discussion, they might also identify other statuses. They should also be able to explain how this master status might affect them in a public speaking situation, a possible stereotype they face, and a standpoint they have because of this potential stereotype.
REF: pgs. 66-69

24. Talk about the two different audiences you can address in a public speaking situation and how you might approach each.

ANS: Students should list voluntary and involuntary audiences. How they address each will depend on information in the book, and to an extent their own styles of speaking.
REF: pgs. 70-71

25. In this public speaking classroom, what three overarching expectations will your audience have of you as a speaker? For each expectation, briefly discuss one way you will fulfill or violate the expectation in an audience centered way.

ANS: Students should identify expectations about form, expectations about the speaker, and expectations about speaker-audience discussions. They should be able to explain how they would either fulfill or violate the expectations of the audience, including being transparent about their master statuses (and either conforming to or deviating from them), either using expected speech forms or violating them with an explanation of why the violation is better for the audience (see example on p. 80) and at least one way they would approach a discussion to stay audience centered (such as considering why someone would ask a question).
REF: pgs. 78-81

Chapter 3

Multiple Choice

1. The process of generating ideas randomly and uncritically, without attention to logic, connections, or relevance.
a. critical thinking
b. informative speaking
c. general purpose
d. brainstorming

ANS: d
REF: pg. 49

2. When a speech's broad goal is to inform, to invite, to persuade, to introduce, to commemorate, or to accept.
a. general purpose
b. specific purpose
c. thesis statement
d. central idea

ANS: a
REF: pg. 52

3. A focused statement that identifies exactly what a speaker wants to accomplish with a speech.
a. general purpose
b. specific purpose
c. thesis statement
d. central idea

ANS: a
REF: pg. 52-53

4. The following statement is an example of what: "I will introduce Master Cho and three of his most noteworthy accomplishments to my audience."
a. general purpose
b. specific purpose
c. thesis statement
d. main point

ANS: b
REF: pg. 52-53

5. A statement that summarizes in a single declarative sentence the main proposition, assumption, or argument you want to express in your speech.
a. general purpose
b. specific purpose
c. thesis statement
d. central idea

ANS: c
REF: pg. 57

6. The following statement is an example of what: "Some of the programs offered by Neighbor-to-Neighbor include mortgage counseling, rental assistance, and transitional housing."
a. general purpose
b. specific purpose
c. thesis statement
d. central idea

ANS: c
REF: pg. 57

True/False

7. Only informative and persuasive speeches require a specific purpose. Commemorative or introductory speeches only require a general purpose.

ANS: False
REF: pg. 56

8. Time limits rarely need to be considered when developing a speech topic.

ANS: False
REF: pg. 45

9. If you are an expert in a certain topic, you are automatically an expert speaker on that topic.

ANS: False
REF: pg. 44

10. Successful public speaking is more likely due to intuition and natural ability than planning and forethought.

ANS: False
REF: pg. 43

11. The following statement is an effective specific purpose statement: "What can be done to improve campus parking for students?

ANS: False
REF: pg. 54-55

Fill in the Blank

12. For the following indicate which statement is the general purpose, the specific purpose and the thesis statement.
a. The three common schools of Marital Arts in the United States include judo, karate, and tae kwon do. _____
b. To inform. _____
c. To inform my audience about the three common schools of Martial Arts in the United States. _____

ANS: a. Thesis statement b. General purpose c. Specific purpose
REF: pgs. 57, 52, 52-3

13. The_____ is the subject of a speech.

ANS: speech topic
REF: pg. 44

14. Using technology, free association, forming categories and clustering are _____ strategies.

ANS: brainstorming
REF: pg. 49

15. The _____ of a speech is its broad goal.

ANS: general purpose
REF: pg. 52

16. The _____ of a speech is a focused statement that identifies exactly what a speaker wants to accomplish with a speech.

ANS: specific purpose
REF: pg. 52-53

17. The _____ is a statement that summarizes in a single declarative sentence the main proposition, assumption, or argument you want to express in your speech.

ANS: thesis statement
REF: pg. 57

List and Define

18. List and briefly explain the three different contexts or reasons people enter the public dialogue.

ANS: Deciding to speak; Being asked to speak; Being required to speak.
REF: pgs. 43-44

19. List and briefly explain three of the constraints of speaking in a classroom setting.

ANS: Preselected purpose, time limits, highly structured assignment, instructor as audience, class members as audience.
REF: pgs. 45

20. Define brainstorming, then identify and explain which type of brainstorming you prefer.

ANS: Brainstorming is a process of generating ideas randomly and uncritically, without attention to logic, connectives, or relevance. See pages 49-51 for the different types of brainstorming from which students can choose.
REF: pgs 49-51

21. Define the term general purpose statement and list two of the kinds of overall goals you might identify in a general purpose statement.

ANS: It is a speech's broad goal, such as to inform, to invite, to persuade, to introduce, to commemorate, to accept.
REF: pg. 52-3

22. Define a specific purpose statement and provide an example.

ANS: It is a focused statement that identifies exactly what a speaker wants to accomplish with a speech. For example: To inform my audience about the services offered to all students at the University Career Center.
REF: pg. 53 for definition, 56 for examples to model.

Essay

23. Discuss one of the contexts in which you have found yourself contributing to the public dialogue. Include an explanation of how that context influenced your speaking goal.

ANS: Students should respond with one of the following: deciding to speak, being asked to speak or being required to speak. Look for their understanding of how their speaking was influenced by the context. For instance, if they were required to speak, then they might say they did not have a choice of a goal because that we determined for them.
REF: pgs. 43-44

24. Briefly discuss the process you went through to narrow your focus (i.e. move from assignment to thesis statement) for your first speech.

ANS: Students here should discuss some of the following: Classroom setting; Assignment requirements; They brainstormed; They articulated their general and specific purpose; They stated their thesis which also helped identify main points. They may not include every step, but they should name and briefly explain at least 3 distinct steps.
REF: pgs. 45-46, 49, 52, 57 (45-57 for complete process information).

25. Choose a topic. Now, discuss how this same topic could be addressed as an informative, persuasive and a commemorative speech.

ANS: Ideas on content should reflect informative, persuasive and commemorative speeches from page 53.
REF: pg. 53

Chapter Four

Multiple Choice

1. The speaker concerned about knowing the positions, perspectives and prior knowledge of their listeners is being audience
a. agreeable.
b. centered.
c. compromised.
d. manipulated.

ANS: b
REF: pg. 65

2. These reflect a person's likes or dislikes of events, people or ideas.
a. standpoint
b. beliefs
c. attitudes
d. values

ANS: c
REF: pg. 68

3. Understanding that an audience is a/an _____ helps speakers stay audience centered.
a. captive audience
b. temporary community
c. technology driven audience
d. group of experts

ANS: b
REF: pg. 70

4. A speaker is informing an audience about different services the community provides for individuals with out health care. An audience member who appears to be Mexican-American asks the speaker "Is there an age requirement to receive services?" The speaker responds: "Your kids will easily qualify, and so will you. I get a lot of Latina single moms like you asking me about services." The young woman in the audience replies: "I have health insurance through the University I am attending. I do not have any children. I am actually asking this question for my grandparents who have no health coverage." This situation best illustrates which of the following concepts?
a. belief
b. ethnocentrism
c. attitude
d. stereotyping

ANS: d
REF: pg. 70

5. Which term best describes what a survey asks or does when they ask an individual about their age, nationality, ethnicity, sex, or religious orientation?
a. standpoint
b. demographic audience analysis
c. close-ended questions
d. master status analysis

ANS: b
REF: pg. 69

6. When a speaker gives a speech about what is good, worthy or important they are relying mainly on
a. attitudes.
b. values.
c. beliefs.
d. norms.

ANS: b
REF: pg. 68

True/False

7. All master statuses are considered equally valuable in US society.

ANS: False
REF: pg. 68

8. An effective speaker stays audience centered by being open to compromising their message.

ANS: False
REF: pg. 65

9. Ethnocentrism is the belief our own cultural perspectives, norms, and ways of organizing society are superior to others.

ANS: True
REF: pg. 68

10. If you are speaking to members of an involuntary audience, then there is no way to capture anyone listener's attention.

ANS: False
REF: pg. 71

11. Chronemics is a form of nonverbal communication that considers issues of time.

ANS: True
REF: pg. 75

Fill in the Blank

12. A/n _____ is a complex and varied group of people the speaker addresses.

ANS: audience
REF: pg. 66

13. _____ are significant positions occupied by a person within society that affect that person's identity in almost all social situations.

ANS: Master statuses
REF: pg. 66

14. A _____ is a perspective from which a person views and evaluates society.

ANS: standpoint
REF: pg. 68

15. A person's perception of an idea being real or not real, true or false is a/an _____.

ANS: belief
REF: pg. 68

16. A _____ question is limited in the number of responses that can be made.

ANS: closed-ended question
REF: pg. 69

17. _____ is working to see and understand the world as another sees it, and can motivate an involuntary audience to welcome you as a speaker.

ANS: Empathy
REF: pg. 72

List and Define

18. List and define the three audience expectations to which speakers adapt.

ANS: Expectations about the speaker, the form of the speech and discussions
REF: pgs. 77, 79, 80

19. Define stereotype and identify one stereotype that people who share one of your master statuses might face.

ANS: A stereotype is a broad generalization about an entire group based on little knowledge or exposure to only certain members of that group. For example, people might think that all women want to have children.
REF: pg. 70

307

20. List and briefly explain the three temporal factors you need to consider when thinking about your speaking environment.

ANS: Time of day; Speaking order; Length of speech
REF: pgs. 75-77

21. Explain what it means to engage in a dialogue.

ANS: To engage in a dialogue is to interact, connect and exchange ideas and opinions with others.
REF: pg. 66

22. Define speaking environment, then list and briefly explain three factors that can affect your speaking environment.

ANS: Size and physical arrangement; Technology; Temporal factors. See text for explanations of each.
REF: pgs. 72, 73-4, 75

Essay

23. Identify one master status that will impact you as a speaker. What is one stereotype that an audience might make about you? What is one standpoint you have related to that stereotype? How might you address your master status and stereotype in your introduction?

ANS: Students are likely to identify race, ethnicity or gender as a master status. Depending on what came up during the class discussion, they might also identify other statuses. They should also be able to explain how this master status might affect them in a public speaking situation, a possible stereotype they face, and a standpoint they have because of this potential stereotype.
REF: pgs. 66-69

24. Talk about the two different audiences you can address in a public speaking situation and how you might approach each.

ANS: Students should list voluntary and involuntary audiences. How they address each will depend on information in the book, and to an extent their own styles of speaking.
REF: pgs. 70-71

25. In this public speaking classroom, what three overarching expectations will your audience have of you as a speaker? For each expectation, briefly discuss one way you will fulfill or violate the expectation in an audience centered way.

ANS: Students should identify expectations about form, expectations about the speaker, and expectations about speaker-audience discussions. They should be able to explain how they would either fulfill or violate the expectations of the audience, including being transparent about their master statuses (and either conforming to or deviating from them), either using expected speech forms or violating them with an explanation of why the violation is better for the audience (see example on p. 80) and at least one way they would approach a discussion to stay audience centered (such as considering why someone would ask a question). REF: pgs. 78-81

Chapter Five

Multiple Choice

1. A list that shows the information you already have about your speech topic and the type of information you need to find.
a. a browser
b. links
c. a research inventory
d. search engines

ANS: c
REF: pg. 85

2. A summary of the text in an article or publication is a/an
a. Internet posting.
b. database.
c. catalog.
d. abstract.

ANS: d
REF: 92

3. When we take in more information than we can process, and know there is more to learn, we are experiencing
a. research inventory results.
b. information overload.
c. libarary fatigue.
d. excessive anxiety.

ANS: b
REF: pg. 85

4. This user-friendly library tool allows the researcher to search a topic by title, author or subject.
a. index
b. abstract
c. catalog
d. full-text database

ANS: c
REF: pg. 91

5. A government document would likely not contain
a. US census statistics.
b. county data, such as public school funding.
c. historical information about state election results.
d. research data funded by private companies.

ANS: d
REF: pg. 93

309

6. An extremely unethical form of presenting someone else's work as your own, created from several different sources.
a. bibliography
b. patch work plagiarism
c. global plagiarism
d. incremental plagiarism

ANS: b
REF: pg. 101

True/False

7. If you find a (~) in a URL, then it is likely that that particular site is multi-authored and comes from a very credible organization.

ANS: False
REF: pg. 89

8. A probe question allows the interviewer to follow up on a previous answer to obtain a more comprehensive response.

ANS: True
REF: pg. 97

9. As a speaker, it is ok for you to embellish the story an interviewee told you in order to make it more exciting to the audience.

ANS: False
REF: pg. 100

10. Gathering more information is beneficial when researching your speech.

ANS: True
REF: pg. 102

11. When conducting an interview you should remember that closed-ended questions are the best questions to ask because they allow the interviewee to elaborate on a topic.

ANS: False
REF: pg. 98

Fill in the Blank

12. Collections of information stored electronically so they are easy to find and retrieve are called_____.

ANS: databases
REF: pg. 92

13. Words you can use to create specific phrases that broaden or narrow your search on the Internet are called _____.

ANS: Boolean operators
REF: pg. 91

14. If you are looking for useful facts and information, such as the depth of Lake Michigan or the meaning of a work, you would consult a/an _____.

ANS: reference work
REF: pg. 94

15. A/an _____ is an alphabetical listing of topics discussed in a publication.

ANS: index
REF: pg. 92

16. A/an _____ is a planned interaction with another person organized around inquiry and response.

ANS: interview
REF: pg. 96

17. A/an _____ is an accurate record of each source used and referenced in your presentation.

ANS: bibliography
REF: pg. 102

List and Define

18. List the six guidelines to evaluating internet sources.

ANS: Is the information reliable? Is the information authoritative? How current is the information? How complete is the information? Is the information relevant? Is the information consistent and unbiased?
REF: pgs. 89-90

19. List four tips for making your interaction with the college librarian a successful experience.

ANS: Complete your research inventory ahead of time; Ask specific questions; Share details of the assignment; Be respectful.
REF: pg. 90-91

20. List and define three of the five kinds of materials available at the library.

ANS: Catalogs, databases, indexes; Government documents; Reference works.
REF: pgs. 91-95

21. List the five main steps for conducting a successful research interview.

ANS: Who to interview; Schedule the interview; Prepare questions for the interview; Conduct the interview; Follow up.
REF: pgs. 96-99

22 List and define the three different types of plagiarism.

ANS: Patchwork plagiarism is constructing a complete speech that you present as your own from portions of several different sources. Global plagiarism is stealing an entire speech from a single source and presenting it as your own. Incremental plagiarism is presenting select portions from a single speech as your own.
REF: pg. 101

Essay

23. Discuss how you might use your own personal knowledge and experience to help you gather research for a speech.

ANS: Students should discuss ways that their experience with a hobby, ritual, job, etc. might help them construct a speech. They might also mention that they would want use the speech to gather experience.
REF: pg. 87

24. Imagine that you had the opportunity to interview anyone in the world for your next speech. Who would you interview? How would you prepare for the interview? For each step in the process, include an example of how you might execute that step for the specific interviewee you chose. (Note: be sure to give the person's name and their relationship to your topic.)

ANS: Students should pick an interviewee, then follow the guidelines presented in the book. Their examples should include some connection between the action they take and the identity of the interviewee. They might choose a celebrity, a politician, or even a family member.
REF: pgs. 96-99

3. Ernesto is planning to do research for his speech on how to support programs for homeless veterans in his city. His audience will be students, parents, and teachers from his high school who want to learn more about this issue. Some audience members might also be interested in raising money for this cause. What are at least three kinds of research you would suggest he include in his speech? What advice or caution might you give him about these kinds of research?

ANS: Students should respond based on the guidelines that have been given in the book and any additional guidelines you have recommended.

Chapter Six

Multiple Choice

1. A speaker uses the following information in a speech: "Every day I walk home from work. Everyday I have to maneuver around bikes, busses, and cars who who do not follow the law when sharing the road with pedestrians." This information best illustrates which of the following?
a. illustration
b. real example
c. hypothetical example
d. supporting material

ANS: b
REF: pg. 110

2. A speaker uses the following information in a speech: "Suppose you skipped breakfast this morning. What would happen to your energy level by 9 or 10 o'clock? You'll   probably feel bored or restless, and maybe sad or unmotivated." This information best   illustrates which of the following?
a. illustration
b. real example
c. hypothetical example
d. supporting material

ANS: c
REF: pg. 110

3. Former president Ronald Reagan was well known for incorporating these stories into his speeches to expertly make a point in a personal way.
a. narratives
b. examples
c. statistics
d. testimony

ANS: a
REF: pg. 113, 114 (specific ex of Reagan)

4. A story that takes only a short time to tell and illustrates a specific point.
a. brief example
b. real example
c. narrative
d. brief narrative

ANS: d
REF: pg. 114

5. If you are interested in finding the midpoint of the set of data, you are looking for the
a. mean.
b. average.
c. mode.
d. median.

ANS: d
REF: pg. 120

6. In a speech about bone marrow donation Jamal says, "I will never forget September 14, 2007 because that was the day that I learned I would need a stranger's bone marrow to save my life."
a. direct quotation
b. expert testimony
c. personal testimony
d. paraphrase

ANS: c
REF: pg. 124

True/False

7. You can always trust statistics because they are unbiased data.

ANS: False
REF: pg. 122

8. When you use hypothetical examples, you want to make sure that they are grounded in fact.

ANS: True
REF: pg. 110

9. A mode is a number that occurs most often in a set of numbers.

ANS: True
REF: pg. 120

10. Testimony is called "quoting others" or "citing the words of other."

ANS: True
REF: pg. 123

11. The denotative meaning of a word is the dictionary definition of a word.

ANS: True
REF: pg. 129

Fill in the Blank

12. An assertion that must be proved is also known as a/an _____.

ANS: claim
REF: pg. 110

13. The two types of examples include _____ and _____.

ANS: real, hypothetical
REF: pg. 110

14. The two types of narratives include _____ and _____.

ANS: brief, extended
REF: pg. 114

15. _____ are summaries that help an audience make sense of large chunks of numerical information.

ANS: Statistics
REF: pg. 117

16. A/an _____ is an exact word-for-word presentation of another's testimony.

ANS: direct quotation
REF: pg. 123

17. A/an _____ is unreasoned distortion of judgment or prejudice about a topic.

ANS: bias
REF: pg. 125

List and Define

18. List and define the three types of testimony.

ANS: Expert; based on an authority; peer: lay, firsthand experience; personal: your own.
REF: pg. 123-124

19. Define paraphrase.

ANS: Paraphrase is a summary of another's testimony in the speaker's own words.
REF: pg. 123

20. Describe the difference between a biased source and an objective source.

ANS: A bias source is an unreasoned distortion of judgment or prejudice about a topic. An objective source has a fair and undistorted view on a question or issue.
REF: pg. 125

21. List and define the two types of definitions for words or phrases. Give an example of how the same word or phrase could have each type of definition.

ANS: Denotative definition is the objective definition of a word or phrase. Connotative definition is the subjective meaning of a word or phrase based on personal experiences and beliefs. For example, the denotative definition of "dog" would probably be a   mammal with four legs, being of different breeds. A connotative definition would be "a person's best friend."
REF: pg. 129

22. Define interextuality and explain what you must do as a speaker for it to be effective.

ANS: Stories that reference other stories or rely on parts of other stories to be complete. To use intertexuality effectively, you must make sure that everyone knows the stories to which you are referring.
REF: pg. 114

Essay

23. What are the four ways that examples can enhance a speech? Consider one or two examples you have used in a speech. Which two ways did you or could you have used these examples to enhance your last speech? (If they have not spoken yet, ask them which two they could use to enhance their upcoming speech).

ANS: To clarify concepts, to reinforce points, to bring concepts to life/elicit emotions, to build your case or make credible generalizations. Students should illustrate their understanding of the tip as they apply it to their own situation.
REF: pg. 110-112

24. What are four ways to use narrative effectively? Think about a speech either in class or outside of class where you heard narrative used in an effective way. Using the criteria identified in the text, explain how the speaker used two of the criteria effectively. (Note: You do not have to retell the narrative.)

ANS: To personalize a point, to challenge your audience to think new ways, to draw your audience in emotionally, to unite with your audience. See pages 114-116 for the criteria. Students should clearly illustrate the criteria as they discuss the speech that they felt was most effective in this area.
REF: pg. 149-152

25. What are the three types of testimony? For each type of testimony, give an example of when it would be best to use it in a speech.

ANS: Expert, peer, personal. Students' examples should clearly illustrate their understanding of when and why to use each type of testimony.
REF: pgs. 123-126

Chapter Seven

Multiple Choice

1. When someone says "That speaker really knows what they are talking about. They have incredible credentials" they are talking about which of the following?
a. logos
b. ethos
c. pathos
d. inferences

ANS: b
REF: pgs. 135-136

2. The use of emotional appeals as proof.
a. logos
b. ethos
c. pathos
d. inferences

ANS: c
REF: pg. 135-136

3. The following claim best illustrates which type of reasoning: "My speech class was easy. My roommate's speech class was easy. My girlfriend's speech class was easy. My brother's speech class will also be easy."
a. inductive reasoning
b. deductive reasoning
c. analogical reasoning
d. causal reasoning

ANS: a
REF: pg. 136

4. The reasoning process that uses a commonly accepted claim to establish a specific claim.
a. Inductive reasoning
b. Deductive reasoning
c. Analogical reasoning
d. Causal reasoning

ANS: b
REF: pg. 139

317

5. The following claim illustrates which type of error in reasoning: "Out of 25 students surveyed from a student body of 1200, all said that parking on campus is a problem. Therefore, 100% of students on campus think parking is a problem."
a. false cause
b. invalid analogy
c. improper sign
d. hasty generalization

ANS: d
REF: pg. 138

6. Assuming one event caused another simply because it happened before the second is what form of faulty reasoning?
a. false cause
b. invalid analogy
c. improper sign
d. hasty generalization

ANS: a
REF: pg. 143

True/False

7. A map of reasoning is a tool to aid the logical arrangement of evidence in a speech.

ANS: True
REF: pg. 147

8. "All United States citizens have the right to vote. Women are citizens of the United States; therefore, women have the right to vote" is an example of a hasty generalization.

ANS: False
REF: pg. 138

9. When using causal reasoning, you should always assume an event has a single cause.

ANS: False
REF: pg. 142

10. Analogical reasoning compares similarities as well as contrasting differences.

ANS: True
REF: pg. 144

11. Competence is how a speaker perceives the knowledge of the audience.

ANS: False
REF: pg. 150

Fill in the Blank

12. The mental leaps we make when we agree that a speaker's evidence supports his or her claims are
_____.

ANS: inferences
REF: pg. 135

13. _____ is the process of reasoning that uses a familiar and commonly accepted claim to establish the truth of a very specific claim.

ANS: Deductive reasoning
REF: pg. 139

14. Finish the following claim:
All people are mortal.
Zhara is a person.
_____.

ANS: Zhara is mortal
REF: pg. 139

15. A/an _____ is something that represents something else.

ANS: sign
REF: pg. 146

16. _____ is the audience's perception of a speaker's competence and character.

ANS: Credibility
REF: pg. 150

17. _____ is the logical arrangement of evidence in a speech.

ANS: Logos
REF: pg. 135

18. _____ is a set of developed statements that allows a speaker to develop evidence and establish the validity of his/her claim.

ANS: Argument
REF: pg. 136

319

List and Define

19. List and define Aristotle's three forms of proof to accomplish sound reasoning.

ANS: Logos: logical arrangement of evidence in a speech; Ethos: the speaker's credibility; Pathos: emotional appeals made by a speaker.
REF: pg. 135-136

20. List and define three types of reasoning.

ANS: Students can choose from the following: inductive reasoning; deductive reasoning; causal reasoning; analogical reasoning; and reasoning by sign.
REF: pgs. 136, 139, 140, 143, 146

21. List and define two types of errors in reasoning.

ANS: Students can choose from: hasty generalization; false cause; invalid analogy.
REF: pgs. 138, 143, 145

22. List and define the four components of a map of reasoning.

ANS: Claim: what I think or want to propose: Grounds: why do I think this or why I want to propose it; Warrant: how I know my grounds support my claims; Backing: how I know my warrant supports the grounds.
REF: pg. 147

23. List and define the two contributing factors to credibility.

ANS: Competence is the audience's view of a speaker's intelligence, expertise, and knowledge of a subject. Character is the audience's view of a speaker's sincerity, trustworthiness, and concern for the well-being of the audience.
REF: pg 150

Essay

24. What are the components of ethos? Think back to a memorable speech that you have given or heard in class. How did the speaker establish ethos? Be sure to give specific examples!

ANS: Students should explain that they understand ethos as credibility, and therefore as competence and character. They should then describe how the speaker proved her/himself credible and demonstrated character.
REF: pg. 150

25. As we have read, there are ethical components for using evidence. What are three choices you can make as a speaker to ensure you are ethical in your use of evidence? Why does the ethical use of evidence matter?

ANS: The tips: Build your credibility, use accurate evidence, verify the structure of your reasoning. Based on the suggestions in this and other chapters, the students should be able to provide reasons why ethics matter when presenting evidence. Reasons may include course concepts such as being audience centered and maintaining character, or contributing to public dialogue in an honest way.
REF: pgs. 149-151

Chapter Eight

Multiple Choice

1. You should not have more than _____ main points and not less than _____ main points in the body of your speech.
a. five/four
b. three/two
c. four/one
d. four/two

ANS: d
REF: pg. 157

2. When a speaker gives an informative speech about their College's progress in the 60's 70's 80's and 90's, they are using _____ pattern of organization.
a. chronological
b. spatial
c. causal
d. problem/solution

ANS: a
REF: pg. 159

3. If a speaker's main points are organized according to location or direction, they are following which type of organizational pattern?
a. chronological
b. spatial
c. causal
d. problem/solution

ANS: b
REF: pg. 160

4. Your speaking outline should
a. contain key words and phrases.
b. contain full sentences.
c. look identical to your preparation outline.
d. avoid delivery cues.

ANS: a
REF: pg. 179

5. This connective highlights an important idea or where you are in your speech.
a. transition
b. internal preview
c. internal summary
d. signpost

ANS: d
REF: pg. 167

6. If you are giving a speech about how to avoid being lonely and make friends on campus by joining clubs, the best pattern for you to use would be
a. chronological.
b. topical.
c. problem-solution.
d. causal.

ANS: c
REF: pg. 161

True/False

7. Your time limit is the most significant consideration affecting the number of main points in your speech.

ANS: True
REF: pg. 157

8. When you use the topical pattern of organization, you seek to explain a cause and effect relationship between ideas or events.

ANS: False
REF: pg. 162

9. Organizing your speech is a way to be audience centered.

ANS: False
REF: pg. 154

10. You should always equally balance the time spent speaking on each of your main points.

ANS: True
REF: pg. 164

11. Transitions summarize the points you have already discussed.

ANS: False
REF: pg. 165

Fill in the Blank

12. The _____ outline contains enough detail to verify the content is well organized and complete but is not the speech word-for-word.

ANS: preparation
REF: pg. 168

13. If you are using the _____ organizational pattern you can use primacy or recency.

ANS: topical
REF: pg. 162

14. _____ are the most important ideas addressed and supported in the speech.

ANS: Main points
REF: pg. 156

15. A _____ is a word or phrase used to link ideas in a speech.

ANS: connective
REF: pg. 165

16. "In discussing the production of batik, I'll explain the four steps: the preparation of the cloth, the mixing of the dyes, the application of the dye, and the setting of the image in   the cloth" is an example of which type of connective: _____.

ANS: internal preview
REF: pg. 166

17. _____ is a way to establish credibility and be ethical because you are giving credit where credit is due.

ANS: Citing sources
REF: pg. 172

18. Delivery cues can be added to the _____ outline.

ANS: speaking
REF: pg. 178

List and Define

19. List and define three of the five types of organizational patterns.

ANS: Students can choose from the following: chronological, spatial, causal, problem and solution, topical.
REF: pgs. 159-163

20. List and explain the three steps for preparing your main points.

ANS: Identify the main points; Use an appropriate number; Determine the order.
REF: pgs. 156- 159

21. List and define two different types of connectives.

ANS: Students can choose from the following: Transitions, internal previews, internal summaries, signposts.
REF: pgs. 165-167

22. List three guidelines for developing a strong preparation outline.

ANS: Use complete sentences; Label parts; Use consistent symbols and indentation; Use at least two sub points per point; Check for balance.
REF: pgs. 172-175

Essay

23. Which type of pattern did you use for your last speech? Why did you choose that pattern? What other pattern could you have chosen? Would that have been as effective? Why or why not?

ANS: In responding to this question, students should mention their purpose statements and possibly their thesis statement. They should explain why they chose the pattern of organization they did choose, and consider how a different pattern would have affected the speech.
REF: pgs. 156-163

24. Discuss two speeches given by your peers in which they used connectives very effectively. Identify the type of connective they used and why it was helpful.

ANS: In their response, it should be clear that students can distinguish between the connectives and why some might be more effective in certain areas of the speech.
REF: pgs. 165-167

25. How does using a speaking outline make you a better speaker? What is one challenge you have with using a speaking outline? How will you overcome it?

ANS: Reasons include being able to make eye contact with/engage the audience, providing you with delivery cues, allowing you to be extemporaneous and being dynamic. Each student will be able to identify his or her specific challenge, and create a solution.
REF: pgs. 178

Chapter Nine

Multiple Choice

1. What is missing in the following introduction of a speech: "Are you looking for a fun, inexpensive way to liven up your wardrobe or home décor? Well, I have something that you will really enjoy! Today I am going to inform you about how to tie dye fabric. I learned to tie dye while at summer camp. It is so much fun. By the end of my speech you will want to tie dye everything you own!"
a. It needs to catch the audience's attention.
b. It needs to reveal the topic to the audience.
c. It needs to establish credibility with the audience.
d. It needs to review the speech for the audience.

ANS: d
REF: pg. 187

2. This is a very important task to be accomplished in your introduction, both piquing curiosity and helping your audience understand how a topic relates to them.
a. Catch the audience's attention.
b. Reveal the topic to the audience.
c. Establish credibility with the audience.
d. Preview the speech for the audience.

ANS: a
REF: pg. 187

3. This component prepares listeners for what to expect and also communicates a sense that you are organized.
a. Catch the audience's attention.
b. Reveal the topic to the audience.
c. Establish credibility with the audience.
d. Preview the speech for the audience.

ANS: d
REF: pg. 187

4. You do this in order to gain the trust of your audience.
a. Catch the audience's attention.
b. Reveal the topic to the audience.
c. Establish credibility with the audience.
d. Preview the speech for the audience.

ANS: c
REF: pg. 187

5. Including this in your conclusion reviews ideas and reminds the audience about important parts of your speech.
a. summary
b. citing a source
c. use of a quotation
d. using a transition

ANS: a
REF: pg. 198

6. In order to remind your audience what the core idea of your speech is, you must include what in your conclusion?
a. an expert quote
b. a journal citation
c. a twist on your argument
d. a restatement of your thesis

ANS: d
REF: pg. 197

True/False

7. One of the most important tasks you have as a speaker is to capture the attention of your audience.

ANS: True
REF: pg. 187

8. You do not have to address your credibility in your introduction if it is obvious to your audience that you know what you are talking about.

ANS: False
REF: pg. 187

9. A powerful introduction can be up to 25% of your entire speech.

ANS: False
REF: pg. 196

10. The more audience-centered your conclusion, the more effective it will be.

ANS: True
REF: pg. 197

11. Returning to content addressed in the introduction can creatively review and give the listeners a sense of completeness.

ANS: True
REF: pg. 199

Fill in the Blank

12. A/an _____ is a brief overview in the introduction of the speech of each of the main points in the speech.

ANS: Preview
REF: pg. 187

13. You can _____ by using a question, a story, a demonstration.

ANS: capture attention
REF: pg. 187

14. A question a speaker asks that an audience is not supposed to answer out loud but rather in their own minds is also called a/an _____.

ANS: rhetorical question
REF: pg. 188

15. When you _____, you tell your audience why they should listen.

ANS: state the importance
REF: pg. 193

16. A/an _____ is a concise restatement of your main points at the end of your speech.

ANS: summary
REF: pg. 198

List and Define

17. List the four objectives you need to accomplish in an introduction.

ANS: Catch the audience's attention; Reveal the topic of my speech; Establish my credibility; Preview my speech.
REF: pg. 197

18. List four of the seven different ways you can prepare a compelling introduction.

ANS: Your students can choose from the following: Ask a question (pg. 188); Tell a story (pg. 189); Recite a quotation or a poem (pg. 189); Give a demonstration (pg. 190); Make an intriguing or startling statement (pg. 192); State the importance of the topic (pg. 193); Share your expertise (pg, 194); State what's to come (pg. 194).
REF: pgs. 188-194

19. List four tips for creating an effective introduction.

ANS: for introductory materials as you do research; Prepare and practice the full introduction in detail; Be brief; Be creative.
REF: pg. 196

20. List the two objectives you need to accomplish in your conclusion.

ANS: Bring the speech to an end; Reinforce my thesis.
REF: pg. 197

21. List three different ways you can prepare a compelling conclusion.

ANS: Students can choose from the following: Summarize main points; Answer your introductory question; Refer back to the introduction; Recite a quotation.
REF: pgs. 198-199

Essay

22. Using the topic of your choice, write an introduction that accomplishes all four objectives on an introduction. (Note: Your introduction should clearly illustrate the objectives, but it does not have to be perfect!)

ANS: Students should be able to write a quick introduction that accomplishes these four objectives. Focus on grading the effort at meeting the objectives when writing under a time limit.
REF: pgs. 187

23. What are four tips that can help you prepare an effective conclusion? Which two are the most challenging for you? What do you do (or will you do) to overcome these challenges?

ANS: Students should incorporate a discussion of the tips for preparing conclusions in the textbook and any additional tips you have outlined for them.
REF: pg. 200

24. Why do the introduction and conclusion of a speech require special consideration when preparing and delivering a speech?

ANS: Students should be able to articulate why they are important in their own words. For the introduction, they should include some version of the idea that intros make an audience more willing to listen, think more highly of the speaker (credibility) and helping the audience understand the speech better (clarity). For the conclusion, they should include some version of the idea of reinforcing the thesis, reminding listeners of main points, and framing the speaker's ideas and arguments in their own way.
REF: pg. 186 for a summary (or other aspects of the chapter)

25. Using a topic of your choice, prepare a conclusion accomplishing the two required objectives. (Note: Your conclusion should clearly illustrate the objectives, but it does not have to be perfect!)

ANS: Students should be able to accomplish both objectives outlined in the textbook. Focus on grading the effort at meeting the objectives when writing under a time limit.
REF: pg, 197

Chapter Ten

1. The word or phrase spoken by a speaker.
a. language
b. symbol
c. referent
d. reference

ANS: b
REF: pg. 204

2. While listening to a speaker describe his memory of a delicious dessert, Manda recalls the taste of the birthday cakes her mother makes. This scenario is an example of which of the following?
a. language
b. symbol
c. referent
d. reference

ANS: d
REF: pg. 204

3. An illogical and confusing comparison between two things.
a. antithesis
b. metaphor
c. simile
d. mixed metaphor

ANS: d
REF: pg. 213

4. Attributing human characteristics to non human objects or concepts.
a. mixed metaphors
b. cliché
c. personification
d. metaphor

ANS: c
REF: pg. 214

5. "Students studied systematically for the speech exam" is an example of
a. repetition.
b. antithesis.
c. alliteration.
d. parallelism.

ANS: c
REF: pg. 217

6. "Ask not what your parents can do for your future, but what you can do for your future" is an example of
a. antithesis.
b. metaphor.
c. simile.
d. personification.

ANS: a
REF: pg. 217

True/False

7. If a word is central to your claim then you should check the dictionary for its definition.

ANS: True
REF: 210

8. We all have the same reference when a word is uttered.

ANS: False
REF: pg. 204

9. Oral style is when you speak like we tend to write in formal writing.

ANS: False
REF: pg. 211

10. Forrest Gump's famous line "Life is like a box of chocolates" is, in fact, a simile.

ANS: True
REF: pg. 212

11. A mnemonic device makes verbal information easier to remember.

ANS: True
REF: pg. 217

Fill in the Blank

12. _____ is a system of verbal or gestural symbols a community uses to communicate with one another.

ANS: Language
REF: pg. 203

13. A _____ word refers to a tangible object.

ANS: concrete
REF: 206

14. A word that refers to ideas or concepts but not specific objects is also known as a/an _____ word.

ANS: abstract
REF: pg. 206

15. A/an _____ is a fixed, distinctive expression whose meaning is not indicated by its individual words.

ANS: idiom
REF: pg. 207

16. When you say "police officers" rather than "policemen" in a speech about the local police force, you are using _____.

ANS: gender inclusive language
REF: pg. 209

17. You use a/n _____ when you compare two things that are different by describing one thing as being something else.

ANS: metaphor
REF: pg. 213

List and Define

18. List and define the three elements of the semantic triangle of meaning.

ANS: Symbol: The word or phrase spoken by the speaker (pg. 246); Referent: the object, concept, or event a symbol represents (pg. 246); Thought or reference is the memory and past experiences that audience members have with an object, concept, or event (pg. 246).
REF: pgs. 204

19. Define concrete and abstract language.

ANS: Concrete language refers to tangible objects (a person, place, or thing). Abstract language refers to ideas or concepts but not specific objects.
REF: pg. 206

20. List and define two devices that create effective, memorable imagery.

ANS: Students can choose from the following: Simile; metaphor; personification. They should not include mixed metaphor because that is ineffective.
REF: pgs. 212-214

21. List and define two devices that help create pleasing rhythm.

ANS: Students can choose from the following: Parallelism; repetition; alliteration; antithesis.
REF: pg. 214-218

22. List the characteristics that make spoken language different than written language.

ANS: Oral language is: More interactive; more casual; more repetitive.
REF: pgs. 211-212

Essay

23. How can you be audience centered when using labels to identify cultural groups? Why does the way you use labels matter?

ANS: Students should articulate that using appropriate labels is respectful to the groups of people they mention in their speech, can help them make a connection with an audience who might identify with that label, and prevents them from perpetuating stereotypes. They might also include a discussion of ethics.
REF: 207-209

24. Using the three elements of I. A. Richards semantic triangle of meaning, diagram a word you or a classmate used in your speech that has more than one connotative meaning. Was the word used clearly in the speech? Why or why not?

ANS: Students should be able to diagram a word using the parts of the triangle and explain whether the word was used effectively. They should include some discussion of whether or not the word remained ambiguous.
REF: pg. 204

25. Think of an idiom you heard or used growing up. How would you explain that idiom to an audience of people who had never heard it before if you were going to use it in a speech?

ANS: Students should know what an idiom is, be able to come up with an idiom and be able to explain in other words what it means. A student may choose one of the idioms mentioned in the book.
REF: pg. 207

Chapter Eleven

Multiple Choice

1. The action and manner of speaking to an audience.
a. delivery
b. gesture
c. language
d. extemporaneous

ANS: a
REF: pg. 221

2. A speech that is carefully prepared and practiced from brief notes.
a. Extemporaneous speech
b. Impromptu speech
c. Manuscript speech
d. Memorized speech

ANS: a
REF: pg. 222

3. A speaking style that is more formal than everyday conversation but remains   spontaneous, relaxed and in contact with the audience.
a. extemporaneous style
b. vocal variety
c. manuscript style
d. conversational style

ANS: d
REF: pg. 223

4. Peoples use of space while communicating.
a. appearance
b. posture
c. proxemics
d. gestures

ANS: c
REF: pg. 235

5. The highness or lowness of a speaker's voice on the musical scale.
a. rate
b. pitch
c. inflection
d. pauses

ANS: b
REF: pg. 228

334

6. Hesitations and brief silences in speech or conversation.
a. rate
b. pitch
c. inflection
d. pauses

ANS: d
REF: pg. 229

True/False

7. The four methods of delivery used by public speakers include extemporaneous, impromptu, conversational and manuscript.

ANS: False (memorized is the fourth, not conversational)
REF: pg. 222-226

8. Most speeches are best delivered from a manuscript.

ANS: False
REF: pgs. 225

9. Memorized speeches are used mainly for toasts, blessings, acceptance speeches, speeches of introduction and in forensics.

ANS: True
REF: pg. 226

10. You should use the same rate of speaking with every audience.

ANS: False
REF: pg. 228

11. Monotone is a way of speaking in which a speaker does not alter her or his pitch.

ANS: True
REF: pg. 229

Fill in the Blank

12. The method of delivery you are required to use the most in this class is _____.

ANS: extemporaneous (but this may vary from instructor to instructor)
REF: pg. 222

13. _____ is the loudness of a speaker's voice.

ANS: Volume
REF: pg. 227

14. _____ is a nonverbal way to greet the audience, gauge their interest and communicate sincerity and honesty.

ANS: Eye contact
REF: pg. 233

15. _____ is the act of saying words correctly according to the accepted standards of a language.

ANS: Pronunication
REF: pg. 231

16. Movements, usually of the hands but sometimes of the full body, that express meaning and emotion or offer clarity to a message are also known as _____.

ANS: gestures
REF: pg. 235

17. _____ is the way we position and carry our bodies.

ANS: Posture
REF: pg. 234

List and Define

18. List and define the four different methods of delivery.

ANS: Extemporaneous; impromptu; manuscript; memorized.
REF: pgs. 222-226

19. List the tips for impromptu delivery.

ANS: Quickly decide on the main points; Introduce main points as I would in my regular speeches; Support main point with sub-subpoints; Summarize my main points.
REF: pg. 224

20. List and briefly define three components of nonverbal delivery.

ANS: Students can choose from the following: Personal appearance (pg. 232); eye contact (pg. 233); facial expressions (pg. 234); posture (pg. 234); gestures (pg. 235); proxemics (pg. 235).
REF: pgs. 232-236

21. List and briefly define three components of verbal delivery.

ANS: Students can choose from the following: Volume (227); rate (228); pitch/inflection (228); pauses (229); articulation (230); pronunciation (231); dialect (231).
REF: pgs. 227-231

22. Define dialect and list four tips a speaker with a dialect unfamiliar to their audience could use to help their listeners better understand her or him.

ANS: Dialect is defined as a pattern of speech that is shared by an ethnic group or people from a specific geographic region. Acknowledge heritage; Give examples of differences you the speaker have encountered; Define unfamiliar terms; Work to soften accent.
REF: pg. 231-232

Essay

23. Compare and contrast the different methods of delivery. Which do you prefer and why?

ANS: Refer to pages 222-227. Students should have an understanding of each method of delivery, and be able to compare the advantages and disadvantages of each, as well as articulating their preferences with a clear reason. A brief summary table can be found on page 227.
REF: pg. 264-267

24. Identify and briefly define three components of verbal delivery that you want to improve upon as a speaker. How will improving these aspects of your verbal delivery make you a better speaker?

ANS: Students should be able to quickly define these verbal components of delivery. They should also be able to explain how improving these components will make them more credible, easier to listen to, more audience centered, etc.
REF: pgs. 227-232

25. Discuss one verbal and one nonverbal habit that you find most distracting as a listener. Discuss a solution tip for each.

ANS: Students should be able to choose a verbal component from pages 227-232 and link with a tip from page 274 and a nonverbal component from pages 232-236.

REF: pg. 227-232, 232-236

Chapter Fifteen

Multiple Choice

1. This question addresses the morality, the "good or "bad" of a persuasive issue.
a. question of policy
b. question of value
c. question of fact
d. question of truth

ANS: b
REF: pg. 309

2. The following specific purpose statement reflects which type of persuasive question: "To persuade my audience to believe a massive meteorite strike caused the extinction of the dinosaurs."
a. question of policy
b. question of value
c. question of fact
d. question of truth

ANS: c
REF: pg. 309

3. This strategy of addressing opposing arguments actually helps enhance speaker credibility.
a. a two-sided message
b. appealing to fear
c. passive agreement
d. using counter arguments

ANS: d
REF: pg. 324

4. Which of the following specific purpose statements is from a persuasive speech seeking passive agreement?
a. To persuade my audience to attend the next city council meeting in support of open-space measures.
b. To persuade my audience to vote for school board members who support bilingual education.
c. To persuade my audience to believe aerobic exercise is fun and significantly enhances a person's quality of life.
d. To persuade my audience to donate time or money to the local Habitat for Humanity chapter.

ANS: c
REF: pg. 314

351

5. This thesis statement reflects which persuasive pattern of organization? "The problems of wildlife overpopulation, disease and other negative consequences caused by feeding big game wildlife can be solved by keeping unnatural food sources away from wild animals."

a. problem-cause-solution
b. topical
c. problem-solution
d. Monroe's Motivated Sequence

ANS: a
REF: pg. 316

6. This five step organizational strategy works especially well for channeling audience motives into action.
a. problem-solution
b. problem-cause-solution
c. comparative advantages
d. Monroe's Motivated Sequence

ANS: d
REF: pg. 321

True/False

7. A persuasive speech attempts to change or reinforce an audience's thoughts, feelings, or actions.

ANS: True
REF: pg. 308

8. A two-sided message is used when there are only two perspectives on an issue and you want to present both sides equally.

ANS: False
REF: pg. 324

9. A well-developed persuasive presentation will have a good chance of success even with an audience closed to change.

ANS: False
REF: pg. 323-324

10. Successful persuasion incorporates language that shows the speaker understand feelings and motivations of others.

ANS: True
REF: pg. 326

11. You should never use fear appeals because they can immobilize your audience.

ANS: False
REF: pg. 326

Fill in the Blank

12. A/an _____ is a speech whose message attempts to change or reinforce an audience's thoughts, feelings, or actions.

ANS: persuasive speech
REF: pg. 308

13. A/an _____ is a question that addresses the merit or morality of an object, action or belief.

ANS: question of value
REF: pg. 309

14. An explicit request that an audience engage in a behavior is a _____.

ANS: call to action
REF: pg. 314

15. The _____ pattern of organization highlights the benefits of one solution over other possible solutions.

ANS: comparative advantages
REF: pg. 320

16. A_____ addresses the best course of action or solution for a problem.

ANS: question of policy
REF: pg. 310

17. A _____ is effective if you make the audience believe that something undesirable will happen if a change does not occur.

ANS: fear appeal
REF: pg. 376

List and Define

18. List and define the different types of persuasive speeches.

ANS: Persuasive speeches on questions of fact (pg. 362); value (pg. 362) and policy (pg. 363).
REF: pgs. 309-310

353

19. List and define the two types of change you can seek from your audience in a persuasive speech on question of policy.

ANS: Immediate action and passive agreement.
REF: pg. 314

20. List three of the four questions an ethical speaker should ask him or herself about his or her topic.

ANS: What is my position on this topic and why do I hold this position? What is my audience's position and why do they hold it? Why am I qualified to persuade my audience on this issue? Is my request for my audience reasonable, and how will my listeners be affected by my message?
REF: pg. 327

21. Define narrative organization. When might you use it?

ANS: When you use two or more stories to construct an argument. This is helpful when personalizing an argument will make an issue easier for the audience to comprehend.
REF: pg. 318

22. Define and list the steps of Monroe's Motivated Sequence.

ANS: Attention, need, satisfaction, visualization and action steps.
REF: pg.321-322

Essay

23. Discuss the differences among informative, invitational, and persuasive speaking. How are they different? How are they similar? Which do you prefer? Why?

ANS: Students should be able to distinguish between the different types of speeches and explain why they prefer one over another.

24. What are the similarities and differences between problem-solution organization and problem-cause-solution organization? When would you chose one over the other?

ANS: A problem-solution speech focuses on convincing an audience that a problem exists, and can be minimized by the solution (314); has two main points which are the problem/solution; the first point defines the problem and makes it relevant to the audience; the second point outlines the solution and may ask for passive agreement, immediate action or both (315); they are good vehicles to make an audience take action. A problem-cause-solution order identifies a problem, explains the causes, and outlines a solution (316); they have three main points (316); they are generally helpful when the speaker thinks the audience would be better persuaded by knowing the cause of the problem, and to clear up misconceptions that might exist (316).
REF: pgs. 314-317

25. Ahmed has heard that you are in a public speaking class, and has come to you for help. He wants to speak about busing at the next school board meeting, but he is unsure how to speak persuasively without alienating his audience. What tips would you give him in order to help him give his best speech?

ANS: Students should illustrate an understanding of how to effectively incorporate the tips into their persuasive speech writing. Be realistic; use evidence fairly; use language that encourages change. Students can also refer to information about ethics.
REF: pgs. 323-327; 327-328

Chapter Sixteen

Multiple Choice

1. The interrelated knowledge, beliefs and values held by a group of individuals defines:
a. logos
b. ethos
c. pathos
d. mythos

ANS: d
REF: pg. 343

2. In a recent speech, Harold claimed, "The reason that test scores are down for school children in our state is because kids play video games after school instead of studying. If we banned video games, test scores across the state would improve dramatically!" This is an example of which kind of fallacy?
a. hasty generalization
b. false cause
c. either-or
d. red herring

ANS: b
REF: pg. 348

3. You are going to listen to a speaker because not only is she an expert in her field, but also because your friends have told you what a smart, engaging and credible speaker she is. You believe the speaker is credible, but you need to hear what they have to say during the course of the speech to decide how credible she really is. Which type of credibility are you most interested in?
a. derived credibility
b. terminal credibility
c. created credibility
d. initial credibility

ANS: a
REF: pg. 337

4. What fallacy is exemplified by the following statement: "If you are not for us, then you must be against us."
a. red herring
b. ad hominem
c. either-or
d. bandwagon

ANS: c
REF: pg. 348

5. What fallacy attacks an individual personally rather than their arguments?
a. red herring
b. ad hominem
c. bandwagon
d. slippery slope

ANS: b
REF: pg. 346

6. Persuasive speakers want to appeal to these internal mental states consisting of feelings.
a. cognitive states
b. emotions
c. bodily states
d. behaviors

ANS: b
REF: pg. 340

True/False

7. When you say to someone, "What do you know, you're a flaming liberal" you are using the red herring fallacy.

ANS: False
REF: pg. 350

8. Derived credibility is credibility the speaker has before giving a presentation.

ANS: False
REF: pg. 337

9. The bandwagon fallacy is commonly used in advertising, where a common claim might be "Everyone is joining our gym, so should you."

ANS: True
REF: pg. 346

10. In a slippery slope argument, the speaker claims that taking one step may or may not lead to an inevitable conclusion.

ANS: False
REF: pg. 351

11. A speaker who persuades by tapping into larger cultural stories about "the way things are" and "the way things should be" is using mythos.

ANS: True
REF: pg. 343

Fill in the Blank

12. _____ is the emotional appeal made by a speaker.

ANS: Pathos
REF: pg. 334

13. _____ is an emotion commonly found in persuasive speeches, even though it is not considered a primary or even a secondary emotion.

ANS: Reverence
REF: pg. 340

14. _____ is the credibility of a speaker before he or she gives a speech.

ANS: Initial credibility
REF: pg. 337

15. A/an _____ speaker uses sensation, theatrics and melodrama to try and persuade their listeners.

ANS: overly manipulative
REF: pg. 341

16. In a recent speech, Wanda said, "As of 2010, older workers will no longer be considered for jobs. My father, who is 50, has been trying to get a job for a year! This shows that older workers are just not going to be hired anymore." This is an example of which fallacy?

ANS: Hasty generalization
REF: pg. 350

17. _____ is an argument that seems valid but is flawed because of unsound evidence or reasoning.

ANS: Fallacy
REF: pg. 346

List and Define

18. List and define the four components of reasoning.

ANS: Logos, the logical arrangement of evidence; ethos, a speaker's credibility; pathos, emotional appeals made by a speaker; mythos, the interrelated knowledge, beliefs and values held by a group of individuals defines.
REF: pg. 334; 343

19. List and define the three types of credibility.

ANS: Initial, the credibility a speaker has before giving a speech; derived, the credibility a speaker develops during a speech; terminal, the credibility a speaker has at the end of a speech.
REF: pg. 337

20. List the three things you can incorporate into a speech to use emotional appeals effectively.

ANS: Stay audience centered; use vivid language; balance emotion and reason.
REF: pgs. 341-343

21. List the three errors in judgment you could make when using emotional appeals.

ANS: Using overly graphic and violent appeals; using frightening or threatening appeals; using overly manipulative appeals.
REF: pgs. 341-342

22. List and define three of the different fallacies.

ANS: Students can choose from: Ad hominem; bandwagon; either-or; red herring and slippery-slope.
REF: pgs. 346-351

Essay

23. Imagine that you are invited to give a speech the seniors at a local high school. You know that you will have to develop your credibility with the audience. How will you develop the three kinds of credibility in this speaking situation?

ANS: Students should identify the three different types of credibility. Their example should be similar to the example outlined on p. 337.
REF: pg. 337

24. Which speeches in our class do you think used logos, ethos, pathos and mythos effectively? Examples can come from your own speeches, from peer speeches, or from sample speeches viewed in class. Provide specific examples of what made them effective.

ANS: Students should know the differences between each as has been defined throughout the chapter. They should also use very clear examples.

25. Using the topic you have selected for your in-class persuasive speech, make a list of the appeals to mythos you might make in the speech (or made in the speech). After you have identified these appeals, consider your audience carefully. Determine which appeals likely resonate (or resonated) strongly with your audience and which may not be appropriate (or may not have been appropriate) given their cultural backgrounds.

ANS: This question comes from the review questions at the end of the chapter. Students should illustrate knowledge of mythos as has been discussed on the text book.
REF: pgs. 343-345

Chapter Seventeen

Multiple Choice

1. A speech that gives the audience a sense of the unique perspective of the person introduced or welcomed.
a. speech of tribute
b. speech of award
c. commemorative speech
d. speeches of introduction

ANS: d
REF: pg. 360

2. A speech that praises, honors, recognizes, or pays tribute to a person, an event, an idea, or an institution.
a. speech of tribute
b. speech of award
c. commemorative speech
d. introductory speech

ANS: c
REF: pg. 362

3. You were just awarded a two thousand dollar scholarship! Your scholarship will be presented at the organization's annual banquet. You have been invited to speak. What type of speech will you give?
a. speech of tribute
b. speech of award
c. acceptance speech
d. introductory speech

ANS: c
REF: pg. 364

4. A speech that is lighthearted that addresses issues or ideas in a humorous way.
a. speech to entertain
b. speech of award
c. acceptance speech
d. introductory speech

ANS: a
REF: pg. 366

5. A speech that specifically honors an individual.
a. speech to entertain
b. speech of tribute
c. acceptance speech
d. commemorative speech

ANS: d
REF: pg. 362

6. The way a speaker uses pauses and delivery for maximum effect that is characteristic of speeches to entertain.
a. volume
b. pitch
c. timing
d. inflection

ANS: c
REF: pg. 367

True /False

7. A successful introductory speech rarely lasts more than three or four minutes.

ANS: True
REF: pg. 361

8. There are two types of commemorative speeches: speeches of tribute and speeches of award.

ANS: True
REF: pg. 362

9. Humor is always successful in speeches because everyone finds the same general ideas funny.

ANS: False
REF: pg. 366

10. Recognizing and crediting others significant to your success is an important component of an acceptance speech.

ANS: True
REF: pg. 364

11. A commemorative speech is usually given in a formal setting.

ANS: True
REF: pg. 362

Fill in the Blank

12. A _____ speech helps an audience celebrate, reflect, remember or commemorate something significant to the group members.

ANS: special occasion
REF: pg. 359

13. A/an _____ speech praises, honors, or pays tribute to a person, an event, an idea, or an institution.

ANS: commemorative
REF: pg. 362

14. When you want to honor someone, you would give a speech of _____.

ANS: tribute
REF: pg. 362

15. A/an _____ is a speech that acknowledges gratitude, appreciation, and pleasure at receiving an honor or gift.

ANS: acceptance speech
REF: pg. 364

16. A speech to _____ makes the audience think as well as laugh.

ANS: entertain
REF: pg. 366

17. _____ is a tool to entertain, not alienate listeners. Use with caution.

ANS: Humor
REF: pg. 366

List and Define

18. List the three guidelines for a successful speech of commemoration.

ANS: Share what is unique and special; express sincere appreciation; tell the truth
REF: pg. 364

19. List the goals in a self-introduction speech.

ANS: State your name and give your credentials; address information about your credibility that relates directly to why you are speaking; express pleasure at being there.
REF: pg. 360

20. List the three guidelines for a successful speech of introduction, of another person.

ANS: Brevity, Accuracy, Appropriateness
REF: pgs. 361-362

21. List the goals of an acceptance speech.

ANS: Thank audience/organization for the award; show your awareness of the significance of the award; acknowledged the people who helped you accomplish what you're being honored for.
REF: pg. 364

22. List the three elements that contribute to making something funny in a speech to entertain.

ANS: Timing; your objective in telling the joke; and the members of the audience.
REF: pg. 367

Essay

23. Imagine that your class you are going to introduce someone you care about to your class. What do you want them to know about this person? Use the guidelines for speeches of introduction to outline a brief introductory speech.

ANS: Students should incorporate the guidelines for introductory speeches: be brief, be accurate, and be appropriate. Responses will vary in length and creativity, but the key is that they demonstrate understanding of these guidelines.
REF: pg. 361

24. Think of an award you have received or would like to receive in the future. If you can't think of one that already exists, create one now that could recognize one of your talents or accomplishments. Write an outline of a speech accepting this award, incorporating the goals outlined in your textbook.

ANS: This essay question is taken form the review question listed in the *Invitation to Public Speaking* web site. Students should illustrate an understanding of how to structure an acceptance speech.
REF: 364

25. You have been invited to give a speech to entertain. What topic might you speak about? What guidelines will you follow? For each guideline, explain how you will speak on your topic in order to meet this guideline. (Hint: imagine you are speaking to a group of people with whom you share commonalities to help answer this question more precisely.)

ANS: The students should use the guidelines on p. 370 to frame their answers. The guidelines are use humor carefully, speak about meaningful issues and pay careful attention to delivery. Their examples should demonstrate understanding of what these concepts mean, and how to use them.

REF: 370

Appendix A

Multiple Choice

1. The process of randomly generating ideas.
a. brainstorming
b. reflective thinking
c. group think
d. chitchat

ANS: a
REF: pg. 381

2. When responding to a hostile question you should
a. ignore the person because they are acting inappropriately.
b. respond to the emotion in the question .
c. confront the person with an argument.
d. remain civil and try to be invitational.

ANS: d
REF: pg. 385

3. At this stage of the reflective thinking process, group members focus on discussing why the problem exists.
a. identification of the problem
b. analysis of the problem
c. implications of possible solutions
d. deciding what is the best solution

ANS: b
REF: pg. 381

4. This group presentation involves each member presenting an individual speech over a common, single topic.
a. oral report
b. panel discussion
c. team presentation
d. meeting

ANS: c
REF: pg. 380

5. The five-step method for structuring a problem solving discussion.
a. brainstorming
b. group think
c. group building and maintenance
d. reflective thinking method

ANS: d
REF: pg. 380

True/False

6. A small group, as defined, has to have between 3 and 15 members.

ANS: True
REF: pg. 376

7. One characteristic of a small group is that only a few group members express their ideas.

ANS: False
REF: pg. 376

8. Minutes are designed to document what was discussed and what decisions were made in the course of a meeting.

ANS: True
REF: pg. 383

9. Engaging in groupthink is a productive way for a group to work when under a time constraint.

ANS: False
REF: pg. 381

10. A panel discussion does not involve an audience.

ANS: False
REF: pg. 379

Fill in the Blank

11. _____is speaking as part of a small collection of individuals.

ANS: Small group speaking
REF: pg. 376

12. _____ happens when group members conform to a single frame of mind without fully and objectively examining all alternatives.

ANS: Group think
REF: pg. 381

13. The _____ lists topics to be discussed in a meeting.

ANS: agenda
REF: pg. 382

14. The _____ session is an excellent format for exploring issues in small groups. These sessions provide an opportunity for group members and their audiences to explore an idea or proposal in more detail, ask for clarity,

ANS: question-and-answer
REF: pg. 383

15. The _____ is a speech given by an individual presenting the group's findings, conclusions or proposals to a larger audience.

ANS: oral report
REF: pg. 378

16. A formal public discussion where several group members share fully prepared speeches over a common topic is a/an_____.

ANS: symposium
REF: pg. 379

List and Define

17. Define small group speaking.

ANS: Speaking to give a presentation to a small collection of individuals or speaking as part of a small group of people.
REF: pg. 376

18. What are the four characteristics of small groups?

ANS: The size (3-15 people); open verbal communication among group members; importance of nonverbal communication; a common goal they work together to achieve.
REF: pg. 376-377

19. List the five guidelines for having an effective meeting.

ANS: Provide an agenda in advance; specify the time and location; be prepared; use an effective procedure for conducting the meeting; distribute meeting minutes to group members.
REF: pg. 382-383

20. List the five steps of the reflective thinking process.

ANS: Identify the problem; Analyze the problem; Suggest possible solutions; Consider implications of possible solutions; Decide on best solution.
REF: pgs. 380

366

21. List three tips for positively dealing with a hostile question.

ANS: Students can choose from: Don't take question personally; Respond with civility; Separate emotion from fact before responding; Address the content, not the emotion/be invitational; Offer evidence for your position.
REF: pg. 385

Essay

22. The text offers six useful techniques for managing the question and answer session of a small group speaking situation. Which two techniques do you think are most important? Why?

ANS: Students may choose from: explain the format (384); listen and clarify (384); keep a positive mindset (385); address the entire group (385); answer with honesty (385-386). Their answer should demonstrate an understanding of the techniques they choose.
REF: pgs. 384-386

23. You are in a small group where each member wants to speak effectively and ethically. What two tips would you give your group about how to accomplish this goal? For each tip, be sure to explain the benefit of the tip, and at least one hazard of not following the tips.

ANS: Students should choose from the following tips: consider the group's purpose and audience when selecting a presentation format (386); use appropriate delivery style and skills (387); organize your presentation (387); use effective visual aids as needed (387). They should be able to articulate a benefit and a hazard.
REF: pg. 386-387

24. What are the three reasons people speak in small groups? Which reason is the one that is most relevant to your current life? Which do you think will be most relevant to you in your future?

ANS: The reasons students should identify are: deciding to speak in groups, being asked to speak in groups, and being required to speak in groups. They should be able to identify a reason that they might speak now (for a class, for a cause they care about, etc.) or in the future (in their career, etc.)
REF: pgs. 377